101 Great, Ready-to-Use Book Lists for Children

101 Great, Ready-to-Use Book Lists for Children

Nancy J. Keane

LIBRARIES UNLIMITED

AN IMPRINT OF ABC-CLIO, LLC
Santa Barbara, California • Denver, Colorado • Oxford, England

Copyright 2012 by ABC-CLIO, LLC

Library of Congress Cataloging-in-Publication Data

Keane, Nancy J.
  101 great, ready-to-use book lists for children / Nancy J. Keane.
    pages cm
  "The book is meant as an extension to the previous work, The big book of children's reading lists (2006)."
  Includes bibliographical references and index.
    ISBN 978–1–61069–083–6 (pbk.) — ISBN 978–1–61069–084–3 (ebook) 1. Children—Books and reading—United States. 2. Children's literature—Bibliography. 3. Children's libraries—Book lists.
4. School libraries—Book lists. I. Keane, Nancy J. Big book of children's reading lists. II. Title. III. Title: One hundred one great, ready-to-use book lists for children. IV. Title: One hundred and one great, ready-to-use book lists for children.
Z1037.K285 2012
028.5′50973—dc23   2011051429

ISBN: 978–1–61069–083–6
EISBN: 978–1–61069–084–3

16 15 14 13 12   1 2 3 4 5

This book is also available on the World Wide Web as an eBook.
Visit www.abc-clio.com for details.

Libraries Unlimited
An Imprint of ABC-CLIO, LLC

ABC-CLIO, LLC
130 Cremona Drive, P.O. Box 1911
Santa Barbara, California 93116-1911

This book is printed on acid-free paper ∞

Manufactured in the United States of America

*Dedicated to my children, Aureta and Alex,
and my grandchildren, Aiden and Jordan.*

Contents

Contents

Acknowledgments

I wish to thank the people who have helped with this endeavor. First, I would like to thank all the authors who gave us these marvelous stories to enjoy. With so many children's books in print, it is always difficult to limit the entries. Without these extraordinary people, this would have been a thankless task. As it was, I have spent numerous entertaining hours wrapped up in the books.

I would also like to thank the many librarians and teachers whom I have the pleasure to contact each day. They have introduced me to books that I might have otherwise missed. The many wonderful, dedicated teachers whom I have had the privilege of knowing also influenced this work tremendously. I have been fortunate to work with a talented group of educators.

I would also like to thank my marvelous editor, Barbara Ittner. She has worked with me from the beginning of this manuscript offering advice and support. She is truly amazing!

Most importantly, I would like to thank my family. My children, Aureta and Alex, and my grandchildren, Aiden and Jordan, are always there to share a story or two.

Introduction

Whether teachers use basal readers, leveled reading, or a literature-based program, there is a need to extend the reading materials for children beyond the current materials. But how do you find those supplemental materials easily? This book represents an attempt to create valuable reading lists to support the extended reading demands.

Every day librarians and teachers plan activities for children that involve using literature. Before starting this task, they may have some books in mind—but perhaps not. It is time consuming to search for books that support the theme of a lesson. Studies have shown that the average librarian has a working repertoire of twenty to thirty titles to recommend at any one time.[1] This book represents an attempt to create valuable reading lists to support adults in their work with children.

An unlimited number of reading lists could be developed to assist professionals in their work. The lists in this book have been chosen in consultation with elementary teachers and public librarians, and through discussions on professional e-mail lists. The book is meant to serve as an extension to the previous work, *The Big Book of Children's Reading Lists* (2006). The book is divided into **School Subject**–related lists, **Character Education/Values**–related lists, **Common Theme**–related lists, **Genres**-related lists, **Family** topics, **Readalike** suggestions, and **Literary Elements.** Additionally, there is a list of Professional Resources. Additional contributors to the book include Jessica Gilcreast and Catherine Cowette.

The books suggested were all in print as of August 2011. Although the emphasis is on books published within the last ten years, older titles are included if they are still in print and represent a valuable addition to the list. Information included for each title includes the author, title, publisher, date of publication, and number of pages. The Lexile level of the book is supplied when available. A short annotation, taken from the Library of Congress cataloging database, is provided as well. The interest level of the book is indicated by IL and a grade level. For example, IL K–3 indicates that the main audience for the book is kindergarten through third grade. IL 3–6 books are appropriate for grades three through six; IL 5–8 books are meant for grades five through eight—that is, upper-level elementary school children. IL AD indicates adult-level material, usually consisting of teacher-level material to use with students. Non-fiction books are designated by the notation "(Non-fiction)." Because six to twelve years of age is a large span in terms of maturity, it is strongly suggested that teachers and librarians review the materials before using them with younger children. It is important to look beyond recommended interest level when suggesting books to students.

We hope that teachers and librarians will find this resource valuable for suggesting reading materials to children. The lists provided in this book can be used in a variety of ways. For example, they can be photocopied and handed out to students as suggested reading. They can be enlarged and posted in the library, put on the library website or published in the library's newsletter, or used to create book displays. Add your school or library logo, or even some copyright free clip art to personalize the list. Have fun. Be creative. Be resourceful.

However you use the lists, it is hoped that you will find them to be valuable resources and aids for suggesting reading materials.

Note

1. Eaton, G. (2002, October 28). How to do a book talk. University of Rhode Island. Retrieved from http://www.uri.edu/artsci/lsc/Faculty/geaton/MSLMAtalk/

Part 1

Character and Values

Being Left Out

Books for Children of All Ages

Bluthenthal, Diana Cain. *I'm Not Invited?* Atheneum Books for Young Readers, c2003. 32p. IL K–3, Lexile: 450
> Minnie is upset when she is not invited to Charles's party and spends her entire week sad as she wonders why her friend did not include her in the fun.

Howe, James. *Horace and Morris But Mostly Dolores.* Atheneum Books for Young Readers, 1999. 32p. IL K–3, Lexile: 410
> Horace, Morris, and Dolores are very good friends and have always done everything together; however, their friendship may be in trouble when Horace and Morris decide to join a no-girls-allowed club and Dolores joins a no-boys-allowed club.

Howe, James. *Horace and Morris Join the Chorus (But What about Dolores?).* Aladdin Paperbacks, 2005. 32p. IL K–3, Lexile: 450
> Delores is upset when her friends are chosen to sing in the chorus, but she finds a way to become part of the performance.

O'Neill, Alexis. *The Recess Queen.* Scholastic Press, 2002. 32p. IL K–3, Lexile: 450
> Mean Jean is the biggest bully on the school playground—until a new girl arrives and challenges Jean's status as the Recess Queen.

Books for Children Ages Eight to Twelve

Criswell, Patti Kelley. *A Smart Girl's Guide to Friendship Troubles: Dealing with Fights, Being Left Out & the Whole Popularity Thing.* Pleasant Co. Publications, c2003. 87p. IL 3–6 (Non-fiction).
> A practical guide to maintaining good friendships and identifying toxic ones that explains how to handle and recover from fights, stop oneself from partaking in bad behaviors such as backstabbing and bullying, and find the right kinds of friends.

Watt, Frances. *The Middle Sheep.* Eerdmans Books for Young Readers, 2010. 71p. IL 3–6
> Maud feels gloomy about being a "middle sheep," and decides that as Extraordinary Ernie's sidekick, she deserves a sidekick, too. That makes Ernie, an only child, feel left out, which leads to bickering between the two of them.

Empathy

Books for Children of All Ages

Bunting, Eve. *Fly Away Home.* Clarion Books, 1991. 32p. IL K–3, Lexile: 450
A homeless boy who lives in an airport with his father, moving from terminal to terminal and trying not to be noticed, is given hope when he sees a trapped bird find its freedom.

DiCamillo, Kate. *Great Joy.* Candlewick Press, 2007. 32p. IL K–3.
Just before Christmas, when Frances sees a sad-eyed organ-grinder and his monkey performing near her apartment, she cannot stop thinking about them, wondering where they go at night, and wishing she could do something to help.

Friedrich, Elizabeth. *Leah's Pony.* Boyds Mills Press, 1996. 32p. IL K–3, Lexile: 580
A young girl sells her pony and uses the money to buy back her father's tractor when the family's belongings are put up for auction.

Havill, Juanita. *Jamaica's Blue Marker.* Houghton Mifflin, c1995. 31p. IL K–3, Lexile: 420
Jamaica thinks her classmate Russell is a pest who is always getting into trouble, but then she discovers he is moving away.

Koller, Jackie French. *No Such Thing.* Boyds Mills Press, 1997. 32p. IL K–3, Lexile: 340
A boy is afraid there is a monster under his bed, until he meets a monster who is afraid there is a boy above his head.

McCloud, Carol. *Have You Filled a Bucket Today?: A Guide to Daily Happiness for Kids.* Ferne Press, c2006. 31p. IL K–3, Lexile: 710 (Non-fiction)
The metaphor of filling a bucket is used to encourage children to practice kind and considerate behavior and teach them the benefits of positive relationships.

O'Neill, Catharine. *Annie and Simon.* Candlewick Press, 2008. 57p. IL K–3, Lexile: 260
These four stories follow the adventures of young Annie, her very patient older brother Simon, and their dog Hazel, as they go on a canoe ride, suffer a bee sting, think about careers, and look for falling stars.

Polacco, Patricia. *The Lemonade Club.* Philomel Books, c2007. 42p. IL K–3, Lexile: 740
After learning that they both have cancer, Marilyn and her teacher, Miss Wichelman, support and encourage each other through their treatments.

Spinelli, Eileen. *Somebody Loves You, Mr. Hatch.* Aladdin Paperbacks, c1991. 32p. IL K–3, Lexile: 550
An anonymous valentine changes the life of the unsociable Mr. Hatch, turning him into a laughing friend who helps and appreciates all his neighbors.

Tessler, Manya. *Yuki's Ride Home.* Bloomsbury Children's Books, 2008. 32p. IL K–3
After an enjoyable day at her grandmother's house, Yuki tries to gather all her courage to ride her bicycle home in the evening fog.

Empathy

Willems, Mo. *Leonardo the Terrible Monster.* Hyperion, c2005. 44p. IL K–3, Lexile: 670
Despite his best efforts, Leonardo the monster simply cannot seem to frighten anyone, until he meets the perfect nervous little boy.

Books for Children Ages Eight to Twelve

Alvarez, Julia. *Return to Sender.* Knopf, c2009. 325p. IL 3–6, Lexile: 890
After his family hires migrant Mexican workers to help save their Vermont farm from foreclosure, eleven-year-old Tyler befriends the oldest daughter in the Mexican family. When he discovers the workers may not be in the country legally, he realizes that real friendship knows no borders.

Draper, Sharon M. *Out of My Mind.* Atheneum Books for Young Readers, c2010. 295p. IL 5–8, Lexile: 700
Considered by many to be mentally retarded, a brilliant, impatient fifth grader with cerebral palsy discovers a technological device that will allow her to speak for the first time.

Estes, Eleanor. *The Hundred Dresses.* Harcourt, 1944. 80p. IL 3–6, Lexile: 870
By winning a medal she is no longer there to receive, a tight-lipped little Polish girl teaches her classmates a lesson. The book includes a note from the author's daughter, Helena Estes.

Graff, Lisa. *The Thing about Georgie: A Novel.* Laura Geringer Books, c2006. 220p. IL 3–6, Lexile: 770
Georgie's dwarfism causes problems, but he could always rely on his parents, his best friend, and classmate Jeanie the Meanie's teasing—until a surprising announcement, a new boy in school, and a class project shake things up.

Graff, Lisa. *Umbrella Summer.* Laura Geringer Books, c2009. 235p. IL 3–6, Lexile: 820
After her brother Jared dies, ten-year-old Annie worries about the hidden dangers of everything, from bug bites to bicycle riding, until she is befriended by a new neighbor who is grieving her own loss.

Haddix, Margaret Peterson. *Because of Anya.* Simon & Schuster Books for Young Readers, c2002. 114p. IL 3–6, Lexile: 710
While ten-year-old Anya faces the difficulties of losing her hair to alopecia, her classmate Keely learns how to stand up for what she knows is right.

Hurwitz, Michele Weber. *Calli Be Gold.* Wendy Lamb Books, c2011. 198p. IL 3–6
Eleven-year-old Calli, the third child in a family of busy high-achievers, likes to take her time and observe rather than rush around. When she meets an awkward, insecure second grader named Noah and is paired with him in the Peer Helper Program, she finds satisfaction and strength in working with him.

Ibbotson, Eva. *The Dragonfly Pool.* Dutton Children's Books, c2008. 377p. IL YA, Lexile: 960
Tally and her friends at Dalderton Boarding School form a dance troupe and travel to Bergania, where she befriends Karil, the crown prince, and helps him flee the Nazis after his father is assassinated.

Empathy

Lynch, Chris. *Cyberia.* Scholastic Press, 2008. 158p. IL 3–6, Lexile: 750
In a future where electronic surveillance has taken the place of love, a veterinarian is charged with putting computer chips in animals to control them. Those creatures choose young Zane, who understands their speech, to release the captives and bring them to a technology-free safety zone.

O'Dell, Scott. *Island of the Blue Dolphins.* Houghton Mifflin, 1990. 177p. IL 5–8
Left alone on a beautiful but isolated island off the coast of California, a young Indian girl spends eighteen years not only merely surviving through her enormous courage and self-reliance, but also finding a measure of happiness in her solitary life.

Schlitz, Laura Amy. *The Night Fairy.* Candlewick Press, 2010. 117p. IL 3–6, Lexile: 630
When Flory the night fairy's wings are accidentally broken and she cannot fly, she has to learn to do everything differently.

From *101 Great, Ready-to-Use Book Lists for Children* by Nancy J. Keane. Santa Barbara, CA: Libraries Unlimited. Copyright © 2012.

Feelings

Books for Children of All Ages

Aliki. *Feelings.* Greenwillow Books, c1984. 32p. IL K–3, Lexile: NP (Non-fiction)
Pictures, dialogs, poems, and stories portray various emotions that we all feel: jealousy, sadness, fear, anger, joy, and love, among others.

Bang, Molly. *When Sophie Gets Angry—: Really, Really Angry—.* Blue Sky Press, c1999. 36p. IL K–3, Lexile: BR
When Sophie gets angry, she goes outside and runs, cries, and climbs her favorite tree. Then, calmed by the breeze, she is soon ready to go back home.

Brown, Marc Tolon. *Arthur's Nose.* Little, Brown, c2001. 40p. IL K–3, Lexile: 350
Arthur the aardvark, unhappy with his nose, decides to see a rhinologist. The book includes pictures that show how Arthur and author/illustrator Marc Brown have changed over the years.

Cain, Janan. *The Way I Feel.* Parenting Press, c2000. 32p. IL K–3, Lexile: NP (Non-fiction)
Illustrations and rhyming text portray children experiencing a range of emotions, including frustration, shyness, jealousy, and pride.

Curtis, Jamie Lee. *Today I Feel Silly & Other Moods That Make My Day.* Joanna Cotler Books, c1998. 34p. IL K–3, Lexile: 250
A child's emotions range from silliness to anger to excitement, coloring and changing each day.

Duffy, Carol Ann. *The Tear Thief.* Barefoot Books, 2007. 34p. IL K–3
In the evening, between supper and bedtime, an invisible fairy slips into homes to steal tears of shame, fear, pain, and sadness. She then climbs to the moon, where she transforms the sackful of droplets into something wonderful.

Everitt, Betsy. *Mean Soup.* Harcourt, c1992. 29p. IL K–3, Lexile: 310
Horace feels really mean at the end of a bad day, until he helps his mother make Mean Soup.

Freymann, Saxton. *How Are You Peeling?: Foods with Moods.* Scholastic, 2004, c1999. 42p. IL K–3, Lexile: BR (Non-fiction)
Photographs of carvings made from vegetables and simple text introduce the world of emotions by presenting questions on anger, sadness, tiredness, and more.

Henkes, Kevin. *A Weekend with Wendell.* Greenwillow Books, c1986. 32p. IL K–3, Lexile: 510
Sophie does not enjoy energetic, assertive Wendell's weekend visit until the very end, when she learns to assert herself and finds out Wendell can be fun to play with after all.

Henkes, Kevin. *Wemberly Worried.* Greenwillow Books, c2000. 32p. IL K–3. Lexile: 170
A mouse named Wemberly, who worries about everything, finds that she has a whole list of things to worry about when she faces the first day of nursery school.

Howe, James. *Horace and Morris But Mostly Dolores.* Atheneum Books for Young Readers, 1999. 32p. IL K–3, Lexile: 410
Horace, Morris, and Dolores are very good friends and have always done everything together; however, their friendship may be in trouble when Horace and Morris decide to join a no-girls-allowed club and Dolores joins a no-boys-allowed club.

Feelings

Keller, Holly. *Nosy Rosie.* Greenwillow Books, c2006. 24p. IL K–3
Rosie the fox's excellent sense of smell is good for finding things, but she stops using it after everyone begins to call her "Nosy Rosie."

Lester, Helen. *Hurty Feelings.* Houghton Mifflin, c2004. 32p. IL K–3, Lexile: 610
Fragility, a hippopotamus whose feelings are easily hurt, meets Rudy, a rude elephant, on the soccer field.

McKissack, Pat. *The Honest-to-Goodness Truth.* Atheneum Books for Young Readers, c2000. 32p. IL K–3, Lexile: 450
After promising never to lie, Libby learns that it's not always necessary to blurt out the whole truth either.

Moser, Adolph. *Don't Pop Your Cork on Mondays!: The Children's Anti-stress Book.* Landmark Editions, c1988. 48p. IL K–3 (Non-fiction)
This book explores the causes and effects of stress and offers practical approaches and techniques for dealing with stress in daily life.

Rayner, Catherine. *Augustus and His Smile.* Good Books, c2006. 26p. IL K–3, Lexile: 620
After searching mountains, forests, oceans, and deserts to find his smile, Augustus the tiger finds it when he looks in a puddle, and realizes that happiness is everywhere around him.

Reid, Camilla. *The Littlest Dinosaur and the Naughty Rock.* Bloomsbury, 2010. 32p. IL K–3
A little dinosaur who is in a bad mood learns a lesson about manners and apologizing from a giant tortoise.

Seeger, Laura Vaccaro. *Walter Was Worried.* Roaring Brook Press, c2005. 34p. IL K–3
Children's faces, depicted with letters of the alphabet, react to the onset of a storm and its aftermath in this picture book, accompanied by simple alliterative text.

Spinelli, Eileen. *Somebody Loves You, Mr. Hatch.* Aladdin Paperbacks, 1991. 32p. IL K–3, Lexile: 550
An anonymous valentine changes the life of the unsociable Mr. Hatch, turning him into a laughing friend who helps and appreciates all his neighbors.

Tomlinson, Jill. *The Owl Who Was Afraid of the Dark.* Egmont Books, 1968. 98p. IL K–3
A baby barn owl named Plop is afraid of the dark until a Boy Scout, a little girl, and other new friends help him understand that the dark can be fun and fascinating.

Vail, Rachel. *Sometimes I'm Bombaloo.* Scholastic, 2002. 32p. IL K–3, Lexile: 450
When Katie Honors feels angry and out of control, her mother helps her to be herself again.

Wild, Margaret. *Harry & Hopper.* Feiwel and Friends, 2011, c2009. 32p. IL K–3
Harry is devastated when he returns home from school to find that his beloved dog, Hopper, will no longer be there to greet him.

Feelings

Books for Children Ages Eight to Twelve

Brown, Susan Taylor. *Hugging the Rock.* Tricycle Press, c2006. 170p. IL 3–6, Lexile: NP
Through a series of poems, Rachel expresses her feelings about her parents' divorce, living without her mother, and her changing attitude toward her father.

Browne, Anthony. *Voices in the Park.* DK Publishing, 1998. 31p. IL 3–6, Lexile: 560
Lives briefly intertwine when two youngsters meet in the park.

Carestio, Michael A. *Black Jack Jetty: A Boy's Journey through Grief.* Magination Press, c2010. 64p. IL 3–6
Visiting his family's summer home on the New Jersey shore, Jack begins to work through his feelings about his father's death in Afghanistan and find his place among the cousins and other relatives whom he had never before met.

Codell, Esme Raji. *Sahara Special.* Hyperion Paperbacks for Children, 2004, c2003. 175p. IL 3–6, Lexile: 660
Struggling with school and her feelings since her father left, Sahara gets a fresh start with a new and unique teacher who supports her writing talents and the individuality of each of her classmates.

Ensor, Barbara. *Thumbelina: Tiny Little Runaway Bride.* Schwartz & Wade Books, c2008. 140p. IL 3–6, Lexile: 890
In this expanded version of the Hans Christian Andersen fairy tale, a tiny girl no bigger than a thumb becomes separated from her overprotective mother, has adventures with various animals, and records her feelings in a diary as she gains self-reliance and searches for someone to love.

Haworth, Danette. *Me & Jack.* Walker & Co., 2011. 232p. IL 3–6
Joshua, the new kid in town whose father works as a recruiter for the U.S. Air Force during the Vietnam War, struggles to make friends and is comforted by Jack, a dog unlike any other who seems to understand Joshua's feelings. When a series of disturbances happen throughout the town and Jack is blamed, however, Joshua finds he must fight to protect everything he loves.

Henkes, Kevin. *Words of Stone.* Greenwillow Books, c1992. 152p. IL 3–6, Lexile: 770
Busy trying to deal with his many fears and his troubled feelings for his dead mother, ten-year-old Blaze finds that his life is changed when he meets the boisterous and irresistible Joselle.

Lubar, David. *My Rotten Life.* Starscape, 2009. 160p. IL 3–6, Lexile: 540
Tired of continually having his feelings hurt by popular students and bullies, fifth-grader Nathan agrees to try an experimental formula, Hurt-Be-Gone, and becomes a half-dead zombie—a condition that has some real advantages, as he soon discovers.

Meehl, Brian. *Out of Patience.* Yearling, 2008, c2006. 292p. IL 3–6, Lexile: 770
Twelve-year-old Jake Waters cannot wait to escape the small town of Patience, Kansas, until the arrival of a cursed toilet plunger causes him to reevaluate his feelings toward his family and its history.

Feelings

Moss, Marissa. *Amelia's Book of Notes & Note Passing: (A Note Notebook).* Simon & Schuster Books for Young Readers, c2006. 76p. IL 3–6, Lexile: 670

The hand-lettered content of this nine-year-old girl's notebook reveals her thoughts and feelings about moving, starting school, and dealing with her older sister, as well as keeping her old best friend and making a new one.

O'Neill, Mary Le Duc. *Hailstones and Halibut Bones.* Doubleday Books for Young Readers, 1989, c1961. 60p. IL 3–6, Lexile: NP

These twelve poems reflect the author's feelings about various colors. This book has become a classic work since its first publication in 1961.

Rosen, Michael. *Michael Rosen's Sad Book.* Candlewick Press, 2005, c2004. 34p. IL 3–6

A man tells about all the emotions that accompany his sadness over the death of his son and explains how he tries to cope with his grief. Sadness effects everyone and sometimes it feels overwhelming. Rosen shows that we cannot let it define us.

Straight, Susan. *The Friskative Dog.* Alfred A. Knopf, c2007. 149p. IL 3–6, Lexile: 770

Sharron's father has disappeared, and she tries to cope with her feelings of loss through the love of a stuffed dog he gave her.

Getting Along

Books for Children of All Ages

Bang, Molly. *When Sophie Gets Angry—: Really, Really Angry—.* Blue Sky Press, c1999. 36p. IL K–3, Lexile: BR
> When Sophie gets angry, she goes outside and runs, cries, and climbs her favorite tree. Then, calmed by the breeze, she is soon ready to go back home.

Becker, Bonny. *A Visitor for Bear.* Candlewick Press, 2008. 56p. IL K–3, Lexile: 430
> Bear's efforts to keep out visitors to his house are undermined by a very persistent mouse.

Howe, James. *Horace and Morris But Mostly Dolores.* Atheneum Books for Young Readers, 1999. 32p. IL K–3, Lexile: 410
> Horace, Morris, and Dolores are very good friends and have always done everything together; however, their friendship may be in trouble when Horace and Morris decide to join a no-girls-allowed club and Dolores joins a no-boys-allowed club.

Keller, Laurie. *Do unto Otters: A Book about Manners.* Holt, 2007. 34p. IL K–3, Lexile: 460
> Mr. Rabbit worries about getting along with his new neighbors, who are otters, until he is reminded of the Golden Rule.

Lester, Helen. *Princess Penelope's Parrot.* Houghton Mifflin, c1996. 32p. IL K–3, Lexile: 710
> An arrogant and greedy princess's chances with a handsome prince are ruined when her parrot repeats to him all the rude comments the princess has made.

McCloud, Carol. *Have You Filled a Bucket Today?: A Guide to Daily Happiness for Kids.* Ferne Press, c2006. 31p. IL K–3, Lexile: 710 (Non-fiction)
> The metaphor of filling a bucket is used to encourage children to practice kind and considerate behavior and teach them the benefits of positive relationships.

Munson, Derek. *Enemy Pie.* Chronicle Books, c2000. 36p. IL K–3, Lexile: 330
> Hoping that the enemy pie that his father makes will help him get rid of his enemy, a little boy finds that instead it helps make a new friend.

O'Neill, Alexis. *The Recess Queen.* Scholastic Press, 2002. 32p. IL K–3, Lexile: 450
> Mean Jean is the biggest bully on the school playground—until a new girl arrives and challenges Jean's status as the Recess Queen.

Proimos, James. *Paulie Pastrami Achieves World Peace.* Little, Brown Books for Young Readers, 2009. 40p. IL K–3, Lexile: 390
> Seven-year-old Paulie, an ordinary boy, brings peace to his home and school through small acts of kindness, but needs help to achieve his goal of world peace.

Ransom, Jeanie Franz. *Don't Squeal unless It's a Big Deal: A Tale of Tattletales.* Magination Press, c2006. 32p. IL K–3
> Mrs. McNeal turns her class of nineteen tattletales into respectful classmates who know how to behave in a true emergency. The book includes a note to parents.

Getting Along

Robbins, Jacqui. *Two of a Kind.* Atheneum Books for Young Readers, c2009. 32p. IL K–3, Lexile: 520
When Anna abandons her best friend, Julisa, to spend time with Kayla and Melanie, whose friendship is considered very special, she soon learns that she has little in common with her new friends.

Scieszka, Jon. *Cowboy & Octopus.* Viking, 2007. 32p. IL K–3, Lexile: 350
A cowboy and an octopus learn a thing or two about friendship as they struggle through a knock-knock joke, ugly hats, and a special dinner of beans.

Seeger, Laura Vaccaro. *Dog and Bear: Two Friends, Three Stories.* Roaring Brook Press, 2007. 32p. IL K–3, Lexile: 320
Three easy-to-read stories reveal the close friendship between Dog and Bear.

Udry, Janice May. *Let's Be Enemies.* HarperTrophy, c1989. 32p. IL K–3, Lexile: 250
Two small boys decide to stop being friends after one of them decides to be the boss. The other boy doesn't want to be bossed around so the two decide to become enemies instead of friends. But find it hard to do.

Willems, Mo. *Happy Pig Day! (Elephant & Piggy).* Hyperion Books, c2011. IL K–3
Piggie celebrates her favorite day of the year, but Gerald the elephant is sad, thinking that he cannot join the fun. Gerald believes that Piggie will not invite him to the party.

Willems, Mo. *Leonardo the Terrible Monster.* Hyperion, c2005. 44p. IL K–3, Lexile: 670
Despite his best efforts, Leonardo the monster simply cannot seem to frighten anyone, until he meets the perfect nervous little boy.

Wilson, Karma. *Bear Feels Scared.* Margaret K. McElderry Books, c2008. 32p. IL K–3, Lexile: 600
Bear's animal friends come to his rescue when he becomes lost and frightened in the woods.

Books for Children Ages Eight to Twelve

Cook, Eileen. *Fourth-Grade Fairy.* Aladdin, 2011. 152p. IL 3–6, Lexile: 550
When fairy-godmother-in-training Willow's wish to attend a human school comes true, she finds getting along with humans to be harder than she expected, but her newly acquired magical talent makes it easy to collaborate with animals.

Morgan, Melissa J. *Freaky Tuesday.* Grosset & Dunlap, c2007. 158p. IL 5–8
The girls of Camp Lakeview keep in touch through their blog as Brynn transfers to Candace's school, where intelligence brings popularity and acting talent does not; Gaby, Val, and Chelsea do volunteer work together; and all of the girls struggle with setting priorities and getting along.

Nails, Jennifer. *Next to Mexico.* Houghton Mifflin, 2008. 235p. IL 5–8, Lexile: 540
Outspoken, impulsive Lylice has skipped fifth grade, but she finds that getting along at Susan B. Anthony Middle School is more difficult than she expected, until she befriends another newcomer to the sixth grade.

Wells, Tina. *Friends Forever?* Harper, c2010. 183p. IL 3–6
Mackenzie is determined to have a great time on the school field trip, but out in the woods, everyone stops getting along and friendships are tested.

Helping

Books for Children Of All Ages

Brisson, Pat. *Wanda's Roses*. Caroline House, Boyds Mills Press, c1994. IL K–3, Lexile: 740
Wanda mistakes a thornbush for a rosebush in the empty lot. She clears away the trash around it and cares for it every day, even though no roses bloom.

Bunting, Eve. *Fly Away Home*. Clarion Books, c1991. 32p. IL K–3, Lexile: 450
A homeless boy who lives in an airport with his father, moving from terminal to terminal and trying not to be noticed, is given hope when he sees a trapped bird find its freedom and he dreams that he too will be free.

Carmi, Giora. *A Circle of Friends*. Star Bright Books, c2003. 32p, IL K–3
When a boy anonymously shares his snack with a homeless man, he begins a cycle of good will.

DiSalvo-Ryan, DyAnne. *Uncle Willie and the Soup Kitchen*. Mulberry Books, 1991. 32p. IL K–3, Lexile: 450
A boy spends the day with Uncle Willie in the soup kitchen, where he works preparing and serving food to the hungry.

Fleming, Candace. *Boxes for Katje*. Farrar, Straus and Giroux, 2003. 36p. IL K–3, Lexile: 460
After a young Dutch girl writes to her new American friend with thanks for the care package sent after World War II, she begins to receive increasingly larger boxes. The entire village eagerly awaits the packages from America.

Fox, Mem. *Wilfrid Gordon McDonald Partridge*. Kane/Miller, 1985. 32p. IL K–3, Lexile: 760
A small boy tries to discover the meaning of "memory" so he can restore that of an elderly friend.

Judge, Lita. *One Thousand Tracings: Healing the Wounds of World War II*. Hyperion Books for Children, c2007. 36p. IL K–3, Lexile: NP (Non-fiction)
The author relates the story of her grandparents' efforts after World War II to send packages of food, clothing, and shoes to their friends in Germany and others in Europe who suffered from the after-effects of the war.

McGovern, Ann. *The Lady in the Box*. Turtle Books, 1999, c1997. 40p. IL K–3, Lexile: 370
When Lizzie and Ben discover a homeless woman living in their neighborhood, they must reconcile their desire to help her with their mother's admonition not to talk to strangers.

McPhail, David. *The Teddy Bear*. H. Holt, 2002. 32p. IL K–3, Lexile: 420
A teddy bear, lost by the little boy who loves him, still feels loved after being rescued by a homeless man.

Robbins, Jacqui. *The New Girl—and Me*. Atheneum Books for Young Readers, c2006. 32p. IL K–3
Two African American girls named Shakeeta and Mia become friends when Shakeeta boasts that she has a pet iguana and Mia learns how to help Shakeeta "feel at home" even when she is in school.

Helping

Books for Children Ages Eight to Twelve

Banerjee, Anjali. *Seaglass Summer.* Wendy Lamb Books, c2010. 163p. IL 3–6, Lexile: 590
While spending a month on an island off the coast of Washington helping in her Uncle Sanjay's veterinary clinic, eleven-year-old Poppy Ray questions her decision to follow in her uncle's footsteps.

Bauer, Joan. *Stand Tall.* Speak, 2005, c2002. 182p. IL 5–8, Lexile: 520
Tree, a six-foot-three-inch twelve-year-old, copes with his parents' recent divorce and his failure as an athlete by helping his grandfather, a Vietnam veteran and recent amputee, and Sophie, a new girl at school.

Dunmore, Helen. *Amina's Blanket.* Crabtree Publishing, 2002, c1996. 42p. IL 3–6
After helping to knit and sew together the squares of a blanket to be sent to a country at war, Josie dreams of what life is like for the girl who will receive the blanket as a gift from Josie's class.

George, Jean Craighead. *Charlie's Raven.* Puffin Books, 2006, c2004. 190p. IL 5–8, Lexile: 710
Charlie, having heard from his Teton Sioux Indian friend that ravens can cure people, brings home a baby raven in hopes of helping his ailing grandfather. His action sets the stage for a learning experience that brings new life to everyone in his family.

Hartnett, Sonya. *The Midnight Zoo.* Candlewick Press, 2011, c2010. 217p. IL 5–8
Twelve-year-old Andrej, nine-year-old Tomas, and their baby sister Wilma flee their Romany encampment when it is attacked by German troops during World War II. In the abandoned town where they take refuge, they find a zoo where the animals tell their stories, helping the children understand what has become of their lives and what it means to be free.

Hobbs, Will. *Jackie's Wild Seattle.* HarperCollins Publishers, c2003. 200p. IL 5–8, Lexile: 660
Fourteen-year-old Shannon and her little brother, Cody, spend the summer with their uncle, helping at a wildlife rescue center named Jackie's Wild Seattle.

Margolis, Leslie. *Girl's Best Friend.* Bloomsbury, 2010. 261p. IL 3–6, Lexile: 620
Maggie Brooklyn Sinclair, who works after school as a dog-walker, looks into a case of kidnapped dogs—even though it may mean helping Ivy, her ex-best friend, recover her rescue dog, Kermit.

Patrick, Denise Lewis. *Cecile's Gift.* American Girl, c2011. 85p. IL 3–6
Cecile Rey, who is spending the summer volunteering with her friend Marie-Grace Gardner at a nearby orphanage, forms a special bond with a young girl named Perrine and decides to try to raise money for the children by helping in a huge benefit.

Pennypacker, Sara. *Clementine.* Hyperion Books for Children, c2006. 133p. IL 3–6, Lexile: 790
While sorting through difficulties in her friendship with her neighbor Margaret, eight-year-old Clementine gains several unique hairstyles while also helping her father in his efforts to banish pigeons from the front of their apartment building.

Helping

Peters, Julie Anne. *Define "Normal": A Novel.* Little, Brown, 2003, c2000. 196p. IL 5–8, Lexile: 350
When she agrees to meet with Jasmine as a peer counselor at their middle school, Antonia never dreams that this girl with the black lipstick and pierced eyebrow will end up helping her deal with the serious problems she faces at home and become a good friend.

Ray, Delia. *Singing Hands.* Clarion Books, c2006. 248p. IL 5–8, Lexile: 960
In the late 1940s, twelve-year-old Gussie, a minister's daughter, learns the definition of integrity while helping with a celebration at the Alabama School for the Deaf—her punishment for misdeeds against her deaf parents and their boarders.

Young, Judy. *The Lucky Star.* Sleeping Bear Press, c2008. 40p. IL 3–6, Lexile: 780
In 1933, facing the hardships of the Great Depression, Ruth learns to follow her mother's example and count her lucky stars when she turns her disappointment over not being able to attend fourth grade into a blessing for her younger sister.

I Am Special

Books for Children of All Ages

Auch, Mary Jane. *The Easter Egg Farm.* Holiday House, c1992. 32p. IL K–3, Lexile: 340
Pauline the hen lays unusual eggs, but Mrs. Pennywort, her owner, thinks they're beautiful, and she and Pauline work together to open an Easter egg farm.

Beaumont, Karen. *I Like Myself!* Harcourt, c2004. 32p. IL K–3
In rhyming text, a child expresses her self-esteem and exults in her unique identity. Bad hair, bad breath? It is OK if you like yourself.

Bloom, Suzanne. *A Splendid Friend, Indeed.* Boyds Mills Press, 2005. 32p. IL K–3, Lexile: BR
When a studious polar bear meets an inquisitive goose, they learn to be friends. Stunning illustrations capture the moods of the two as they move towards friendship.

Carlson, Nancy L. *I Like Me!* Viking Kestrel, 1988. 32p. IL K–3, Lexile: 400
By admiring her finer points and showing that she can take care of herself and have fun even when there's no one else around, a charming pig proves the best friend you can have is yourself.

Chaconas, Dori. *Dancing with Katya.* Peachtree, c2006. 32p. IL K–3
In the late 1920s, Anna tries to help her younger sister Katya regain her strength and joy in life after being crippled by polio.

Chodos-Irvine, Margaret. *Ella Sarah Gets Dressed.* Harcourt, c2003. 32p. IL K–3, Lexile: 810
Despite the advice of others in her family, Ella Sarah persists in wearing the striking and unusual outfit of her own choosing.

Couric, Katie. *The Blue Ribbon Day.* Doubleday, c2004. 32p. IL K–3
When Carrie is disappointed not to make the school soccer team, she turns her attention to creating a science fair project.

Heide, Florence Parry. *The Day of Ahmed's Secret.* Mulberry Books, 1990. 32p. IL K–3, Lexile: 810
Ahmed rides his donkey cart throughout the city of Cairo, hurrying to finish his work so that he can return home and share his secret with his family.

Herron, Carolivia. *Nappy Hair.* Dragonfly Books, 1999. 32p. IL K–3, Lexile: 200
Various people at a backyard picnic offer their comments on a young girl's tightly curled, "nappy" hair. The story is told in the call-and-response tradition of story telling.

Hoffman, Mary. *Amazing Grace.* Dial Books for Young Readers, 1991. 26p. IL K–3, Lexile: 680
Although a classmate says that she cannot play Peter Pan in the school play because she is African American, Grace discovers that she can do anything she sets her mind to.

Lalli, Judy. *I Like Being Me: Poems for Children about Feeling Special, Appreciating Others, and Getting Along.* Free Spirit, c1997. 54p. IL K–3
This collection of poems deals with being kind, solving problems, learning from mistakes, telling the truth, dealing with feelings, being a friend, and more.

I Am Special

Lovell, Patty. *Stand Tall, Molly Lou Melon.* G. P. Putnam's, c2001. 32p. IL K–3, Lexile: 560
Even when the class bully at her new school makes fun of her, Molly remembers what her grandmother told her and she feels good about herself.

Mills, Claudia. *Ziggy's Blue-Ribbon Day.* Farrar, Straus and Giroux, 2005. 32p. IL K–3, Lexile: 560
Ziggy does not do well in the school track and field day events, but he feels much better after his classmates recognize his drawing talent.

Rahaman, Vashanti. *Read for Me, Mama.* Boyds Mills Press, 1997. 32p. IL K–3. Lexile: 540
A young boy who loves to read helps his mother on the road to literacy.

Books for Children Ages Eight to Twelve

Codell, Esme Raji. *Sahara Special.* Hyperion Paperbacks for Children, 2004, c2003. 175p. IL 3–6, Lexile: 660
Struggling with school and her feelings since her father left, Sahara gets a fresh start with a new and unique teacher who supports her writing talents and the individuality of each of her classmates.

Dowell, Frances O'Roark. *Chicken Boy.* Aladdin Paperbacks, 2007, c2005. 201p. IL 5–8, Lexile: 860
Since the death of his mother, Tobin's family and school life have been in disarray. When he starts raising chickens with his seventh-grade classmate, Henry, everything starts to fall into place.

Ehrenhaft, Daniel. *The Last Dog on Earth.* Dell Yearling, 2004, c2003. 230p. IL 5–8, Lexile: 620
Fourteen-year-old Logan Moore, lacking direction and self-esteem, develops a strong bond with Jack, a stray dog. Their relationship is threatened when a deadly disease emerges that causes canines to turn vicious before they die, and humans react to the problem in a typically irrational manner.

Hutchings, Juliana. *A Horse to Remember.* Raven Publishing, c2007. 176p. IL 5–8
Hilary's family moves from Delaware to a small town in Tennessee, where she forms a connection with a wild stallion that seems as lonely and out of place as she is, and decides to secretly train the horse to save it from the slaughterhouse.

Korman, Gordon. *Liar, Liar, Pants on Fire.* Scholastic, 1999, c1997. 86p. IL 3–6, Lexile: 460
Zoe, an imaginative third grader, thinks that she has to make things up to be interesting, until a good friend and an eagle convince her that she does not have to lie to be special.

Stevenson, Robin. *Impossible Things.* Orca Book Publishers, 2008. 177p. IL 5–8, Lexile: 530
Cassidy Silver is accustomed to being the biggest freak in the seventh grade, but things start to change when Victoria, a new girl at school, chooses to be her friend, and the confidence she gains from having a friend spills over into other areas of Cassidy's life.

Trembath, Don. *Emville Confidential.* Orca Book Publishers, 2007. 188p. IL 5–8
Baron has always dreamed of following in the footsteps of his favorite detectives. When a new client asks Baron's backyard detective agency for help, Baron believes he may finally have a chance to prove he is as tough and in control as his heroes.

I Am Special

Weeks, Sarah. *Oggie Cooder.* Scholastic, 2009, c2008. 172p. IL 3–6, Lexile: 880
  Quirky fourth grader Oggie Cooder goes from being shunned to being everyone's best friend when his uncanny ability to chew slices of cheese into the shapes of states wins him a slot on a popular television talent show. He soon learns the perils of being a celebrity—and having a neighbor girl as his manager.

Kindness

Books for Children of All Ages

Brumbeau, Jeff. *The Quiltmaker's Gift.* Scholastic Press, 2001, c2000. 48p. IL K–3, Lexile: 630
When a generous quilt maker finally agrees to make a quilt for a greedy king but only under certain conditions, she causes him to undergo a change of heart.

Crimi, Carolyn. *Don't Need Friends.* Dragonfly Books, 2001, c1999. 32p. IL K–3, Lexile: 290
After his best friend moves away, Rat rudely rebuffs the efforts of the other residents of the junkyard to be friendly, until he and a grouchy old dog decide that they need each other.

Edwards, Nancy. *Glenna's Seeds.* Child & Family Press, c2001. 24p. IL K–3
When Glenna gives away a packet of flower seeds, it sets off a chain of kind events among her neighbors.

Edwards, Pamela Duncan. *The Leprechaun's Gold.* Katherine Tegen, c2004. 32p. IL K–3, Lexile: 770
A leprechaun intervenes when a greedy young harpist sabotages a royal contest.

Henkes, Kevin. *Chrysanthemum.* Greenwillow, c1991. 32p. IL K–3, Lexile: 460
Chrysanthemum loves her name—until she starts going to school and the other children make fun of it.

Henkes, Kevin. *Lilly's Big Day.* Greenwillow Books, c2006. 32p. IL K–3, Lexile: 660
When her teacher announces that he is getting married, Lilly the mouse sets her heart on being the flower girl at his wedding.

Kirk, David. *Little Miss Spider: At Sunny Patch School.* Scholastic Press/Callaway, 2000. 33p. IL K–3, Lexile: NP
On her first day at school, Little Miss Spider worries that she cannot do what the others can, but she soon learns that she has a special quality all her own.

McBratney, Sam. *I'm Sorry.* HarperCollins, c2000. 32p. IL K–3
Two young friends have a fight that is resolved when they apologize to each other.

Meddaugh, Susan. *Martha Walks the Dog.* Houghton Mifflin, c1998. 32p. IL K–3, Lexile: 270
Martha, the talking dog, rescues the neighborhood from a noisy neighbor and his bully dog, Bob.

Murphy, Mary. *How Kind!* Candlewick Press, 2002. 26p. IL K–3
This boardbook tells a story about treating others with kindness. Acts of kindness can be infectious and may lead to more.

Peet, Bill. *The Ant and the Elephant.* Houghton Mifflin, c1972. 46p. IL K–3, Lexile: 720
Of all the animals the elephant rescues, only the tiny ant returns the favor.

Pinkney, Jerry. *The Lion & the Mouse.* Little, Brown and Co. Books for Young Readers, 2009. 34p. IL K–3
In this wordless retelling of an Aesop fable, an adventuresome mouse proves that even small creatures are capable of great deeds when he rescues the King of the Jungle.

Kindness

Polacco, Patricia. *Welcome Comfort.* Philomel Books, c1999. 32p. IL K–3, Lexile: 520
Welcome Comfort, a lonely foster child, is assured by his friend the school custodian that there is a Santa Claus, but he does not discover the truth until one wondrous and surprising Christmas Eve.

Rylant, Cynthia. *An Angel for Solomon Singer.* Orchard Books, 1992. 30p. IL K–3, Lexile: 1120
A lonely New York City resident finds companionship and good cheer at the Westway café, where dreams come true.

San Souci, Robert D. *The Talking Eggs: A Folktale from the American South.* Dial Books for Young Readers, c1989. 32p. IL K–3, Lexile: 940
In this Southern folktale, kind Blanche, following the instructions of an old witch, gains riches, while her greedy sister makes fun of the old woman and is duly rewarded.

Silverstein, Shel. *The Giving Tree.* HarperCollins Publishers, c1992. 57p. IL K–3, Lexile: 530
A young boy grows to manhood and old age while experiencing the love and generosity of a tree that gives to him without thought of return.

Steptoe, John. *The Story of Jumping Mouse: A Native American Legend.* Lothrop, Lee & Shepard Books, c1984. 40p. IL K–3, Lexile: 500
The gifts of Magic Frog and his own hopeful and unselfish spirit bring Jumping Mouse to the Far-Off Land where no mouse goes hungry.

Wallace, Nancy Elizabeth. *The Kindness Quilt.* M. Cavendish Children, c2006. 41p. IL K–3
Minna does a lot of thinking about her project to do something kind, make a picture about what she did, and share it with her classmates, but finally comes up with an idea that spreads to the whole school.

Yashima, Taro. *Crow Boy.* Viking Press, c1955. 37p. IL K–3, Lexile: 760
The story of a strange, shy little boy in a Japanese village school who is ignored by his classmates until suddenly, and almost too late, a new teacher shows them that Crow Boy has much to offer.

Books for Children Ages Eight to Twelve

Chicken Soup for the Kid's Soul 2: Read-Aloud or Read-Alone Character-Building Stories for Kids Ages 6–10. Health Communications, c2006. 234p. IL 3–6, Lexile: 790
These character-building stories, intended for children ages six to ten, cover such themes as kindness, honesty, courage, friendship, learning from experiences, and striving to succeed.

Osborne, Mary Pope. *Dark Day in the Deep Sea.* Random House, c2008. 106p. IL 3–6, Lexile: 520
Eight-year-old Jack and his seven-year-old sister, Annie, learn about the ocean, solve the mystery of its fabled sea monster, and gain compassion for their fellow creatures after joining a group of nineteenth-century explorers aboard the H.M.S. *Challenger*.

Paterson, Katherine. *The Tale of the Mandarin Ducks.* Puffin Books, 1990. 40p. IL 3–6, Lexile: 930
A pair of mandarin ducks, separated by a cruel lord who wishes to possess the drake for his colorful beauty, reward a compassionate couple who risk their lives to reunite the ducks.

Kindness

Polacco, Patricia. *An Orange for Frankie.* Philomel Books, c2004. 40p. IL 3–6, Lexile: 780
  Frankie and his eight brothers and sisters learn lessons about giving, family, and tradition during a snowy Michigan Christmas long ago.

Polacco, Patricia. *Welcome Comfort.* Philomel Books, c1999. 32p. IL K–3, Lexile: 520
  Welcome Comfort, a lonely foster child, is assured by his friend the school custodian that there is a Santa Claus, but he does not discover the truth until one wondrous and surprising Christmas Eve.

Wallace, Bill. *A Dog Called Kitty.* Aladdin Paperbacks, 2002, c1980. 153p. IL 3–6, Lexile: 710
  Ricky, who has been afraid of dogs ever since he was attacked by a rabid dog as a young child, allows compassion to overrule his fears when a starving, scruffy pup shows up at the farm.

Listening

Books for Children of All Ages

Binkow, Howard. *Howard B. Wigglebottom Learns to Listen.* Thunderbolt Publishing, c2005. 32p. IL K–3
Howard B. Wigglebottom has a great deal of difficulty listening, which gets him into a great deal of trouble.

Cook, Julia. *The Worst Day of My Life Ever!* Boys Town Press, c2011. 32p. IL K–3
Readers learn the steps that are part of the fundamental social skills of listening and following instructions. When the hero, RJ, learns to use these skills the right way, he has the best day of his life.

Dahl, Michael. *In One Ear, Out the Other.* Picture Window Books, c2011. 32p. IL K–3
Bud the monster is not a good listener, but when he almost misses a party at his own house, he finally figures out a way to solve his problem.

Davoll, Barbara. *Christopher and His Friends.* Tyndale House, c2003. 117p. IL K–3
A young mouse and his friends learn about the importance of listening to those who are wise, calming angry friends, dealing with bullies, controlling one's tongue, and encouraging one another.

Gran, Julia. *Big Bug Surprise.* Scholastic Press, 2007. 32p. IL K–3, Lexile: 610
Prunella knows so much about insects that people get bored listening to her talk, but when her classroom fills up with bees during show-and-tell, Prunella saves the day. The book includes facts about insects.

Hargreaves, Roger. *Little Miss Chatterbox.* Price Stern Sloan, 2011. 32p. IL K–3
Little Miss Chatterbox loses a series of jobs because of her tendency to talk on and on when she should be listening to her customers' requests, until she finds just the right job for her.

Lester, Helen. *Listen, Buddy.* Houghton Mifflin, c1995. 32p. IL K–3, Lexile: 520
A lop-eared rabbit named Buddy finds himself in trouble with the Scruffy Varmint because he never listens.

Meier, Joanne D. *It's Time to Listen.* Child's World, c2009. 32p. IL K–3
Herbie Bear loves library time, but must sit very quietly to hear his favorite stories.

Neasi, Barbara J. *Listen to Me.* Children's Press, c2001. 31p. IL K–3, Lexile: 290
When Mom and Dad are too busy to talk and to listen, a boy and his grandmother enjoy conversations and spending time together.

O'Connor, Jane. *Fancy Nancy and the Delectable Cupcakes.* Harper, c2010. 25p. IL K–3, Lexile: 350
Nancy's failure to pay attention gets her into trouble when she makes cupcakes for the school bake sale.

Perkins, Al. *The Ear Book.* Beginner Books, 2007. 29p. IL K–3
A boy and his dog have fun listening to many sounds, including popcorn popping, flutes tooting, hands clapping, and fingers snapping.

Listening

Poth, Karen. *Larry Learns to Listen.* Zonderkidz, c2003. 14p. IL K–3
Larry learns a lesson about listening when his great new video game stops working because he did not heed his friends' advice to read the directions.

Willis, Jeanne. *Shhh!* Hyperion Paperbacks for Children, 2007. 25p. IL K–3
A shrew tries to share the wonderful secret to peace on Earth, but has trouble being heard.

Books for Children Ages Eight to Twelve

DiCamillo, Kate. *The Miraculous Journey of Edward Tulane.* Candlewick Press, 2006. 198p. IL 3–6, Lexile 700
Edward Tulane, a cold-hearted and proud toy rabbit, loves only himself–until he is separated from the little girl who adores him and travels across the country, acquiring new owners and listening to their hopes, dreams, and histories.

Katula, Bob. *Larryboy and the Awful Ear Wacks Attacks.* Zonderkidz, c2002. 96p. IL 3–6
Larryboy, a heroic cucumber with plunger ears, comes to the rescue when Alvin the Onion unleashes the awful ear wacks that interfere with being a good listener.

Lottridge, Celia Barker. *The Listening Tree.* Fitzhenry & Whiteside, c2011. 172p. IL 3–6
When Ellen and her mother board with Aunt Gladys in the city, Ellen finds comfort in the old tree near her window, and realizes she must overcome her fears of the outside world when she overhears a disturbing plot.

Soderberg, Erin. *Monkey See, Monkey Zoo.* Bloomsbury, 2010. 148p. IL 3–6, Lexile: 890
After listening to a young boy describe his life, Willa the monkey escapes from her zoo home and, together with some friendly chipmunks, goes in search of him in the human city.

Whelan, Gloria. *The Listeners.* Sleeping Bear Press, c2009. 40p. IL 3–6
After a day of picking cotton in late 1860, Ella May, a young slave, joins her friends Bobby and Sue at their second job of listening outside the windows of their master's house for useful information.

Manners

Books for Children of All Ages

Allard, Harry. *Miss Nelson Is Missing!* Houghton Mifflin, c1977. 32p. IL K–3, Lexile: 340
The kids in Room 207 take advantage of their teacher's good nature—until she disappears and they are faced with a vile substitute.

Candell, Arianna. *Mind Your Manners in School.* Barrons Educational Series, 2005. 35p. IL K–3 (Non-fiction)
Brief stories describe classroom friendships, the importance of silence when the teacher is giving a lesson, the friendly way for borrowing and sharing storybooks, picking up toys after playtime, and other typical school situations.

Elliott, Laura. *Hunter's Best Friend at School.* HarperCollins, c2002. 32p. IL K–3, Lexile: 610
Hunter the raccoon is not sure what he should do when his best friend Stripe starts acting up at preschool.

Gantos, Jack. *Rotten Ralph's Show and Tell.* Houghton Mifflin, c1989. 30p. IL K–3, Lexile: 610
Sarah takes her rotten cat Ralph to school for show-and-tell; he behaves terribly, as usual, and spoils everyone's show.

Henkes, Kevin. *Lilly's Purple Plastic Purse.* Greenwillow, c1996. 32p. IL K–3, Lexile: 540
Lilly loves everything about school, especially her teacher, but when he asks her to wait a while before showing the class her new purse, she does something for which she is very sorry later.

Javernick, Ellen. *What if Everybody Did That?* Marshall Cavendish Children, 2010. 32p. IL K–3
A child learns that there are consequences for thoughtless behavior, from feeding popcorn to a bear at the zoo to dropping an empty can out of a car window.

Shannon, David. *David Goes to School.* Blue Sky Press, c1999. 32p. IL K–3, Lexile: BR
David's activities in school include chewing gum, talking out of turn, and engaging in a food fight, causing his teacher to say over and over, "No, David!"

Books for Children Ages Eight to Twelve

Bell, Alison. *Zibby Payne & the Red Carpet Revolt.* Lobster Press, c2008. 94p. IL 3–6, Lexile: 790
Zibby, after being caught chewing gum at an assembly, gets stuck taking a manners course led by the class diva Amber. When Amber tries to turn the sixth-grade dance into a fancy ball, Zibby just has to revolt.

Espeland, Pamela. *Dude, That's Rude!: (Get Some Manners)* Free Spirit Publishing, c2007. 117p. IL 5–8 (Non-fiction)
This practical guide focuses on basic manners and the difference between what is appropriate and what is not.

Hirsch, Odo. *Darius Bell and the Glitter Pool.* Kane Miller, 2010, c2009. 214p. IL 3–6
The Bell family ancestors, showered with honors, gifts, and land, established a tradition of bestowing a substantial gift upon the town every twenty-five years. When Darius's father's turn comes, the

Manners

Bells do not have enough money to buy an impressive gift and are planning to donate a wheelbarrow full of vegetables—until Darius finds something glorious in the wake of an earthquake that he believes is the answer.

Holm, Jennifer L. *Boston Jane: An Adventure*. Yearling, 2010, c2001. 247p. IL 3–6
Schooled in the lessons of etiquette for young ladies of 1854, Miss Jane Peck of Philadelphia finds little use for manners during her long sea voyage to the Pacific Northwest and while living among the American traders and Chinook Indians of Washington Territory.

Kipling, Rudyard. *How the Rhinoceros Got His Skin*. Abdo Publishing, 2005, c1995. 28p. IL 3–6
This classic tale by Rudyard Kipling describes how the rhinoceros's lack of manners resulted in his baggy skin and bad temper.

Series

Winkler, Henry. *Hank Zipzer*. Grosset & Dunlap, c2003. 154p. IL 3–6
Hank Zipzer vows to do well in fourth grade, but his resolve is tested when his teacher demands he write a paper on what he did on his summer vacation, he brings home another bad report card, his sister's iguana lays eggs in his science project, and he is chosen to lead his softball team to victory in the all-important school Olympiad.

Personal Safety

Books for Children of All Ages

Gibbons, Gail. *Fire! Fire!* HarperCollins, c1984. 40p. IL K–3, Lexile: 590 (Non-fiction)
This account examines fire fighters who battle fires in the city, in the country, in the forest, and on the waterfront.

Girard, Linda Walvoord. *Who Is a Stranger and What Should I Do?* Whitman, 1985. 32p. IL K–3 (Non-fiction)
This book explains how to deal with strangers in public places, on the telephone, and in cars, emphasizing situations in which the best thing to do is run away or talk to another adult.

Joyce, Irma. *Never Talk to Strangers.* Golden Book, 2009, c1967. 26p. IL K–3
Illustrations and rhyming text teach children the rule about not speaking to strangers.

Nelson, Robin. *Staying Safe in Emergencies.* Lerner Publications, c2006. 32p. IL K–3 (Non-fiction)
This introduction to the concept of an emergency, presented in simple text with illustrations, explains what an emergency is, what to do, how to call 911, how to treat cuts, and more.

Pancella, Peggy. *Bicycle Safety.* Heinemann Library, c2005. 32p. IL K–3 (Non-fiction)
Examines bicycle safety, explains why it is important, and discusses choosing the right bike and equipment, checking equipment, wearing the right clothing and reflectors at night, and following the rules of the road.

Pancella, Peggy. *Fire Safety.* Heinemann Library, c2005. 32p. IL K–3 (Non-fiction)
Describes the rules of fire safety for young readers, looking at good and bad fires, identifying some of the things that can start fires, and explaining exactly what to do in the event of a house fire.

Pancella, Peggy. *Home Safety.* Heinemann Library, c2005. 32p. IL K–3 (Non-fiction)
Discusses principles for staying safe at home.

Pancella, Peggy. *Water Safety.* Heinemann Library, c2005. 32p. IL K–3 (Non-fiction)
An illustrated account focusing on swimming and boating safety in various environments such as pools, rivers, and oceans.

Rathmann, Peggy. *Officer Buckle and Gloria.* Putnam's, c1995. 34p. IL K–3
The children at Napville Elementary School always ignore Officer Buckle's safety tips, until a police dog named Gloria accompanies him when he gives his safety speeches.

Books for Children Ages Eight to Twelve

Anderson, Judith. *Know the Facts about Personal Safety.* Rosen Central, 2010. 48p. IL 5–8 (Non-fiction)
Explains the many threats to personal safety that children and teens face and offers suggestions on how they can stay safe in dangerous situations.

Personal Safety

Brown, Marc Tolon. *Dinosaurs, Beware!: A Safety Guide.* Little, Brown, c1982. 30p. IL 3–6 (Non-fiction)
> Approximately sixty safety tips are demonstrated by dinosaurs in situations at home, during meals, camping, in the car, and in other familiar places.

Grayson, Robert. *Managing Your Digital Footprint.* Rosen Central, 2011. 48p. IL 5–8 (Non-fiction)
> Discusses the meaning of a digital footprint, or online identity, and such topics as personal communication and privacy issues, and the social effects that electronic communication can have on the users of this technology.

Hunter, Nick. *Internet Safety.* Heinemann Library, c2012. 56p. IL 5–8 (Non-fiction)
> This discussion of issues and controversies related to Internet safety in the early twenty-first century describes the dangers and risks in using the Internet, explores the ways that criminals access information and the role of the government in protecting citizens, and provides tips and advice on staying safe and protecting your personal identity while using the Internet.

Levete, Sarah. *Keeping Safe.* Stargazer Books, 2007. 32p. IL 3–6 (Non-fiction)
> Offers advice to children on how to stay safe, answering questions about safety at home, at school, at play, and on the Internet, and explaining how to deal with strangers and what to do if there is a problem.

Pendziwol, Jean. *No Dragons for Tea: Fire Safety for Kids (and Dragons).* Kids Can Press, c1999. 32p. IL 3–6, Lexile: NP
> A little girl learns an important lesson about fire safety when her house catches fire after a dragon sneezes.

Politeness

Books for Children of All Ages

Banks, Marty Mokler. *The Splatters Learn Some Manners*. Harvest House Publishers, c2009. 32p. IL K–3

The rude and messy Splatter family receives lessons on politeness, table manners, and cleanliness when the Duchess invites them to dinner.

Cuyler, Margery. *Kindness Is Cooler, Mrs. Ruler.* Simon & Schuster Books for Young Readers, c2007. 41p. IL K–3

Mrs. Ruler guides her students in discovering ways of being kind to their family members, their community, and one another.

Gallo, Tina. *It's Nice to Be Nice!* Simon Spotlight, c2009. 24p. IL K–3

The YGG gang learns the importance of politeness when Brobee gives his friend Foofa a flower and she forgets to say "Thank you." Also, when Brobee asks his friend Muno for help without saying "Please," Plex the magic robot steps in to explain how to be nice.

McNaughton, Janet Elizabeth. *Brave Jack and the Unicorn.* Tundra Books, c2005. 32p. IL K–3

Jack, held to be inferior to his handsome and clever brothers, wins the day and the hand of a princess with his kind heart and deeds.

Meiners, Cheri J. *Be Polite and Kind.* Free Spirit Publishing, c2004. 35p. IL K–3 (Non-fiction)

Demonstrates ways of showing politeness, speaking kindly, using basic courtesies, and respecting the feelings of others. The book includes role-playing activities.

Raatma, Lucia. *Politeness.* Bridgestone Books, c2002. 24p. IL K–3 (Non-fiction)

Explains the virtue of politeness and describes ways to show politeness in the home, school, and community.

Spence, Kenlyn Foster. *Astronaut Noodle on Planet Velocity.* BelleBooks, 2005. 31p. IL K–3

Astronaut Noodle, on a mission to take pictures of the Planet Velocity, encounters people who are too busy to say hello or be kind and tries to convince them to slow down and enjoy life.

Books for Children Ages Eight to Twelve

Milne, A. A. *When We Were Very Young.* Dutton Children's Books, 2008. 99p. IL 3–6, Lexile: NP

A collection of poems reflecting the experiences of a little English boy growing up in the early part of the twentieth century.

Respect

Books for Children of All Ages

Bunting, Eve. *So Far from the Sea.* Clarion Books, c1998. 30p. IL K–3, Lexile: 590
When seven-year-old Laura and her family visit Grandfather's grave at the Manzanar War Relocation Center, the Japanese American child leaves behind a special symbol.

Cuyler, Margery. *Kindness Is Cooler, Mrs. Ruler.* Simon & Schuster Books for Young Readers, c2007. 41p. IL K–3
Mrs. Ruler guides her students in discovering ways of being kind to their family members, their community, and one another.

Fleischman, Paul. *Weslandia.* Candlewick Press, 2002, c1999. 34p. IL K–3, Lexile: 820
Wesley's garden produces a crop of huge, strange plants that provide him with clothing, shelter, food, and drink, thereby helping him create his own civilization and changing his life.

Hallinan, P. K. *Heartprints.* Ideals Children's Books, 2002, c1999. 24p. IL K–3
When the children are kind and help others, they leave heartprints along the way.

Hamilton, Martha. *The Hidden Feast: A Folktale from the American South.* August House LittleFolk, 2006. 32p. IL K–3
The barnyard animals have a good time at their neighbors' party until dinner is served, when the feast appears to be disappointing and Rooster rudely storms off before discovering a hidden treat.

Lester, Helen. *Hooway for Wodney Wat.* Houghton Mifflin, c1999. 32p. IL K–3, Lexile: 360
All of his classmates make fun of Rodney because he cannot pronounce his name, but it is Rodney's speech impediment that drives away the class bully.

Lovell, Patty. *Stand Tall, Molly Lou Melon.* G. P. Putnam's, c2001. 32p. IL K–3, Lexile: 560
Even when the class bully at her new school makes fun of her, Molly remembers what her grandmother told her and she feels good about herself.

McKinley, Cindy. *One Smile.* Illumination Arts, c2002. 33p. IL K–3
When a child smiles at a stranger, she sets off a chain of kindness that eventually comes full circle.

Mills, Andy. *Shapesville.* Gurze Books, c2003. 32p. IL K–3
A celebration focuses on the many different sizes, shapes, and colors of the people who live in Shapesville, where everyone is different and each is a star. The book includes discussion questions and a note to parents and educators.

O'Neill, Alexis. *The Recess Queen.* Scholastic Press, 2002. 32p. IL K–3, Lexile: 450
Mean Jean is the biggest bully on the school playground—until a new girl arrives and challenges Jean's status as the Recess Queen.

Pearson, Emily. *Ordinary Mary's Extraordinary Deed.* Gibbs Smith, c2002. 32p. IL K–3
A young girl's good deed is multiplied as it is passed on by those who have been touched by the kindness of others.

Respect

Raatma, Lucia. *Respect.* Cherry Lake Publishing, c2009. 24p. IL K–3 (Non-fiction)
Describes respect as a virtue and suggests ways in which children can recognize and practice being respectful.

Woodson, Jacqueline. *The Other Side.* Putnam's, c2001. 32p. IL K–3, Lexile: 300
Two girls, one white and one African American, gradually get to know each other as they sit on the fence that divides their town.

Books for Children Ages Eight to Twelve

Bianco, Margery Williams. *The Velveteen Rabbit.* Abdo Publishing, 1995. 40p. IL 3–6
By the time the velveteen rabbit is dirty, worn out, and about to be burned, he has almost given up his hope of ever finding the magic he needs to become real.

Cowley, Marjorie. *The Golden Bull.* Charlesbridge, c2008. 206p. IL 5–8, Lexile: 760
Brother and sister Jomar and Zefa must learn to respect each other's strengths and build a new relationship when they are sent from their home by their father to the city of Ut in ancient Mesopotamia, where Jomar becomes an apprentice to a master goldsmith who is embellishing a magnificent lyre to be used in the temple.

Giovanni, Nikki. *The Grasshopper's Song: An Aesop's Fable Revisited.* Candlewick Press, 2008. 50p. IL 3–6, Lexile: 660
Angry that his singing is unappreciated by the Ants who relied on his music to make their summer work easier, Jimmy Grasshopper decides to sue them for lacking respect and not acknowledging his usefulness in their lives.

Janet Mary, Grandma. *Grandpa's Fishin' Friend.* My Grandma and Me Publishers, c2006. 32p. IL 3–6
A young boy spends a sunny afternoon fishing with his grandfather. Together they develop a bond of love and respect as they search for a large-mouth bass they call Albert Einstein.

Taylor, Mildred D. *Roll of Thunder, Hear My Cry.* Puffin, 1991, c1976. 276p. IL 5–8, Lexile: 920
An African American family in Depression-era Mississippi battles the odds to hold onto their property and their self-respect.

Wallace, Bill. *Skinny-Dipping at Monster Lake.* Aladdin Paperbacks, 2004, c2003. 212p. IL 3–6, Lexile: 630
When twelve-year-old Kent helps his father in a daring underwater rescue, he wins the respect he has always craved.

Stealing

Books for Children of All Ages

Anthony, David. *Holiday Holdup.* Sigil Publishing, c2009. 128p. IL K–3
Twins Abigail and Andrew and their younger sister Zoe battle candy bandits who sneak into homes and try to steal the presents under families' Christmas trees.

Brett, Jan *Trouble with Trolls.* G. P. Putnam's Sons, c1992. 32p. IL K–3, Lexile: 580
While climbing Mt. Baldy, Treva outwits some trolls who want to steal her dog.

Brimner, Larry Dane. *The Sparkle Thing.* Children's Press, c2001. 31p. IL K–3, Lexile: 350
Gabby takes a pretty sparkle thing from the market without paying for it and must face the consequences.

Castan, Javier Saez. *The Three Hedgehogs: A Pantomime in Two Acts and a Colophon.* Douglas & McIntyre, 2004. 32p. IL K–3
A trio of hungry hedgehogs eat several apples from a farm woman's orchard, are chased down for theft, and find help in arguing against the charges from an unexpected source.

Douglas, Erin. *Get That Pest!* Green Light Readers/Harcourt, 2000. 24p. IL K–3, Lexile: 90
When a farmer and his wife discover that something is stealing the eggs laid by their ten red hens, they set up elaborate traps to catch the thief.

Geisert, Arthur. *Pigaroons.* Houghton Mifflin, 2004. 32p. IL K–3
The River Patrollers are tired of the Pigaroons always stealing things. When the thieves steal a block of ice and carve it for the annual ice festival, the River Patrollers find an ingenious way to fight back.

Hogrogian, Nonny. *One Fine Day.* Simon & Schuster Books for Young Readers, c1971. 32p. IL K–3, Lexile: 1080
After the old woman cuts off his tail when he steals her milk, the fox must go through a long series of transactions before she will sew it back on again.

Kimmel, Eric A. *Anansi and the Magic Stick.* Holiday House, c2001. 32p. IL K–3, Lexile: 170
Anansi the Spider steals Hyena's magic stick so he won't have to do the chores. When the stick's magic won't stop, however, Anansi gets more than he bargained for.

McCully, Emily Arnold. *Marvelous Mattie: How Margaret E. Knight Became an Inventor.* Farrar, Straus and Giroux, 2006. 32p. IL K–3 Lexile: 720 (Non-fiction)
Describes inventor Margaret E. Knight's childhood, explaining how her interest in mechanical innovations began, and tells the story of her invention of a paper bag maker and her legal battle for the patent after someone stole her idea.

Moffatt, Judith. *Who Stole the Cookies?* Grosset & Dunlap, c1996. 32p. IL K–3, Lexile: BR
Each in a series of animals denies taking the cookies, but the true thief turns up in a cave.

Stealing

Pinkwater, Daniel Manus. *Irving and Muktuk: Two Bad Bears.* Houghton Mifflin, c2001. 32p. IL K–3, Lexile: 820

Two muffin-loving polar bears make a yearly attempt to use stealth and subterfuge to get muffins at the Yellowtooth Blueberry Muffin Festival.

Rankin, Laura. *Ruthie and the (Not So) Teeny Tiny Lie.* Bloomsbury Children's Books, 2007. 32p. IL K–3, Lexile: 490

Ruthie loves tiny things, so when she finds a tiny camera on the playground, she is very happy. After she lies and says the camera belongs to her, however, nothing seems to go right.

Seuss, Dr. *How the Grinch Stole Christmas.* Random House, 2007. 85p. IL K–3

Dr. Seuss's classic holiday story describes a mean old creature who learns a lesson when he tries to keep Christmas from coming.

Slobodkina, Esphyr. *Caps for Sale: A Tale of a Peddler, Some Monkeys, and Their Monkey Business.* HarperCollins, 1985, c1947. 45p. IL K–3, Lexile: 480

A band of mischievous monkeys steals every one of a peddler's caps while he takes a nap under a tree.

Yolen, Jane. *Piggins.* Harcourt, c1987. 32p. IL K–3, Lexile: 450

During a dinner party, the lights go out and Mrs. Reynard's beautiful diamond necklace is stolen, but Piggins the butler quickly discovers the real thief.

Books for Children Ages Eight to Twelve

Adler, David A. *Cam Jansen: The Mystery of the Gold Coins.* Puffin Books, 1982. 57p. IL 3–6

While using her photographic memory to find her missing science fair project, Cam accidentally locates two valuable gold coins.

Freeman, Martha. *Who Stole Halloween?* Holiday House, c2005. 232p. IL 3–6, Lexile: 710

When nine-year-old Alex and his friend Yasmeen investigate the disappearance of cats in their neighborhood, they stumble onto a larger mystery involving a haunted house and a ghostly cat.

Krensky, Stephen. *The Mystery of the Stolen Bike.* Little, Brown, c1998. 59p. IL 3–6, Lexile: 440

Francine is embarrassed by her hand-me-down bike, but when it is stolen, her friends rally to find the thief.

McKissack, Pat. *Tippy Lemmey.* Aladdin Paperbacks, 2003. 59p. IL 3–6, Lexile: 380

Leandra, Paul, and Jeannie keep trying to avoid a dog named Tippy Lemmey, until they discover that the animal is not really their enemy.

O'Connor, Barbara. *How to Steal a Dog: A Novel.* Farrar, Straus and Giroux, 2007. 170p. IL 3–6, Lexile: 700

Living in the family car in their small North Carolina town after their father leaves them virtually penniless, Georgina is desperate to improve their situation and unwilling to accept her overworked

Stealing

mother's calls for patience. She persuades her younger brother to help her in an elaborate scheme to get money by stealing a dog and then claiming the reward that the owners are bound to offer.

Roy, Ron. *The Missing Mummy.* Random House, c2001. 82p. IL 3–6, Lexile: 510

Dink, Josh, and Ruth Rose help catch the thieves who have stolen the treasure from a museum's mummy exhibit.

Warner, Gertrude Chandler. *The Mystery at the Dog Show.* A. Whitman, c1993. 121p. IL 3–6, Lexile: 600

The Alden children suspect someone of trying to sabotage the local dog show. Just who is shaving the prize dogs?

Trustworthiness

Books for Children of All Ages

Andersen, H. C. *The Emperor's New Clothes*. Houghton Mifflin, c1977. 44p. IL K–3
A vain emperor is duped into parading through town without clothes by a pair of swindlers posing as tailors.

Berendes, Mary. *The Boy Who Cried Wolf*. Child's World, c2011. 24p. IL K–3
A boy tending sheep on a lonely mountainside thinks it a fine joke to cry "wolf" and watch the people come running, until one day a wolf is really there and no one answers his call.

Burton, Virginia Lee. *Mike Mulligan and His Steam Shovel*. Houghton Mifflin, 1967. 44p. IL K–3, Lexile: 820
Although Mike Mulligan's steam shovel, Mary Anne, is too old-fashioned to compete with newer models, the people of Popperville find a way to keep the pair working.

Demi. *The Empty Pot*. H. Holt, c1990. 32p. IL K–3, Lexile: 630
When Ping admits that he is the only child in China unable to grow a flower from the seeds distributed by the Emperor, he is rewarded for his honesty.

Hoban, Russell. *A Bargain for Frances*. HarperCollins, 1970. 62p. IL K–3, Lexile: 470
Thelma usually outsmarts Frances, until Frances decides to teach her a lesson about friendship.

Lionni, Leo. *Swimmy*. Knopf, c1991. 32p. IL K–3, Lexile: 640
Swimmy, a small black fish, finds a way to protect a school of small red fish from their natural enemies.

Marshall, James. *George and Martha*. Houghton Mifflin, c2000. 46p. IL K–3. Lexile: 500
Relates several episodes in the friendship of two hippopotamuses.

Monjo, F. N. *The Drinking Gourd: A Story of the Underground Railroad*. HarperCollins, 1993, c1970. 62p. IL K–3, Lexile: 370
Sent home alone for misbehaving in church, Tommy discovers that his house is a station on the Underground Railroad.

Ness, Evaline. *Sam, Bangs & Moonshine*. Holt, c1966. 40p. IL K–3
A fisherman's daughter learns to distinguish between her dream world and reality when her cat and a friend are threatened by danger.

Peet, Bill. *Cowardly Clyde*. Houghton Mifflin, c1979. 38p. IL K–3, Lexile: 730
For a war horse, Clyde is an abysmal coward. He finally decides that even if he can't be brave, then at least he can act brave.

Piper, Watty, pseud. *The Little Engine That Could*. Philomel Books in association with Grosset & Dunlap, c2005. 48p. IL K–3, Lexile: 680
Although she is not very big, the Little Blue Engine agrees to try to pull a stranded train full of toys over the mountain.

Trustworthiness

Rosenthal, Amy Krouse. *Cookies: Bite-Size Life Lessons*. HarperCollins, c2006. 33p. IL K–3, Lexile: 760 (Non-fiction)
   Defines words such as "cooperate," "patient," "proud," "modest," "respect," "compassionate," and others with sentences about cookies.

Silverstein, Shel. *The Giving Tree*. HarperCollins Publishers, c1992. 57p. IL K–3, Lexile: 530
   A young boy grows to manhood and old age while experiencing the love and generosity of a tree that gives to him without thought of return.

Small, Mary. *Being Trustworthy: A Book about Trustworthiness*. Picture Window Books, c2006. 24p. IL K–3, Lexile: 480 (Non-fiction)
   Explains that earning trust is not always easy but is worth the effort, and presents several examples of how to show one's trustworthiness to parents, friends, teachers, and others.

Soto, Gary. *Too Many Tamales*. Putnam, c1993. 32p. IL K–3, Lexile: 670
   Maria tries on her mother's wedding ring while helping make tamales for a Christmas family get-together. Panic ensues when, hours later, she realizes the ring is missing.

Yashima, Taro. *Crow Boy*. Viking Press, c1955. 37p. IL K–3, Lexile: 760
   The story of a strange, shy little boy in a Japanese village school who is ignored by his classmates until suddenly, and almost too late, a new teacher shows them that Crow Boy has much to offer.

Books for Children Ages Eight to Twelve

Citra, Becky. *Missing*. Orca Book Publishers, 2011. 179p. IL 5–8
   When Thea's father gets a job at a guest ranch in Cariboo, she earns the trust of an abused horse, solves an old mystery, and makes a new friend.

Hand, Elizabeth. *Maze of Deception*. Scholastic, c2003. 137p. IL 3–6, Lexile: 520
   Young Boba Fett forms an uneasy alliance with rival bounty hunter Aurra Sing in an attempt to find the fortune that Boba's late father has hidden on the planet of Aargau.

Hayes, Joe. *Juan Verdades, The Man Who Couldn't Tell a Lie = El Hombre Que No Sabia Mentir*. Cinco Puntos Press, 2010. 32p. IL 3–6
   A retelling, in English and Spanish, of the tale of a wealthy rancher who is so certain of the honesty of his foreman that he wagers his ranch on it.

Korman, Gordon. *The Danger*. Scholastic, c2003. 150p. IL 3–6, Lexile: 700
   Four adolescents try to raise a British ship that sank in the Caribbean in 1665 with a cargo of gold on board. However, they cannot trust anyone, not even themselves.

Kropp, Paul. *The Countess and Me*. Fitzhenry & Whiteside, c2002. 144p. IL 5–8
   When he first meets Countess von Loewen, Jordan finds himself obliging her by burying a quartz skull she claims is cursed. She is not your typical neighbor, but soon she employs him as her gardener and believes in him as no one ever has. Jordan must now confront his own self-worth and value.

Trustworthiness

Levinson, Marilyn. *No Boys Allowed!* Scholastic, 2005, c1993. 137p. IL 5–8, Lexile: 750
After her father leaves the family to marry a younger woman, eleven-year-old Cassie Landauer feels she can't trust any male—including her best friend—until her great-uncle helps her put the changes in her life in perspective.

Moss, Marissa. *Amelia's Science Fair Disaster.* Simon & Schuster Books for Young Readers, c2008. IL 3–6
Seventh grader Amelia hopes she will be able to work with her best friend Page on the group science fair project. When she is actually paired with Felix and Sadie, Amelia fears that she will be unable to trust them with completing the project.

Oldfield, Jenny. *Secret Whispers.* Hodder Children's Books, 2007. 142p. IL 3–6
Krista enlists the help of Lee Harris, a boy with the ability to communicate with horses, to help her earn the trust of Sugar, a lonely, neglected pony that has just arrived at the stables.

Smith, Roland. *The White House.* Sleeping Bear Press, c2010. 256p. IL 5–8, Lexile: 670
Q and Angela attempt to learn the truth about the supposed death of Angela's real mother, who used to be a Secret Service agent, while trying to figure out who they can trust.

Taylor, Theodore. *The Trouble with Tuck.* Dell Yearling, 2000, c1981. 107p. IL 3–6, Lexile: 880
A young girl trains her blind dog to follow and trust a seeing-eye companion dog.

Tripp, Valerie. *Josefina Saves the Day: A Summer Story.* Pleasant Co., c2000. 77p. IL 3–6, Lexile: 690
In 1825, when Josefina trusts a trader in Santa Fe with an important deal, she makes a surprising discovery about this young American, who leaves town without paying her.

Webb, Holly. *Dogmagic.* Scholastic, 2009, c2008. 129p. IL 3–6, Lexile: 730
Eleven-year-old Lottie and her familiar, Sofie the dachshund, wonder whether she can trust her new friend Ruby with the secret of her uncle's magical pet shop.

Part 2

Literary Elements

Alliteration in Picture Books

Atwood, Margaret Eleanor. *Bashful Bob and Doleful Dorinda.* Bloomsbury Children's Books, 2006. 31p. IL K–3, Lexile: 960

A story told mainly with words that begin with the letters "b" and "d" in which bashful Bob, abandoned and raised by dogs, meets doleful Dorinda, who deals with dirty dishes, and the two become friends and eventually heroes.

Atwood, Margaret Eleanor. *Princess Prunella and the Purple Peanut.* Workman Publishing, c1995. 32p. IL K–3, Lexile: 530

Prunella, a proud, prissy princess, plans to marry a pinheaded prince who will pamper her—until a wise old woman's spell puts a purple peanut on the princess's pretty nose.

Base, Graeme. *Animalia.* H. N. Abrams, 1986. 32p. IL K–3, Lexile: 860

An alphabet book with fantastic and detailed pictures, bearing such labels as "Lazy lions lounging in the local library."

Bayer, Jane. *A My Name Is Alice.* Dial Books for Young Readers, 1984. 30p IL K–3, Lexile: 370

The well-known jump rope ditty, which is built on letters of the alphabet, is illustrated with animals from all over the world.

Buzzeo, Toni. *Dawdle Duckling.* Puffin Books, 2003. 32p. IL K–3, Lexile: 460

Mama Duck tries to keep Dawdle Duckling together with his siblings, but he wants to dawdle and dream, preen and play, splash and spin.

Crimi, Carolyn. *Henry & the Buccaneer Bunnies.* Candlewick Press, 2005. 34p. IL K–3, Lexile: 910

Captain Barnacle Black Ear, baddest of the Buccaneer Bunnies, is ashamed of his book-loving son, Henry—until the day a great storm approaches.

Edwards, Pamela Duncan. *Clara Caterpillar.* HarperCollins, c2001. 33p. IL K–3, Lexile: 660

By camouflaging herself, Clara Caterpillar, who becomes a cream-colored butterfly, courageously saves Catisha, the crimson-colored butterfly, from a hungry crow.

Edwards, Pamela Duncan. *Dinorella: A Prehistoric Fairy Tale.* Hyperion Books for Children, c1997. 32p. IL K–3, Lexile: 530

In this story, loosely based on that of Cinderella but featuring dinosaurs, the Duke falls in love with Dinorella when she rescues him from the dreaded deinonychus at the Dinosaur Dance.

Edwards, Pamela Duncan. *Four Famished Foxes and Fosdyke.* HarperCollins, c1995. 32p. IL K–3, Lexile: 570

An alliterative tale about four fox kits who go hunting for meat in the barnyard, while their gourmet brother fixes a vegetarian feast.

Edwards, Pamela Duncan. *Some Smug Slug.* HarperCollins, c1996. 32p. IL K–3, Lexile: 620

A smug slug that will not listen to the animals around it comes to an unexpected end.

Fox, Mem. *Feathers and Fools.* Harcourt, c1989. 34p. IL K–3, Lexile: 960

A modern fable about some peacocks and swans who allow the fear of their differences to become so great that they end up destroying each other.

Alliteration in Picture Books

Gerstein, Mordicai. *The Absolutely Awful Alphabet.* Harcourt, c1999. 32p. IL K–3, Lexile: 690
An illustrated alphabet book for young readers that features outrageous characters in the shape of each letter.

Palatini, Margie. *The Web Files.* Hyperion Books for Children, c2001. 32p. IL K–3, Lexile: 220
Ducktective Web and his partner try to quack the case of the pilfered peck of perfectly picked pickled peppers. This is a take off on the Dragnet TV show and adults will enjoy the humor as much as children.

Seeger, Laura Vaccaro. *Walter Was Worried.* Roaring Brook Press, c2005. 34p. IL K–3, Lexile: 210
Children's faces, depicted with letters of the alphabet, react to the onset of a storm and its aftermath in this picture book, accompanied by simple alliterative text.

Sendak, Maurice. *Alligators All Around: An Alphabet.* Harper & Row, c1962. 32p. IL K–3, Lexile: NP
The letters of the alphabet are introduced by alligators engaged in a variety of activities.

Shaw, Nancy. *Sheep on a Ship.* Houghton Mifflin, 1989. 32p. IL K–3, Lexile: 160
Sheep on a deep-sea voyage run into trouble when it storms; they are glad to come paddling into port.

Steig, William. *Wizzil.* Farrar, Straus and Giroux, 2000. 32p, IL K–3, Lexile: 690
A bored witch causes trouble when she decides to take revenge on an old man, but her mischief leads to a happy ending.

Stevens, Janet. *The Great Fuzz Frenzy.* Harcourt, c2005. 48p. IL K–3, Lexile: 420
When a tennis ball lands in a prairie dog town, the residents find that their newfound frenzy for fuzz creates a fiasco.

Van Allsburg, Chris. *The Alphabet Theatre Proudly Presents "The Z Was Zapped": A Play in Twenty-Six Acts.* Houghton Mifflin, c1987. 56p. IL K–3, Lexile: BR
Depicts how A was in an avalanche, B was badly bitten, C was cut to ribbons, and the other letters of the alphabet suffered similar mishaps.

Allegories

Books for Children of All Ages

Berger, Barbara. *Grandfather Twilight.* Philomel Books, c1984. 28p. IL K–3
At the day's end, Grandfather Twilight walks in the forest to perform his evening task, bringing the miracle of night to the world.

Bunting, Eve. *Riding the Tiger.* Clarion Books, c2001. 32p. IL K–3
Ten-year-old Danny is bored and lonely when he hops on the back of the exciting and somewhat scary tiger that offers him a ride. He soon discovers that it's easier to get on the tiger than it is to get off.

Bunting, Eve. *Terrible Things: An Allegory of the Holocaust.* Jewish Publication Society, c1989. 32p. IL K–3
In this allegory, the author's reaction to the Holocaust, the animals of the forest are carried away, one type after another, by the Terrible Things. They do not realize that if they would all stick together and not look the other way, such terrible things might not happen.

Kellogg, Steven. *The Island of the Skog.* Dial Books for Young Readers, c1973. 32p. IL K–3, Lexile: 530
To escape the dangers of urban life, Jenny and her friends sail away to an island, only to be faced with a new problem—its single inhabitant, the Skog.

Lucado, Max. *Because I Love You.* Crossway Books, c1999. 31p. IL K–3, Lexile: 370
Shaddai, a wise and loving man, builds a wonderful village for his children. When one of them chooses to go out into the dangerous wilderness, however, Shaddai does not abandon him.

Spinelli, Eileen. *Coming through the Blizzard: A Christmas Story.* Simon & Schuster Books for Young Readers, c1999. 26p. IL K–3
With a blizzard raging, a minister wonders who will come for Christmas services. He learns that Christmas comes to a small church in unexpected ways.

Van Allsburg, Chris. *The Stranger.* Houghton Mifflin, c1986. 31p. IL K–3, Lexile: 640
The enigmatic origins of the stranger whom Farmer Bailey hits with his truck and brings home to recuperate seem to have a mysterious relation to the changing season.

Wagner, Jenny. *John Brown, Rose and the Midnight Cat.* Puffin, 1977. 32p. IL K–3, Lexile: 420
Rose's dog feels he can look after her without any help from a cat, but Rose has different ideas.

Books for Children Ages Eight to Twelve

Achebe, Chinua. *How the Leopard Got His Claws.* Candlewick Press, 2011. 40p. IL 3–6
A fable explaining how the leopard got his claws and teeth and why he rules the forest with terror.

Crowther, Peter. *Dr. Jekyll and Mr. Hyde.* Skyview Books, 2009. 64p. IL 5–8
A retelling of the story of a doctor who is transformed into a murderous madman when he takes a secret drug of his own creation.

Allegories

Macaulay, David. *Baaa.* Houghton Mifflin, 1985. 61p. IL 3–6, Lexile: 560
After the last person has gone from the earth, sheep take over the world but make the same mistakes as humans. Eventually they, too, disappear.

Meade, Starr. *Keeping Holiday.* Crossway Books, 2008. 192p. IL 5–8
Each year Dylan's family visits Holiday, and this time his determination to bring home the feelings and experiences of that special place leads Dylan and his cousin Clare on a journey through such places as the Forest of Life and Winterland as they seek the Founder and the true Holiday.

Needle, Jan. *Moby-Dick, or, The Whale.* Candlewick Press, 2009, c2006. 182p. IL 5–8
An abridged and illustrated version of Herman Melville's classic that tells the story of Captain Ahab and his obsession with the capture and killing of the great white whale that mutilated him, Moby Dick.

Van Allsburg, Chris. *The Wretched Stone.* Houghton Mifflin, c1991. 31p. IL 5–8, Lexile: 580
A strange glowing stone picked up on a sea voyage captivates a ship's crew and has a terrible transforming effect on them.

Analogies

Books for Children of All Ages

Brisson, Pat. *Beach Is to Fun: A Book of Relationships*. Holt, 2004. 34p. IL K–3, Lexile: 120
A day at the beach is the occasion for this rhyming look at the relationships between things. "Sea is to salty as candy is to sweet. / Hat is to head as sandals are to feet."

Jonas, Ann. *The Trek*. Mulberry Books, 1985. 32p. IL K–3, Lexile: 250
The city streets become a jungle, then a desert, as a child forges her way to school, observing and avoiding all the wild animals posing as trees, chimneys, fences, and even fruit.

Lionni, Leo. *Matthew's Dream*. Knopf, 1991. 32p. IL K–3, Lexile: 560
A visit to an art museum inspires a young mouse to become a painter. Matthew transforms his small room into a museum to house his "mouseterpieces."

Lionni, Leo. *Swimmy*. Knopf, c1991. 32p. IL K–3, Lexile: 640
Swimmy, a small black fish, finds a way to protect a school of small red fish from their natural enemies.

Steig, William. *Rotten Island*. D. R. Godine, 1969. 32p. IL K–3, Lexile: 790
Rotten Island has always been a paradise for nasty creatures, until one awful day a beautiful flower begins to grow, threatening to spoil the island forever.

Wisniewski, David. *Golem*. Clarion Books, c1996. 32p. IL K–3, Lexile: 690
A saintly rabbi miraculously brings to life a clay giant, who helps him watch over the Jews of sixteenth-century Prague.

Wisniewski, David. *Tough Cookie*. Lothrop, Lee & Shepard Books, c1999. 28p. IL 3–6, Lexile: 90
When his friend Chips is snatched and chewed, Tough Cookie sets out to stop Fingers. In this tale told in the form of an old Bogart film, Tough Cookie is decked out in a yellow trench coat and fedora.

Yolen, Jane. *Welcome to the Green House*. Putnam & Grosset, 1997, c1993. 32p IL K–3, Lexile: 770
Describes the tropical rainforest and the life found there. The rainforest is shown as being filled with relentless noise, the movement of the animals, and amazing plant life.

Cause and Effect

Books for Children of All Ages

Aardema, Verna. *Bringing the Rain to Kapiti Plain: A Nandi Tale.* Dial Books for Young Readers, c1981. 32p. IL K–3, Lexile: NP
A cumulative rhyme relating how Ki-pat brought rain to the drought-stricken Kapiti Plain.

Aardema, Verna. *Why Mosquitoes Buzz in People's Ears: A West African Tale.* Dial Books for Young Readers, c1975. 32p. IL K–3, Lexile: 770
This tale reveals the meaning of the mosquito's buzz.

Brown, Margaret Wise. *The Runaway Bunny.* HarperCollins, 1942. 38p. IL K–3, Lexile: 600
A little rabbit who wants to run away tells his mother how he will escape, but she is always right behind him.

Carle, Eric. *The Grouchy Ladybug.* HarperCollins, 1977. 42p. IL K–3. Lexile: 560
A grouchy ladybug who is looking for a fight challenges everyone she meets, regardless of their size or strength.

Carle, Eric. *The Very Hungry Caterpillar.* Philomel Books, c1987. 18p. IL K–3, Lexile: 460
Follows the progress of a hungry little caterpillar as he eats his way through a varied and very large quantity of food until, full at last, he forms a cocoon around himself and goes to sleep. Die-cut pages illustrate what the caterpillar ate on successive days.

Christelow, Eileen. *Five Little Monkeys Jumping on the Bed.* Clarion, c1989. 32p. IL K–3, Lexile: 310
In this counting book, one by one, the little monkeys jump on the bed, only to fall off and bump their heads.

Giff, Patricia Reilly. *Today Was a Terrible Day.* Puffin Books, 1980. 25p. IL K–3, Lexile: 460
The story follows the humorous mishaps of a second grader who is learning to read.

Hogrogian, Nonny. *One Fine Day.* Simon & Schuster Books for Young Readers, c1971. 32p. IL K–3, Lexile: 1080
After the old woman cuts off his tail when he steals her milk, the fox must go through a long series of transactions before she will sew it back on again.

Hutchins, Pat. *Rosie's Walk.* Simon & Schuster, c1968. 32p. IL K–3, Lexile: NP
Although unaware that a fox is after her as she takes a walk around the farmyard, Rosie the hen still manages to lead him into one accident after another.

Keats, Ezra Jack. *The Snowy Day.* Viking Press, 1962. 32p. IL K–3, Lexile: 500
This story follows the adventures of a little boy in the city on a very snowy day.

Kellogg, Steven. *Chicken Little.* HarperCollins, c1985. 32p. IL K–3, Lexile: 690
Chicken Little and his feathered friends, alarmed that the sky seems to be falling, are easy prey for hungry Foxy Loxy, who poses as a police officer in hopes of tricking the birds into his truck.

Noble, Trinka Hakes. *The Day Jimmy's Boa Ate the Wash.* Dial Press, c1980. 32p. IL K–3. Lexile: 540
Jimmy's boa constrictor wreaks havoc on the class trip to a farm.

Cause and Effect

Numeroff, Laura Joffe. *If You Give a Moose a Muffin.* Laura Geringer Book, c1991. 32p. IL K–3, Lexile: 590
Shows the chaos that can ensue if one gives a moose a muffin and starts him on a cycle of urgent requests.

Numeroff, Laura Joffe. *If You Give a Mouse a Cookie.* Laura Geringer Books, c1985. 32p. IL K–3, Lexile: 660
Relates the cycle of requests a mouse is likely to make after you give him a cookie, taking the reader through a young child's day.

Numeroff, Laura Joffe. *If You Give a Pig a Pancake.* Laura Geringer Book, c1998. 32p. IL K–3, Lexile: 570
Shows the chaos that can happen in the house when you give a pig a pancake.

Peet, Bill. *Big Bad Bruce.* Houghton Mifflin, c1977. 38p. IL K–3, Lexile: 890
Bruce, a bear bully, never picks on anyone his own size—until he is diminished in more ways than one by a small but very independent witch.

Peet, Bill. *Pamela Camel.* Houghton Mifflin, c1984. 30p. IL K–3, Lexile: 1070
A tired and dejected circus camel finds long-sought-after recognition along a railroad track.

Steig, William. *Sylvester and the Magic Pebble.* Simon and Schuster Books for Young Readers, 1969. 36p. IL K–3, Lexile: 700
Sylvester the donkey finds a magic pebble that grants his every wish. In a moment of fright, he wishes he were a rock, and then cannot hold the pebble to wish himself back to normal again.

Viorst, Judith. *Alexander and the Terrible, Horrible, No Good, Very Bad Day.* Atheneum, c1972. 32p. IL K–3, Lexile: 970
On a day when everything goes wrong for him, Alexander is consoled by the thought that other people have bad days, too.

Wood, Audrey. *The Napping House.* Harcourt, c1984. 32p. IL K–3, Lexile: NP
In this cumulative tale, a wakeful flea atop a number of sleeping creatures causes a commotion, with just one bite.

Books for Children Ages Eight to Twelve

Cleary, Beverly. *Muggie Maggie.* Morrow Junior Books, c1990. 70p. IL 3–6, Lexile: 730
Maggie resists learning cursive writing in the third grade, until she discovers that knowing how to read and write cursive promises to open up an entirely new world of knowledge for her.

DePaola, Tomie. *The Legend of the Bluebonnet: An Old Tale of Texas.* Putnam, 1983. 30p. IL 3–6, Lexile: 740
A retelling of the Comanche Indian legend of how a little girl's sacrifice brought the flower called the bluebonnet to Texas.

Smith, Robert Kimmel. *Chocolate Fever.* Puffin Books, 2006, c1972. 93p. IL 3–6, Lexile: 680
After eating too much chocolate, Henry breaks out in brown bumps that help him foil some hijackers and teach him a valuable lesson about self-indulgence.

Chain Reaction

Books for Children of All Ages

Cuyler, Margery. *That's Good! That's Bad!* Henry Holt, 1991. 32p. IL K–3, Lexile: 370
A little boy has a series of adventures and misadventures with a bunch of wild animals. He soon learns which are good, and which are not so good.

Kimmel, Eric A. *Easy Work!: An Old Tale.* Holiday House, c1998. 32p. IL K–3, Lexile: 530
Thinking his work in the fields is harder than his wife's work in the house, Mr. McTeague trades places with her for one day.

Love, Ann. *The Prince Who Wrote a Letter.* Childs Play, 1992. 32p. IL K–3, Lexile: 550
Idle gossip in the castle of King Clifford starts a rumor that almost causes a war with the next kingdom.

Numeroff, Laura Joffe. *If You Give a Mouse a Cookie.* Laura Geringer Books, 2000, c1985. 32p. IL K–3, Lexile: 660
Relates the cycle of requests a mouse is likely to make after you give him a cookie, taking the reader through a young child's day.

Shannon, David. *The Rain Came Down.* Blue Sky Press, c2000. 32p. IL K–3, Lexile: 370
An unexpected rain shower causes quarreling among the members of a small community. The rain makes everyone in town a bit cranky.

Books for Children Ages Eight to Twelve

Ferreiro-Esteban, Carmen. *Two Moon Princess.* Tanglewood, 2007. 323p. IL 5–8, Lexile: 810
Andrea, a reluctant, tomboyish princess from the Kingdom of Zeltia—a world resembling medieval Spain—is transported from a forbidden cave into modern California. When she accidentally returns to her home with the wrong person, it sets off a chain reaction that threatens her family and their kingdom.

Parker, Laurie. *The Turtle Saver.* Quail Ridge Press, c2002. 40p. IL 3–6
A story told in rhyming verse, accompanied by color illustrations, shows how one act of kindness—a man stopping his truck to move a turtle out of the road—can start a chain reaction of good-heartedness.

Rice, David L. *Because Brian Hugged His Mother.* Dawn Publications, c1999. 32p. IL 3–6, Lexile: 710
When Brian hugs and kisses his mother one morning, the act starts a chain reaction of kindness and consideration that spreads throughout the town and eventually comes back to him.

Circular

Books for Children of All Ages

Arnold, Tedd. *No Jumping on the Bed!* Puffin Books, 1987. 32p. IL K–3, Lexile: 850
  Walter lives near the top floor of a tall apartment building, where one night his habit of jumping on his bed leads to a tumultuous fall through floor after floor, collecting occupants all the way down.

Brett, Jan. *The Umbrella.* G. P. Putnam's Sons, c2004. 32p. IL K–3, Lexile: 680
  Carlos goes into the cloud forest to look for animals, but he manages to miss seeing them, even though they have an adventure with his umbrella.

Brown, Marcia. *Once a Mouse—: A Fable Cut in Wood.* Atheneum Books for Young Readers, c1961. 32p. IL K–3, Lexile: 530
  As it changes from mouse, to cat, to dog, to tiger, a hermit's pet also becomes increasingly vain.

Carle, Eric. *The Tiny Seed.* Simon & Schuster Books for Young Readers, c1987. 32p. IL K–3, Lexile: 400 (Non-fiction)
  A simple description of a flowering plant's life cycle through the seasons.

Carmi, Giora. *A Circle of Friends.* Star Bright Books, c2003. 32p. IL K–3
  When a boy anonymously shares his snack with a homeless man, he begins a cycle of good will.

Connor, Leslie. *Miss Bridie Chose a Shovel.* Houghton Mifflin, c2004. 32p. IL K–3, Lexile: 1170
  When Miss Bridie emigrates to America in 1856, she chooses to bring a shovel along with her, which proves to be a useful tool throughout her life.

Cooney, Barbara. *Miss Rumphius.* Viking Press, 1982. 32p. IL K–3, Lexile: 680
  After making her girlhood dreams of world travel and living by the sea come true, a retired librarian follows her grandfather's old advice of doing something to make the world more beautiful, and then passes that wisdom on to her grandniece.

Egielski, Richard. *Buz.* Laura Geringer Books, c1995. 32p. IL K–3, Lexile: 380
  When a little boy swallows a bug along with his cereal, pandemonium breaks out as the bug searches for an escape, the boy searches for an antidote, and two Keystone Cop pills search for the bug.

Fleming, Denise. *Time to Sleep.* Holt, 1997. 32p. IL K–3, Lexile: 310
  When Bear notices that winter has nearly arrived, he hurries to tell Snail, after which each animal tells another, until finally the now-sleeping Bear is awakened in his den with the news.

Grifalconi, Ann. *The Village of Round and Square Houses.* Little, Brown, c1986. 32p. IL K–3, Lexile: 850
  A grandmother explains to her listeners why in their village on the side of a volcano the men live in square houses and the women live in round ones.

Hoberman, Mary Ann. *A House Is a House for Me.* Puffin Books, 2007. 48p. IL K–3
  Lists in rhyme the "houses" of various things, such as a garage for a car, a glove for a hand, and a pocket for pennies.

Circular

Hogrogian, Nonny. *One Fine Day.* Simon & Schuster Books for Young Readers, c1971. 32p. IL K–3, Lexile: 1080

> After the old woman cuts off his tail when he steals her milk, the fox must go through a long series of transactions before she will sew it back on again.

Horning, Sandra. *The Giant Hug.* A. A. Knopf, c2005. 34p. IL K–3, Lexile: 830

> When Owen sends a real hug to his grandmother for her birthday, he inadvertently brings cheer to the postal workers as they pass the hug along.

Jonas, Ann. *Round Trip.* Greenwillow Books, c1983. 32p. IL K–3, Lexile: 330

> Black-and-white illustrations and text record the sights on a day trip to the city and back home again to the country. The trip to the city is read from front to back and the return trip, from back to front, upside down.

Lester, Helen. *It Wasn't My Fault.* Houghton Mifflin, 1985. 30p. IL K–3, Lexile: 420

> When accidents happen to Murdley Gurdson, they are usually his own fault. When a bird lays an egg on Murdley's head one day, however, he tries hard to find someone else to blame.

Macaulay, David. *Black and White.* Houghton Mifflin, 1990. 32p. IL 3–6, Lexile: 610

> Four brief "stories" about parents, trains, and cows—or is it really all one story? The author recommends careful inspection of words and pictures to both minimize and enhance confusion.

Martin, Bill. *Chicka Chicka Boom Boom.* Simon & Schuster Books for Young Readers, c1989. 34p. IL K–3, Lexile: 530

> An alphabet rhyme/chant that relates what happens when the entire alphabet tries to climb a coconut tree.

Munsch, Robert N. *50 Below Zero.* Annick Press, c1986. 22p. IL K–3, Lexile: 290

> Jason is forced to take matters into his own hands when his father's sleepwalking becomes ridiculous.

Munsch, Robert N. *Love You Forever.* Firefly, c1987. 32p. IL K–3, Lexile: 780

> Describes the relationship of a mother and child as the child grows into a man and has a baby of his own.

Numeroff, Laura Joffe. *If You Give a Moose a Muffin.* Laura Geringer Book, c1991. 32p. IL K–3, Lexile: 590

> Shows the chaos that can ensue if one gives a moose a muffin and starts him on a cycle of urgent requests.

Numeroff, Laura Joffe. *If You Give a Mouse a Cookie.* Laura Geringer Books, 1985. 32p. IL K–3, Lexile: 660

> Relates the cycle of requests a mouse is likely to make after you give him a cookie, taking the reader through a young child's day.

Numeroff, Laura Joffe. *If You Give a Pig a Pancake.* Laura Geringer Book, c1998. 32p. IL K–3, Lexile: 570

> Shows the chaos that can happen in the house when you give a pig a pancake.

Circular

Polacco, Patricia. *Welcome Comfort.* Philomel Books, c1999. 32p. IL K–3, Lexile: 520

Welcome Comfort, a lonely foster child, is assured by his friend the school custodian that there is a Santa Claus, but he does not discover the truth until one wondrous and surprising Christmas Eve.

Priceman, Marjorie. *How to Make an Apple Pie and See the World.* Knopf, 1996, c1994. 32p. IL K–3, Lexile: 590

Because the market is closed, the reader is led around the world to gather the ingredients for making an apple pie. The book includes a recipe.

Provensen, Alice. *A Day in the Life of Murphy.* Simon & Schuster Books for Young Readers, c2003. 32p. IL K–3, Lexile: 40

Murphy, a farm terrier, describes a day in his life as he gets fed in the kitchen, hunts mice, goes to the veterinarian, returns to the house for dinner, investigates a noise outside, and retires to the barn for sleep.

Silverman, Erica. *Big Pumpkin.* Aladdin Paperbacks, 1992. 32p. IL K–3, Lexile: 350

A witch trying to pick a big pumpkin on Halloween discovers the value of cooperation when she gets help from a series of monsters.

Van Allsburg, Chris. *Jumanji.* Houghton Mifflin, c1981. 31p. IL K–3, Lexile: 620

Left on their own for an afternoon, two bored and restless children find more excitement than they bargained for in a mysterious and mystical jungle adventure board game.

Ward, Jennifer. *The Seed and the Giant Saguaro.* Rising Moon, c2003. 32p. IL K–3, Lexile: NP

A packrat, carrying fruit from the giant saguaro, is chased by various desert animals and inadvertently helps spread the cactus's seed. The book includes information on saguaros.

Wheeler, Lisa. *Bubble Gum, Bubble Gum.* Little, Brown, c2004. 32p. IL K–3, Lexile: NP

After a variety of animals get stuck, one by one, in bubble gum melting in the road, they must survive encounters with a big blue truck and a burly black bear.

Wiesner, David. *Flotsam.* Clarion Books, c2006. 40p. IL K–3, Lexile: NP

In this colorful picture book, a young, science-minded boy goes to the beach to collect and examine anything floating that has been washed ashore and discovers an underwater camera that contains a collection of unusual pictures.

Willems, Mo. *Don't Let the Pigeon Drive the Bus!* Hyperion Books for Children, c2003. 34p. IL K–3, Lexile: 120

A pigeon that longs to drive a bus sees a chance to make its dream come true when the bus driver takes a short break.

Wood, Audrey. *The Napping House.* Harcourt, c1984. 32p. IL K–3, Lexile: NP

In this cumulative tale, a wakeful flea atop a number of sleeping creatures causes a commotion, with just one bite.

Comparing and Contrasting Characters

Books for Children of All Ages

Becker, Bonny. *A Visitor for Bear.* Candlewick Press, 2008. 56p. IL K–3, Lexile: 430
Bear's efforts to keep visitors out of his house are undermined by a very persistent mouse.

DePaola, Tomie. *Nana Upstairs & Nana Downstairs.* Puffin Books, c1973. 32p. IL K–3, Lexile: 530
Four-year-old Tommy enjoys his relationship with both his grandmother and great-grandmother, but eventually learns to face their inevitable deaths.

Dyer, Sarah. *Clementine and Mungo.* Bloomsbury Children's Books, 2004. 27p. IL K–3
Clementine gives creative answers to the many questions that her younger brother Mungo asks.

Henkes, Kevin. *Chester's Way.* Greenwillow Books, c1988. 32p. IL K–3, Lexile: 570
Chester and Wilson share the same exact way of doing things, until Lilly moves into the neighborhood and shows them that new ways can be just as good.

Henkes, Kevin. *Sheila Rae, the Brave.* Greenwillow Books, c1987. 32p. IL K–3, Lexile: 440
When brave Sheila Rae, who usually looks out for her sister Louise, becomes lost and scared one day, Louise comes to the rescue.

Polacco, Patricia. *Pink and Say.* Philomel Books, c1994. 48p. IL K–3, Lexile: 590
Chronicles the friendship of Pink, a fifteen-year-old African American Union soldier, and Say, his poor white comrade, as one nurses the other back to health from a battle wound and the two of them are imprisoned at the Andersonville Civil War prison. Based on a true story.

Rosoff, Meg. *Jumpy Jack & Googily.* Holt, 2008. 32p. IL K–3
Jumpy Jack the snail is terrified that there are monsters around every corner despite the reassurances of his best friend, Googily.

Seuss, Dr. *Horton Hatches the Egg.* Random House, c1968. 55p. IL K–3, Lexile: 460
A lazy bird hatching an egg wants a vacation, so she asks Horton, the elephant, to sit on her egg—which he does through all sorts of hazards, until he is rewarded for doing what he said he would.

Stanley, Diane. *Saving Sweetness.* Puffin, 1996. 32p. IL K–3, Lexile: 660
The sheriff of a dusty western town rescues Sweetness, an unusually resourceful orphan, from nasty old Mrs. Sump and her terrible orphanage.

Series

Willems, Mo. *Elephant and Piggie Series.* Hyperion Books for Children, 2007– . IL K–3
These sweet and surprising stories are a much needed breath of fresh air in the early reader arena. They feature the interaction between two lovable and funny characters—an optimistic and sometimes reckless pig and a cautious, pessimistic elephant. Each book has been vetted by an early learning specialist.

Comparing and Contrasting Characters

Books for Children Ages Eight to Twelve

Clifford, Eth. *Help! I'm a Prisoner in the Library.* Houghton Mifflin, c1979. 105p. IL 3–6, Lexile: 630
Two girls spend an adventurous night trapped inside the public library during a terrible blizzard.

Grimes, Nikki. *Dark Sons*. Zondervan, 2010. 190p. IL 5–8
Alternating poems compare and contrast the conflicted feelings of Ishmael, son of the Biblical patriarch Abraham, and Sam, a teenager in New York City, as they try to come to terms with being abandoned by their fathers and with the love they feel for their younger stepbrothers.

Pirotta, Saviour. *The Lonely Princess: An Indian Fairy Tale; And Also Rapunzel.* Sea-to-Sea, 2008. IL 3–6
Presents two tales to compare and contrast. In the first folktale, which comes from India, a powerful sage imprisons his beloved daughter in a floating palace after he catches a man gazing at her. In the second story, which comes from Germany, a beautiful girl with long golden hair is imprisoned in a lonely tower by a witch.

Contractions

Books for Children of All Ages

Carr, Jan. *Greedy Apostrophe: A Cautionary Tale*. Holiday House, c2007. 32p. IL K–3, Lexile: 660
   Greedy Apostrophe runs all over town inserting himself in places where he does not belong, causing great confusion.

Cleary, Brian P. *I'm and Won't, They're and Don't: What's a Contraction?* Millbrook Press, c2010. 31p. IL 3–6, Lexile: 490
   Contains illustrated rhymes that are designed to explain the concept of contractions.

Donohue, Moira Rose. *Alfie the Apostrophe*. Whitman, 2006. 32p. IL K–3, Lexile: 540
   Alfie the Apostrophe feels unsure of himself until he shows off his abilities for creating possessives and making contractions at the Punctuation Talent Show.

Shaskan, Trisha Speed. *If You Were a Contraction*. Picture Window Books, c2009. 24p. IL K–3, Lexile: 350
   Illustrated sentences about a family of pigs introduce contractions.

Descriptive Words

Books for Children of All Ages

Beck, Carolyn. *Buttercup's Lovely Day.* Orca Book, 2008. 32p. IL K–3
Buttercup the cow describes her day and everything that she loves about the life she leads, from morning until night and all that happens in between.

Heller, Ruth. *A Cache of Jewels and Other Collective Nouns.* Putnam & Grosset Group, 1987. 48p. IL K–3
Rhyming text and illustrations introduce a variety of collective nouns such as a "drift of swans" and a "clutch of eggs."

Heller, Ruth. *Fantastic! Wow! and Unreal!: A Book about Interjections and Conjunctions.* Puffin, 2000, c1998. 32p. IL K–3
Introduces and explains various interjections and conjunctions, including "awesome," "alas," and "yet."

Heller, Ruth. *Many Luscious Lollipops: A Book about Adjectives.* Putnam & Grosset Group, 1989. 44p. IL K–3, Lexile: NP
Brief text in rhyme and pictures introduce adjectives and their uses.

Heller, Ruth. *Merry-Go-Round: A Book about Nouns.* Putnam & Grosset, 1990. 46p. IL K–3, Lexile: NP
Rhyming text and illustrations present explanations of the various types of nouns and rules for their usage.

MacLachlan, Patricia. *All the Places to Love.* HarperCollins, c1994. 32p. IL K–3, Lexile: 920
A young boy describes the favorite places that he shares with his family on his grandparent's farm and in the nearby countryside.

Books for Children Ages Eight to Twelve

Barron, T. A. *The Day the Stones Walked: A Tale of Easter Island.* Philomel Books, c2007. 32p. IL 3–6, Lexile: 630
Pico does not believe the old stories that say the moai—the stone statues of his village—come alive and protect the people in times of trouble, until a great wave comes and he faces grave danger. The book includes facts about tsunamis, Easter Island, and the effects of deforestation.

Creech, Sharon. *Hate That Cat.* Joanna Cotler Books, c2008. 153p. IL 3–6, Lexile: NP
Jack is studying poetry again in school, and he continues to write poems reflecting his understanding of famous works and how they relate to his life.

Creech, Sharon. *Love That Dog.* Joanna Cotler Books, c2001. 86p. IL 3–6, Lexile: 1010
A young student, who comes to love poetry through a personal understanding of what different famous poems mean to him, surprises himself by writing his own inspired poem.

Descriptive Words

Dahl, Roald. *The BFG.* Farrar, Straus and Giroux, 1982. 219p. IL 3–6, Lexile: 720
Kidsnatched from her orphanage by a BFG (Big Friendly Giant), who spends his life blowing happy dreams to children, Sophie concocts with him a plan to save the world from nine other human-gobbling cannybull giants.

Law, Ingrid. *Savvy.* Dial Books for Young Readers, c2008. 342p. IL 5–8, Lexile: 1070
Recounts the adventures of Mibs Beaumont, whose thirteenth birthday has revealed her "savvy"— a magical power unique to each member of her family—just as her father is injured in a terrible accident.

Spinelli, Eileen. *Where I Live.* Dial Books for Young Readers, c2007. 112p. IL 3–6, Lexile: NP
In a series of poems, Diana writes about her life before and after her father loses his job and she and her family move far away to live with Grandpa Joe.

Epistolary

Books for Children of All Ages

Ada, Alma Flor. *Dear Peter Rabbit.* Aladdin Paperbacks, 1994. 32p. IL K–3, Lexile: 780
Presents letters between such fairy tale characters as Goldilocks, Baby Bear, Peter Rabbit, and the Three Pigs.

Ada, Alma Flor. *With Love, Little Red Hen.* Aladdin Paperbacks, 2001. 34p. IL K–3,
A series of letters describe the actions of Goldilocks, Peter Rabbit, the Three Pigs, Little Red Hen, and other storybook characters when Little Red Hen and her chicks become the target of the unsavory Wolf and his cousin, Fer O'Cious.

Ada, Alma Flor. *Yours Truly, Goldilocks.* Aladdin Paperbacks, 1998. 30p. IL K–3, Lexile: 810
Presents the correspondence of Goldilocks, the Three Pigs, Baby Bear, Peter Rabbit, and Little Red Riding Hood as they plan to attend a housewarming party for the pigs and avoid the evil wolves in the forest.

Ahlberg, Janet. *The Jolly Christmas Postman.* Little Brown, c1991. 32p. IL K–3, Lexile: NP
Follows the postman from door to door as he delivers Christmas cards and other surprises to familiar figures such as Red Riding Hood and Humpty Dumpty, and presents pockets holding the actual cards and other deliveries—including a puzzle—that shape the story.

Christelow, Eileen. *Letters from a Desperate Dog.* Clarion Books, c2006. 32p. IL K–3
Feeling misunderstood and unappreciated by her owner, Emma the dog asks for advice from the local canine advice columnist.

Durant, Alan. *Dear Santa Claus.* Candlewick Press, 2005. 28p. IL K–3
Holly writes a letter to Santa, and he responds and answers all her questions about his work and, ultimately, gives her a very special gift. The book includes pull-out letters and other items.

Fleming, Candace. *Boxes for Katje.* Farrar, Straus and Giroux, 2003. 36p. IL K–3, Lexile: 460
After a young Dutch girl writes to her new American friend in thanks for the care package sent after World War II, she begins to receive increasingly larger boxes.

Holabird, Katharine. *Angelina's Invitation to the Ballet.* Viking, 2003. 28p. IL K–3
Contains special envelopes, invitations, letters, notes, and a story about Angelina Ballerina, who wins two tickets to the Cindermouse Ballet.

James, Simon. *Dear Mr. Blueberry.* Aladdin Paperbacks, 1991. 27p. IL K–3, Lexile: 660
A young girl and her teacher correspond about the whale she has discovered in her pond.

Kelly, Irene. *A Small Dog's Big Life: Around the World with Owney.* Holiday House, c2005. 32p. IL K–3
Letters tell the story of Owney, a dog who became mascot of the Albany, New York, post office in 1888 and traveled around the world. The book includes historical notes.

Nolen, Jerdine. *Plantzilla.* Silver Whistle/Harcourt, c2002. 32p. IL K–3, Lexile: 460
In a series of letters, a boy, his science teacher, and his parents discuss the progress of a very unusual, sometimes frightening plant that becomes more human as the summer progresses.

Epistolary

Nolen, Jerdine. *Plantzilla Goes to Camp.* Simon & Schuster Books for Young Readers, c2006. 32p. IL K–3

> Through a series of letters, a boy, his parents, and others discuss Camp Wannaleavee, the camp bully, and Plantzilla, which has been forbidden to come with the boy to camp but misses his caretaker and arrives in time to become the camp hero.

Orloff, Karen Kaufman. *I Wanna Iguana.* Putnam, c2004. 32p. IL K–3, Lexile: 460

> Alex and his mother write notes back and forth in which Alex tries to persuade her to let him have a baby iguana for a pet.

Ruelle, Karen Gray. *Dear Tooth Fairy.* Holiday House, c2006. 32p. IL K–3

> When her tooth becomes loose, Emily excitedly writes to the Tooth Fairy and tries to help the tooth fall out.

Stevens, Janet. *Help Me, Mr. Mutt!: Expert Answers for Dogs with People Problems.* Harcourt, c2008. 50p. IL K–3, Lexile: 350

> Dogs across the United States write to Mr. Mutt, a people expert, for help with their humans.

Stewart, Sarah. *The Gardener.* Farrar, Straus and Giroux, 1997. 36p. IL K–3, Lexile: 570

> A series of letters relating what happens when, after her father loses his job, Lydia Grace goes to live with her Uncle Jim in the city but takes her love for gardening with her.

Teague, Mark. *Dear Mrs. Larue: Letters from Obedience School.* Scholastic Press, 2002. 32p. IL K–3, Lexile: 500

> Gertrude LaRue receives typewritten and paw-written letters from her dog Ike, entreating her to let him leave the Igor Brotweiler Canine Academy and come back home.

Books for Children Ages Eight to Twelve

Amato, Mary. *The Naked Mole-Rat Letters.* Holiday House, c2005. 266p. IL 3–6, Lexile: 670

> Twelve-year-old Frankie sends fabricated e-mail letters in an attempt to end her widowed father's long-distance romance with a Washington, D.C., zookeeper.

Blos, Joan W. *Letters from the Corrugated Castle: A Novel of Gold Rush California, 1850–1852.* Atheneum Books for Young Readers, c2007. 310p. IL 5–8, Lexile: 1000

> In this epistolary novel set in the 1850s, which thirteen-year-old Eldora, who was raised in Massachusetts as an orphan, moves with her guardians to San Francisco. There, she begins teaching English to two "Mexicano" children, befriends a boy who is searching for gold, and finds herself face-to-face with her influential mother.

Byars, Betsy Cromer. *The SOS File.* Henry Holt, 2004. 71p. IL 3–6, Lexile: 600

> The students in Mr. Magro's class submit stories for the SOS file about their biggest emergencies, and then they read them aloud for extra credit.

Epistolary

Holm, Jennifer L. *Middle School Is Worse Than Meatloaf: A Year Told through Stuff.* Atheneum Books for Young Readers, c2007. IL 3–6, Lexile: NP

> Ginny makes a to-do list for her seventh-grade year, which includes landing a role in the school play, trying to make friends, ignoring her horoscope, and going to see her grandpa Joe in Florida. Unfortunately, she always seems to come up short in accomplishing any of her goals.

Klise, Kate. *Regarding the Fountain: A Tale, in Letters, of Liars and Leaks.* Avon Books, c1998. 138p. IL 5–8, Lexile: 830

> When the principal asks a fifth grader to write a letter about the purchase of a new drinking fountain for their school, he finds that all sorts of chaos results.

Moriarty, Jaclyn. *The Year of Secret Assignments.* Arthur A. Levine Books, 2004. 340p. IL YA, Lexile: 890

> Three female students from Ashbury High write to three male students from rival Brookfield High as part of a pen pal program, leading to romance, humiliation, revenge plots, and war between the schools.

Parks, Rosa. *Dear Mrs. Parks: A Dialogue with Today's Youth.* Lee & Low Books, c1996. 111p. IL 3–6, Lexile: 850 (Non-fiction)

> In this correspondence between Rosa Parks and various children, the "Mother of the Modern-Day Civil Rights Movement" answers questions and encourages young people to reach their highest potential.

Wrede, Patricia C. *Sorcery and Cecelia, or, The Enchanted Chocolate Pot: Being the Correspondence of Two Young Ladies of Quality Regarding Various Magical Scandals in London and the Country.* Harcourt, c2003. 316p. IL YA, Lexile: 720

> In 1817 England, two young cousins—Cecilia, who lives in the country, and Kate, who lives in London—write letters to keep each other informed of their exploits. Their dialog takes a sinister turn when they find themselves confronted by evil wizards.

Yee, Lisa. *So Totally Emily Ebers.* Arthur A. Levine Books, c2007. 280p. IL 3–6, Lexile: 660

> In a series of letters to her absent father, twelve-year-old Emily Ebers deals with moving cross-country, her parents' divorce, a new friendship, and her first serious crush.

Flashbacks

Books for Children of All Ages

Ahlberg, Allan. *Previously.* Candlewick Press, 2007. 32p. IL K–3
The adventures of various nursery rhyme and fairy tale characters, including Goldilocks, Jack and Jill, the frog prince, Cinderella, and the gingerbread man, are retold in backward sequence, with each tale interrelated to the others.

Buzzeo, Toni. *The Sea Chest.* Dial Books for Young Readers, c2002. 32p. IL K–3, Lexile: 1040
A young girl listens as her great-aunt, a lighthouse keeper's daughter, tells of her childhood living on a Maine island, and of the infant who washed ashore after a storm.

Cooney, Barbara. *Miss Rumphius.* Viking Press, 1982. 32p. IL K–3, Lexile: 680
After making her girlhood dreams of world travel and living by the sea come true, a retired librarian follows her grandfather's old advice of doing something to make the world more beautiful, and then passes that wisdom on to her grandniece.

Fox, Mem. *Wilfred Gordon McDonald Partridge.* Kane/Miller, 1984. 32p. IL K–3, Lexile: 760
A small boy tries to discover the meaning of "memory" so he can restore that of an elderly friend.

Levinson, Riki. *Watch the Stars Come Out.* Puffin, 1985. 32p. IL K–3, Lexile: 460
Grandma tells about her mama's journey to America by boat, many years ago.

Noble, Trinka Hakes. *The Day Jimmy's Boa Ate the Wash.* Dial Press, c1980. 32p. IL K–3. Lexile: 540
Jimmy's boa constrictor wreaks havoc on the class trip to a farm.

Pryor, Bonnie. *The House on Maple Street.* HarperCollins, 1987. 32p. IL K–3, Lexile: 650
During the course of three hundred years, many people have passed by or lived on the spot now occupied by a house numbered 107 Maple Street.

Say, Allen. *Grandfather's Journey.* Houghton Mifflin, c1993. 32p. IL K–3, Lexile: 650
A Japanese American man recounts his grandfather's journey to America, which he later also undertakes, and the feeling of being torn by a love for two different countries.

Viorst, Judith. *Alexander, Who Used to Be Rich Last Sunday.* Atheneum, 1978. 32p. IL K–3, Lexile: 570
Although Alexander and his money are soon parted, he comes to realize all the things that can be done with a dollar.

Books for Children Ages Eight to Twelve

Bunting, Eve. *Blue and the Gray.* Scholastic, 1996. 32p. IL 3–6, Lexile: 620
As an African American boy and his white friend watch the construction of a house that will make them neighbors on the site of a Civil War battlefield, they agree that their homes are monuments to that war.

Fourth Wall

Books for Children of All Ages

Carle, Eric. *From Head to Toe.* HarperCollins, c1997. 26p. IL K–3, Lexile: 80 (Non-fiction)
Encourages the reader to exercise by following the movements of various animals.

Muntean, Michaela. *Do Not Open This Book.* Scholastic Press, 2006. 34p. IL K–3
As Pig tries to write a book, he chastises the reader who keeps interrupting him by turning the pages.

Stevenson, James. *No Laughing, No Smiling, No Giggling.* Farrar, Straus and Giroux, 2004. 32p. IL K–3, Lexile: 280
The reader joins Freddy Fafnaffer the pig as he deals with Mr. Frimdimpny, a crocodile who never laughs and who decides on the rules for reading this book.

Stone, Jon. *The Monster at the End of This Book.* Golden Books, 2004. 24p. IL K–3
Grover worries page by page about meeting the monster at the end of this book. The anticipation of what he will find builds throughout the book.

Tullet, Herve. *Press Here.* Handprint Books, 2010. 62p. IL K–3
Instructs the reader on how to interact with the illustrations to manipulate yellow, blue, and red dots.

Watt, Melanie. *Chester.* Kids Can Press, c2007. 32p. IL K–3, Lexile: 350
A self-centered cat named Chester keeps interrupting his owner as she tries to write a story about a mouse.

Wiesner, David. *The Three Pigs.* Clarion Books, c2001. 40p. IL K–3, Lexile: NP
The three pigs escape the wolf by going into another world where they meet the cat and the fiddle, the cow that jumped over the moon, and a dragon.

Willems, Mo. *Don't Let the Pigeon Drive The Bus!* Hyperion Books for Children, c2003. 34p. IL K–3, Lexile: 120
A pigeon that longs to drive a bus sees a chance to make its dream come true when the bus driver takes a short break.

Willems, Mo. *We Are in a Book!* Hyperion Books for Children, c2010. 57p. IL K–3
Piggie realizes that she and Gerald the elephant are in a book and that she can make the reader say words, but when Gerald comes to understand the danger of the book ending, Piggie comes up with a solution to get the reader to keep reading.

Books for Children Ages Eight to Twelve

Browne, Anthony. *Voices in the Park.* DK Publishing, 1998. 31p. IL 3–6, Lexile: 560
Lives briefly intertwine when two youngsters meet in the park. This story is told from four perspectives that show different views of the event.

Fourth Wall

Holm, Jennifer L. *Babymouse. 1, Queen of the World!* Random House, c2005. 91p. IL 3–6
An imaginative mouse dreams of being queen of the world, but will settle for an invitation to the most popular girl's slumber party.

Scieszka, Jon. *The Stinky Cheese Man and Other Fairly Stupid Tales.* Viking, 1992. 51p. IL K–3, Lexile: 520
Madcap revisions of familiar fairy tales. Readers may be surprised to read the alternate versions of classics such as the familiar nursery tales "Little Red Riding Hood," "The Princess and the Pea," and "Jack and the Beanstalk."

Glossaries

Bruel, Nick. *Bad Kitty Gets a Bath.* Roaring Brook Press, 2008. 125p. IL K–3, Lexile: 650
Takes a humorous look at the normal way cats bathe, the reasons why it is inappropriate for humans to bathe that way, and the challenges of trying to give a cat a real bath with soap and water. Includes fun facts, a glossary, and other information.

Cowley, Joy. *Gracias, the Thanksgiving Turkey.* Scholastic, 2005, c1996. 32p. IL K–3, Lexile: 470
Trouble ensues when Papa gets Miguel a turkey to fatten up for Thanksgiving and Miguel develops an attachment to the bird.

Day, Alexandra. *Frank and Ernest.* Green Tiger Press, 1988. 40p. IL K–3
An elephant and a bear take over a diner and find out about responsibility and food language.

Dodds, Dayle Ann. *Minnie's Diner: A Multiplying Menu.* Candlewick Press, 2004. 40p. IL K–3, Lexile: NP
This rhyming tale describe five boys and their father who forget about their chores on the farm as they enjoy Minnie's good cooking, with each requesting double what the previous one ordered.

Elya, Susan Middleton. *Bebe Goes to the Beach.* Harcourt, c2008. 32p. IL K–3
A baby and his mother spend a day at the beach. Includes Spanish words, interspersed in the rhyming text, which are defined in a glossary.

Horowitz, Dave. *Five Little Gefiltes.* G. P. Putnam's Sons, c2007. 32p. IL K–3
Five little gefilte fish sneak out of their jar and explore the world, causing their poor mother great worry. The book includes a note about gefilte fish and a glossary of Yiddish words.

Joosse, Barbara M. *Mama, Do You Love Me?* Chronicle Books, c1991. 26p. IL K–3, Lexile: 420
An Inuit child learns that her mother's love is unconditional when she disobeys and journeys across the Arctic, from village to ice floe, in search of her puppy.

O'Connor, Jane. *Fancy Nancy.* HarperCollins, c2006. 32p. IL K–3, Lexile: 420
A young girl believes that everything should be fancy. From her tiara to her sparkly shoes, she is always fancy. Now she helps her family to be fancy for one special night.

Scieszka, Jon. *Baloney (Henry P.).* Viking, 2001. 34p. IL K–3, Lexile: 400
A transmission received from outer space in a combination of different Earth languages tells of an alien schoolboy's fantastic excuse for being late to school again.

Books for Children Ages Eight to Twelve

Casanova, Mary. *The Klipfish Code.* Houghton Mifflin, 2007. 227p. IL 3–6, Lexile: 770
Sent with her younger brother to Godoy Island to live with her aunt and grandfather after German troops bomb Norway in 1940, ten-year-old Merit longs to join her parents in the Resistance. When her aunt, a teacher, is taken away two years later, she resents even more the Nazis' presence and her grandfather's refusal to oppose them. The book includes historical facts and a glossary.

Glossaries

Knight, Joan. *Charlotte in Giverny.* Chronicle Books, c2000. 62p. IL 3–6, Lexile: 800
> While living in France in 1892, Charlotte, a young American girl, writes a journal about her experiences, including her interactions with the Impressionist painters at the artist colony of Giverny. The book includes profiles of the artists who are mentioned in the journal and a glossary of French words.

Lamstein, Sarah. *Big Night for Salamanders.* Boyds Mills Press, c2010. 40p. IL 3–6
> A boy and his parents go out into the rainy spring night to help salamanders cross a busy road on their annual migration to the vernal pools in which they breed. The book includes a glossary and facts about the life cycle of the salamander.

Mackall, Dandi Daley. *Rudy Rides the Rails: A Depression Era Story.* Sleeping Bear Press, Thomson/Gale, c2007. 36p. IL 3–6
> In 1932, during the Depression in Ohio, thirteen-year-old Rudy, who is determined to help his family weather the hard times, hops a train going west to California and experiences the hobo life.

Marsden, Carolyn. *When Heaven Fell.* Candlewick Press, 2007. 183p. IL 3–6, Lexile: 710
> When her grandmother reveals that the daughter whom she had given up for adoption is coming from America to visit her Vietnamese family, nine-year-old Binh is convinced that her newly discovered aunt is wealthy and will take care of all the family's needs.

McDonough, Yona Zeldis. *The Doll Shop Downstairs.* Viking, c2009. 118p. IL 3–6
> When World War I breaks out, nine-year-old Anna thinks of a way to save her family's beloved New York City doll repair shop. The book includes a brief author's note about the history of the Madame Alexander doll, a glossary, and a timeline.

Shefelman, Janice Jordan. *Anna Maria's Gift.* Random House, c2010. 104p. IL 3–6, Lexile: 470
> In 1715 Italy, eight-year-old Anna Maria Lombardini arrives at a Venice orphanage with few possessions except the special violin her father made for her. When her teacher, Antonio Vivaldi, favors her over a fellow student, the beloved instrument winds up in a canal. The book includes a glossary and a historical note.

Hyperbole

Books for Children of All Ages

Arnold, Tedd. *Hi! Fly Guy.* Scholastic, c2005. 30p. IL K–3, Lexile: 280
When Buzz captures a fly to enter in The Amazing Pet Show, his parents and the judges tell him that a fly cannot be a pet, but Fly Guy proves them wrong.

Bang, Molly. *When Sophie Gets Angry—: Really, Really Angry—.* Blue Sky Press, c1999. 36p. IL K–3, Lexile: BR
When Sophie gets angry, she goes outside and runs, cries, and climbs her favorite tree. Then, calmed by the breeze, she is soon ready to go back home.

Barrett, Judi. *Cloudy with a Chance of Meatballs.* Atheneum, 1978. 32p. IL K–3, Lexile: 730
Life is delicious in the town of Chewandswallow, where it rains soup and juice, snows mashed potatoes, and blows storms of hamburgers—until the weather takes a turn for the worse.

Barrett, Judi. *Things That Are Most in the World.* Aladdin Paperbacks, 2001, c1998. 32p. IL K–3. Lexile: 840
The reader who wants to know what are the quietest, silliest, smelliest, and wiggliest things in the world finds imaginative answers to these and other questions about superlatives.

Bertrand, Lynne. *Granite Baby.* Farrar, Straus and Giroux, 2005. 34p. IL K–3
Five talented New Hampshire sisters try to care for a baby that one of them has carved out of granite.

Gag, Wanda. *Millions of Cats.* G. P. Putnam's, c1956. 32p. IL K–3, Lexile: 730
An old man sets out in search of a pet for his lonely wife and returns with millions of cats, all of which to be the most beautiful of the bunch.

Hawkes, Kevin. *The Wicked Big Toddlah.* Knopf, c2007. 34p. IL K–3
The first year of giant baby Toddie's life is full of amusing situations as his caregivers figure out how to bathe, feed, and change him.

Hopkinson, Deborah. *Apples to Oregon: Being the (Slightly) True Narrative of How a Brave Pioneer Father Brought Apples, Peaches, Pears, Plums, Grapes, and Cherries (and Children) Across the Plains.* Atheneum Books for Young Readers, c2004. 34p. IL K–3, Lexile: 840
A pioneer father transports his beloved fruit trees and his family to Oregon in the mid-nineteenth century. The book is loosely based on the life of Henderson Luelling.

Hutchins, Pat. *The Very Worst Monster.* Mulberry Books, c1985. 32p. IL K–3, Lexile: 450
Hazel sets out to prove that she—not her baby brother—is the worst monster anywhere.

Isaacs, Anne. *Swamp Angel.* Dutton, c1994. 38p. IL K–3, Lexile: 1020
Along with other amazing feats, Angelica Longrider, also known as Swamp Angel, wrestles a huge bear, known as Thundering Tarnation, to save the winter supplies of the settlers in Tennessee.

James, Simon. *Baby Brains.* Candlewick Press, 2007, c2004. 26p. IL K–3, Lexile: 710
Mr. and Mrs. Brains know their new baby is very intelligent, but they soon realize that he is still just a baby.

Hyperbole

Morris, Carla. *The Boy Who Was Raised by Librarians*. Peachtree, c2007. 32p. IL K–3, Lexile 720
Melvin discovers that the public library is the place where he can find just about anything—including three librarians who help in his quest for knowledge.

Nolen, Jerdine. *Thunder Rose*. Harcourt, c2003. 32p. IL K–3, Lexile 910
Unusual from the day she is born, Thunder Rose performs all sorts of amazing feats, including building metal structures, taming a stampeding herd of steers, capturing a gang of rustlers, and turning aside a tornado.

Osborne, Mary Pope. *New York's Bravest*. Knopf, Distributed by Random House, c2002. 32p. IL K–3, Lexile: 350
Tells of the heroic deeds of the legendary New York firefighter, Mose Humphreys.

Reiss, Mike. *Late for School*. Peachtree, 2009, c2003. 32p. IL K–3, Lexile: NP
A boy who has never been late to school encounters some very strange obstacles as he hurries on his way, only to discover when he arrives that he is a day early.

Schur, Maxine. *Gullible Gus*. Clarion Books, c2009. 45p. IL 3–6, Lexile: 760
Cowboy Gus gets teased a lot because he tends to believe everything that the other cowboys tell him, so he visits Fibrock, a town full of liars, hoping to be cured. There, he encounters Hokum Malarkey, who tells him three outrageous stories.

Simms, Laura. *Rotten Teeth*. Houghton Mifflin, c1998. 32p. IL K–3, Lexile: 490
When Melissa takes a big glass bottle of authentic pulled teeth from her father's dental office for a show-and-tell presentation, she becomes a first-grade celebrity.

From *101 Great, Ready-to-Use Book Lists for Children* by Nancy J. Keane. Santa Barbara, CA: Libraries Unlimited. Copyright © 2012.

Metaphors

Books for Children of All Ages

Bunting, Eve. *A Turkey for Thanksgiving.* Clarion, c1991. 31p. IL K–3, Lexile: 410
 Mr. and Mrs. Moose try to invite a turkey to their Thanksgiving feast.

Cooney, Barbara. *Chanticleer and the Fox.* HarperCollins Publishers, c1986. 36p. IL K–3, Lexile: 840
 A sly fox tries to outwit a proud rooster through the use of flattery.

Fleischman, Paul. *Sidewalk Circus.* Candlewick Press, 2007, c2004. 32p. IL K–3
 A young girl watches as the activities across the street from her bus stop become a circus.

Houston, Gloria. *My Great-Aunt Arizona.* HarperCollins, c1992. 32p. IL 3–6, Lexile: 660
 An Appalachian girl, Arizona Houston Hughes, grows up to become a teacher who influences generations of school children.

Johnston, Tony. *Cat, What Is That?* David R. Godine, 2008, c2001. 32p. IL K–3
 An illustrated picture book with rhyming text that describes the behavior and characteristics of cats.

Pattou, Edith. *Mrs. Spitzer's Garden.* Harcourt, c2001. 32p. IL K–3
 With her sure, loving, gardener's touch, Mrs. Spitzer nurtures the students in her classroom each year.

Ringgold, Faith. *Tar Beach.* Crown Publishers, c1991. 32p. IL K–3, Lexile: 790
 A young girl dreams of flying above her Harlem home, claiming all she sees for herself and her family. The book is based on the author's quilt painting of the same name.

Rylant, Cynthia. *In November.* Harcourt, c2000. 32p. IL K–3, Lexile: 440
 Describes the autumn activities and traditions that November's cooling temperatures bring.

Van Allsburg, Chris. *The Stranger.* Houghton Mifflin, c1986. 31p. IL K–3, Lexile: 640
 The enigmatic origins of the stranger whom Farmer Bailey hits with his truck and brings home to recuperate seem to have a mysterious relation to the changing season.

Yolen, Jane. *Owl Moon.* Philomel Books, c1987. 32p. IL K–3, Lexile: 630
 On a winter's night under a full moon, a father and daughter trek into the woods to see the Great Horned Owl.

Books for Children Ages Eight to Twelve

Babbitt, Natalie. *The Search for Delicious.* Square Fish/Farrar, Straus and Giroux, 2007, c1969. 176p. IL 5–8, Lexile: 910
 The prime minister is compiling a dictionary. When no one at court can agree on the meaning of "delicious," the king sends his twelve-year-old messenger to poll the country.

Coerr, Eleanor. *Sadako and the Thousand Paper Cranes.* G. P. Putnam's, c1977. 80p. IL 3–6, Lexile: 630 (Non-fiction)
 Hospitalized with the dreaded atom bomb disease, leukemia, a child in Hiroshima races against time to fold one thousand paper cranes to verify the legend that by doing so a sick person will become healthy.

Onomatopoeia

Books for Children of All Ages

Bunting, Eve. *Smoky Night.* Harcourt Brace, c1994. 36p. IL K–3, Lexile: 360
When riots break out in the streets of their Los Angeles neighborhood, a young boy and his mother learn the value of getting along with others no matter what their background or nationality.

Flack, Marjorie. *Angus and the Ducks.* Farrar, Straus and Giroux, 1997, c1930. 32p. IL K–3
A curious Scottish terrier decides to investigate the strange noise coming from the other side of the hedge.

Franco, Betsy. *Summer Beat.* Margaret K. McElderry Books, c2007. 34p. IL K–3
Two friends celebrate the sounds and sights of summer. They find delight in even the simple sounds of bees and the joy of blowing bubbles.

Gershator, Phillis. *Listen, Listen.* Barefoot Books, c2007. 34p. IL K–3
Illustrations and rhyming text explore the sights and sounds of nature in each season of the year.

Guiberson, Brenda Z. *The Emperor Lays an Egg.* Henry Holt, 2001. 32p. IL K–3, Lexile: 840 (Non-fiction)
Follows the activities of mother and father emperor penguins as they share the duties involved in laying and nurturing eggs, and then caring for the newly hatched penguins.

MacLennan, Cathy. *Chicky Chicky Chook Chook.* Boxer Books, Distributed by Sterling Publishing, 2007. 28p. IL K–3
Chicks, kittens, and bees play in the summer sunshine until a thunderstorm interrupts their idyllic day.

Raschka, Christopher. *Charlie Parker Played Be Bop.* Orchard Paperbacks, 1997, c1992. 32p. IL K–3, Lexile: 140 (Non-fiction)
Introduces the musical style of jazz known as bebop as played by the legendary African American saxophonist Charlie Parker.

Rylant, Cynthia. *The Great Gracie Chase: Stop That Dog!* Blue Sky Press, c2001. 32p. IL K–3, Lexile: 410
A cumulative tale about a small dog named Gracie whose quiet life is disrupted by some noisy painters.

Usui, Kanako. *The Fantastic Mr. Wani.* Tiger Tales, 2005. 36p. IL K–3
As Mr. Wani, a crocodile, hurries to get to the Froggies party, he literally runs into a number of other animals along the way.

Wheeler, Lisa. *Old Cricket.* Atheneum Books for Young Readers, c2003. 32p. IL K–3, Lexile: 730
Old Cricket doesn't feel like helping his wife and neighbors to prepare for winter, so he pretends to have all sorts of ailments that require the doctor's care, but hungry Old Crow has other ideas.

Onomatopoeia

Wilson, Karma. ***Bear Snores on.*** Spotlight, Margaret K. McElderry Books, 2002. 34p. IL K–3, Lexile: 280

On a cold winter night, many animals gather to party in the cave of a sleeping bear, who awakes and protests that he has missed the food and the fun.

Yashima, Taro. ***Umbrella.*** Viking, c1986. 30p. IL K–3, Lexile: 480

Momo eagerly waits for a rainy day so she can use the red boots and umbrella she received on her third birthday.

Yolen, Jane. ***Welcome to the Green House.*** Putnam & Grosset, 1993. 32p. IL K–3, Lexile: 770 (Non-fiction)

Describes the tropical rainforest and the life found there. Yolen shows us the rainforest through poems and illustrations.

Personification

Books for Children of All Ages

Burton, Virginia Lee. *The Little House.* Houghton Mifflin, c1969. 40p. IL K–3, Lexile: 890
A country house is unhappy when the city, with all its buildings and traffic, grows up around her.

Burton, Virginia Lee. *Mike Mulligan and His Steam Shovel.* Houghton Mifflin, 1967. 44p. IL K–3, Lexile: 820
Although Mike Mulligan's steam shovel, Mary Anne, is too old-fashioned to compete with newer models, the people of Popperville find a way to keep the pair working.

Cowan, Catherine. *My Life with the Wave.* HarperCollins, c1997. 32p. IL 3–6, Lexile: 840
A young boy brings home a wave after a trip to the seashore, but after a while the novelty of having a wave in the house wears off on everyone.

Cronin, Doreen. *Click, Clack, Moo: Cows That Type.* Simon & Schuster Books for Young Readers, c2006. 32p. IL K–3, Lexile: 160
When Farmer Brown's cows find a typewriter in the barn, they start making demands, and eventually go on strike when the farmer refuses to give them what they want.

Ets, Marie Hall. *Gilberto and the Wind.* Puffin, 1963. 32p. IL K–3, Lexile: 460
Gilberto is a small boy whose companion is the wind—an unpredictable friend who might roar, whisper, be silent, or tear things apart.

Fox, Mem. *Night Noises.* Harcourt, 1989. 32p. IL K–3, Lexile: 430
Old Lily Laceby dozes by the fire with her faithful dog at her feet as strange night noises herald a surprising awakening.

George, Kristine O'Connell. *Old Elm Speaks: Tree Poems.* Clarion Books, c1998. 48p. IL K–3, Lexile: NP
This collection of short, simple poems presents images relating to trees in various circumstances and throughout the seasons.

Grey, Mini. *Traction Man Is Here!* Knopf, Distributed by Random House, 2005. 32p. IL K–3, Lexile: 730
Traction Man, a boy's courageous action figure, has a variety of adventures with Scrubbing Brush and other objects in the house.

Keller, Laurie. *Open Wide: Tooth School Inside.* H. Holt, 2000. 34p. IL K–3, Lexile: 360 (Non-fiction)
Through a classroom setting in which teeth are the students, presents information about the structure and care of teeth and the services provided by dentists.

Leedy, Loreen. *Follow the Money!* Holiday House, c2002. 32p. IL K–3, Lexile: 130 (Non-fiction)
A quarter describes all the ways it is used from the time it is minted until it is taken back to a bank.

Locker, Thomas. *Water Dance.* Harcourt Brace, c1997. 32p. IL 3–6, Lexile: 310
Water speaks of its existence in such forms as storm clouds, mist, rainbows, and rivers. The book includes factual information on the water cycle.

Personification

McKissack, Pat. *Flossie & the Fox.* Dial Books for Young Readers, c1986. 32p. IL K–3, Lexile: 610
A wily fox, notorious for stealing eggs, meets his match when he encounters a bold little girl in the woods who insists upon proof that he is a fox before she will be frightened.

McMullan, Kate. *I Stink!* Joanna Cotler Books, c2002. 34p. IL K–3, Lexile: BR
A big-city garbage truck makes its rounds, consuming everything from apple cores and banana peels to leftover ziti with zucchini.

Rylant, Cynthia. *The Great Gracie Chase: Stop That Dog!* Blue Sky Press, c2001. 32p. IL K–3, Lexile: 410
A cumulative tale about a small dog named Gracie whose quiet life is disrupted by some noisy painters.

Rylant, Cynthia. *The Old Woman Who Named Things.* Harcourt Brace, c1996. 32p. IL K–3, Lexile: 760
An old woman who has outlived all her friends is reluctant to become too attached to the stray dog that visits her each day.

Silverstein, Shel. *The Giving Tree.* HarperCollins Publishers, c1992. 57p. IL K–3, Lexile: 530
A young boy grows to manhood and old age experiencing the love and generosity of a tree that gives to him without thought of return.

Steig, William. *Sylvester and the Magic Pebble.* Simon and Schuster Books for Young Readers, 1969. 36p. IL K–3, Lexile: 700
Sylvester the donkey finds a magic pebble that grants his every wish. When in a moment of fright he wishes he were a rock, he then cannot hold the pebble to wish himself back to normal again.

Teague, Mark. *Dear Mrs. Larue: Letters from Obedience School.* Scholastic Press, 2002. 32p. IL K–3, Lexile: 500
Gertrude LaRue receives typewritten and paw-written letters from her dog Ike, entreating her to let him leave the Igor Brotweiler Canine Academy and come back home.

Van Allsburg, Chris. *Two Bad Ants.* Houghton Mifflin, c1988. 31p. IL K–3, Lexile: 780
When two bad ants desert from their colony, they experience a dangerous adventure that convinces them to return to their former place of safety.

Prediction

Books for Children of All Ages

Banyai, Istvan. *Zoom.* Viking, 1995. 64p. IL K–3
This wordless picture book presents a series of scenes, each one from farther away, showing, for example, a girl playing with toys, which is actually a picture on a magazine cover, which is part of a sign on a bus, and so on.

Blake, Quentin. *Clown.* H. Holt, 1998, c1995. 32p. IL K–3
After being discarded and tossed into a garbage can, Clown makes his way through town and has a series of adventures as he tries to find a new home for himself.

Brett, Jan. *The Mitten: A Ukrainian Folktale.* G. P. Putnam's Sons, 2009, c1989. 32p. IL K–3, Lexile: 800
Several animals sleep snugly in Nicki's lost mitten—until the bear sneezes. This children's classic has been enjoyed by children of all ages.

Halpern, Monica. *How Many Seeds?* Steck-Vaughn, c1999. 8p. IL K–3 (Non-fiction)
Simple text and pictures help students learn about the number of seeds in different types of fruit.

Krauss, Ruth. *The Carrot Seed.* HarperCollins, c1973. 25p. IL K–3
Despite everyone's dire predictions, a little boy has faith in the carrot seed he plants.

Numeroff, Laura Joffe. *If You Give a Mouse a Cookie.* Laura Geringer Books, 1985. 32p. IL K–3, Lexile: 660
Relates the cycle of requests a mouse is likely to make after you give him a cookie, taking the reader through a young child's day.

Park, Barbara. *Junie B., First Grader: Shipwrecked.* Random House, c2004. 88p. IL K–3
Junie B.'s journal entries start with Room One's stomach virus excitement, the first-grade Columbus Day play, and getting the part of the *Pinta,* the fastest ship in Columbus's fleet.

Portis, Antoinette. *Not a Box.* HarperCollins, c2006. 32p. IL K–3
To an imaginative little bunny, a box is not always just a box.

Portis, Antoinette. *Not a Stick.* HarperCollins, c2008. 32p. IL K–3
An imaginative young pig shows some of the many things that a stick can be.

Prelutsky, Jack. *If Not for the Cat.* Greenwillow Books, c2004. 40p. IL K–3, Lexile: NP
An illustrated collection of haiku-style poems about different animals.

Teague, Mark. *Dear Mrs. Larue: Letters from Obedience School.* Scholastic Press, 2002. 32p. IL K–3, Lexile: 500
Gertrude LaRue receives typewritten and paw-written letters from her dog Ike, entreating her to let him leave the Igor Brotweiler Canine Academy and come back home.

Van Allsburg, Chris. *The Mysteries of Harris Burdick.* Houghton Mifflin, 1984. 31p. IL K–3, Lexile: 760
Presents a series of loosely related drawings, each accompanied by a title and a caption that the reader may use to make up his or her own story.

From *101 Great, Ready-to-Use Book Lists for Children* by Nancy J. Keane. Santa Barbara, CA: Libraries Unlimited. Copyright © 2012.

Prediction

Van Allsburg, Chris. *The Stranger.* Houghton Mifflin, c1986. 31p. IL K–3, Lexile: 640
The enigmatic origins of the stranger whom Farmer Bailey hits with his truck and brings home to recuperate seem to have a mysterious relation to the changing season.

Wiesner, David. *Flotsam.* Clarion Books, c2006. 40p. IL K–3, Lexile: NP
In this colorful picture book, a young, science-minded boy goes to the beach to collect and examine anything floating that has been washed ashore and discovers an underwater camera that contains a collection of unusual pictures.

From *101 Great, Ready-to-Use Book Lists for Children* by Nancy J. Keane. Santa Barbara, CA: Libraries Unlimited. Copyright © 2012.

Satire

Books for Children of All Ages

Creech, Sharon. *A Fine, Fine School.* Joanna Cotler Books, c2001. 32p. IL K–3, Lexile: 300
When a principal loves his school so much that he wants the children to attend classes every day of the year, it's up to his students to show him that free time is a good thing, too.

Cronin, Doreen. *Click, Clack, Moo: Cows That Type.* Simon & Schuster Books for Young Readers, c2006. 32p. IL K–3, Lexile: 160
When Farmer Brown's cows find a typewriter in the barn, they start making demands, and eventually go on strike when the farmer refuses to give them what they want.

Cronin, Doreen. *Duck for President.* Simon & Schuster Books for Young Readers, c2004. 40p. IL K–3, Lexile: 680
When Duck gets tired of working for Farmer Brown, his political ambition eventually leads to his being elected president.

Scieszka, Jon. *The Stinky Cheese Man and Other Fairly Stupid Tales.* Viking, 1992. 51p. IL K–3, Lexile: 520
Madcap revisions of familiar fairy tales.

Seuss, Dr. *Yertle the Turtle and Other Stories.* Random House, c1986. 82p. IL K–3, Lexile: 520
Contains three modern fables in verse: "Yertle the Turtle," "Gertrude McFuzz," and "The Big Brag."

Teague, Mark. *Dear Mrs. Larue: Letters from Obedience School.* Scholastic Press, 2002. 32p. IL K–3, Lexile: 500
Gertrude LaRue receives typewritten and paw-written letters from her dog Ike, entreating her to let him leave the Igor Brotweiler Canine Academy and come back home.

Books for Children Ages Eight to Twelve

Goldman, William. *The Princess Bride: S. Morgenstern's Classic Tale of True Love and High Adventure.* Harcourt, 2007, c1973. 414p. IL YA
Westley, a farm boy, goes off to seek his fortune shortly after declaring his love for Buttercup, the most beautiful woman in the world. Their relationship is put to the test when Westley's ship is captured by pirates and Buttercup is summoned to become the bride of the prince.

Rex, Adam. *The True Meaning of Smekday.* Disney/Hyperion Books, 2009, c2007. 423p. IL 5–8, Lexile: 740
Twelve-year-old Gratuity "Tip" Tucci is left to fend for herself after Earth is colonized by aliens and her mother is abducted. She must try to stop another alien invasion with only the help of a cat named Pig and an alien named J. Lo.

Satire

Swift, Jonathan. *Gulliver's Travels.* Puffin Books, 1997. 345p. IL 5–8
  The voyages of an Englishman carry him to a land where people are only six inches high, a land populated by giants, an island filled with sorcerers, and a land where horses are masters of human-like creatures.

Urban, Linda. *A Crooked Kind of Perfect.* Harcourt, c2007. 213p. IL 3–6, Lexile: 730
  Ten-year-old Zoe Elias longs to play the piano, but must resign herself to learning the organ instead. She finds that her musicianship has a positive impact on her workaholic mother, her jittery father, and her school social life.

Wells, H. G. *The First Men in the Moon.* Dover Publications, 2001. 161p. IL 5–8
  In this novel, which was originally published in 1901, Cavor, a scientist, and his materialistic companion Bedford travel to the moon in a ship built by Cavor. There, the pair encounter a hostile race of biologically engineered creatures.

Sequencing

Books for Children of All Ages

Andersen, H. C. *The Emperor's New Clothes.* Houghton Mifflin, c1977. 44p. IL K–3
A vain emperor is duped into parading through town without clothes by a pair of swindlers posing as tailors.

Andersen, H. C. *The Princess and the Pea.* North-South Books, 1985. 24p. IL K–3, Lexile: 580
A young girl feels a pea through twenty mattresses and twenty featherbeds, which proves she is a real princess.

Asbjornsen, Peter Christen. *The Three Billy Goats Gruff.* Clarion, c1973. 31p. IL K–3, Lexile: 500
Three clever billy goats outwit a big ugly troll that lives under the bridge they must cross on their way up the mountain.

Aston, Dianna Hutts. *A Seed Is Sleepy.* Chronicle Books, c2007. 34p. IL K–3, Lexile: 750 (Non-fiction)
This introduction to seeds explains their varying shapes and sizes, the locations where they are found, and their life cycles.

Barry, Robert E. *Mr. Willowby's Christmas Tree.* Random House Children's Books, 1991. 32p. IL K–3
Mr. Willowby's Christmas tree is too tall, so he trims off the top and gives it to the upstairs maid for her tree; she finds it too tall, so she cuts off the top, which the gardener uses for his tree; but it is too tall. . . .

Brett, Jan. *Berlioz the Bear.* Putnam, c1991. 32p. IL K–3, Lexile: 540
Berlioz the bear and his fellow musicians are due to play for the town ball, but the mule pulling their bandwagon refuses to move. A strange buzzing in Berlioz's double bass turns into a surprise that saves the day.

Brett, Jan. *Gingerbread Baby.* G. P. Putnam's, c1999. 32p. IL K–3, Lexile: 430
A young boy and his mother bake a gingerbread baby, which escapes from their oven and leads a crowd on a chase similar to the one in the familiar tale about a not-so-clever gingerbread man.

Bunting, Eve. *Sunflower House.* Harcourt Brace, c1996. 32p. IL K–3, Lexile: 530
A young boy creates a summer playhouse by planting sunflowers and saves the seeds to make another house the next year.

Burton, Virginia Lee. *Mike Mulligan and His Steam Shovel.* Houghton Mifflin, 1967. 44p. IL K–3, Lexile: 820
Although Mike Mulligan's steam shovel, Mary Anne, is too-old fashioned to compete with newer models, the people of Popperville find a way to keep the pair working.

Buzzeo, Toni. *Little Loon and Papa.* Dial Books for Young Readers, c2004. 32p. IL K–3
Motivated by a challenging situation and his supportive father, Little Loon finally learns to dive.

Carle, Eric. *The Very Hungry Caterpillar.* Philomel Books, c1987. 18p. IL K–3
Follows the progress of a hungry little caterpillar as he eats his way through a varied and very large quantity of food until, full at last, he forms a cocoon around himself and goes to sleep. Die-cut pages illustrate what the caterpillar ate on successive days.

Sequencing

Cronin, Doreen. *Click, Clack, Moo: Cows That Type.* Simon & Schuster Books for Young Readers, c2006. 32p. IL K–3, Lexile: 160
> When Farmer Brown's cows find a typewriter in the barn, they start making demands, and eventually go on strike when the farmer refuses to give them what they want.

Cronin, Doreen. *Duck for President.* Simon & Schuster Books for Young Readers, c2004. 40p. IL K–3, Lexile: 680
> When Duck gets tired of working for Farmer Brown, his political ambition eventually leads to his being elected president.

Cronin, Doreen. *Giggle, Giggle, Quack.* Simon & Schuster Books for Young Readers, c2006. 32p. IL K–3, Lexile: 330
> When Farmer Brown goes on vacation, leaving his brother Bob in charge, Duck makes trouble by changing all of his instructions to notes the animals like much better.

DePaola, Tomie. *Charlie Needs a Cloak.* Aladdin Paperbacks, c1973. 32p. IL K–3, Lexile: 500 (Non-fiction)
> A shepherd shears his sheep, cards and spins the wool, weaves and dyes the cloth, and sews a beautiful new red cloak.

Donaldson, Julia. *The Gruffalo.* Dial Books for Young Readers, c1999. 28p. IL K–3, Lexile: 200
> A clever mouse uses the threat of a terrifying creature to keep from being eaten by a fox, an owl, and a snake—only to have to outwit that creature as well.

Ernst, Lisa Campbell. *Stella Louella's Runaway Book.* Simon & Schuster Books for Young Readers, c1998. 34p. IL K–3, Lexile: 640
> As she tries to find the book that she must return to the library that day, Stella gathers a growing group of people who have all enjoyed reading the book.

Frost, Helen. *Monarch and Milkweed.* Atheneum Books for Young Readers, c2008. 34p. IL K–3, Lexile: 970 (Non-fiction)
> Illustrations and text describe the life cycle of the monarch butterfly and its link with the milkweed plant.

Kimmel, Eric A. *I Took My Frog to the Library.* Puffin Books, 1992. 28p. IL K–3, Lexile: 430
> A young girl brings her pets to the library—with predictably disastrous results.

Levenson, George. *Pumpkin Circle: The Story of a Garden.* Tricycle Press, c1999. 38p. IL K–3, Lexile: NP (Non-fiction)
> Rhyming text and photographs follow a pumpkin patch as it grows and changes, from seeds to plants, to pumpkins ready to harvest, to jack-o-lanterns, and then to seeds again.

Lobel, Arnold. *Frog and Toad All Year.* HarperCollins, c1976. 64p. IL K–3, Lexile: 300
> Two friends share experiences in each season of the year.

London, Jonathan. *Froggy Gets Dressed.* Viking, 1992. IL K–3, Lexile: 300
> Rambunctious Froggy hops out into the snow for a winter frolic but is called back by his mother to put on some necessary articles of clothing.

Sequencing

Lowry, Lois. *Gooney Bird Greene*. Yearling, 2004, c2002. 88p. IL 3–6, Lexile: 590
A most unusual new student who loves to be the center of attention entertains her teacher and fellow second graders by telling absolutely true stories about herself, including how she got her name.

Martin, Bill. *The Ghost-Eye Tree*. Holt, 1985. 32p. IL K–3, Lexile: NP
Walking down a dark lonely road on an errand one night, a brother and sister argue over who is afraid of the dreaded Ghost-Eye tree.

McClintock, Marshall. *A Fly Went by*. Beginner Books, c1986. 62p. IL K–3, Lexile: 270
A sheep with its foot caught in a tin can sets off a chase, with a fly in the lead.

McKissack, Pat. *Flossie & the Fox*. Dial Books for Young Readers, c1986. 32p. IL K–3, Lexile: 610
A wily fox, notorious for stealing eggs, meets his match when he encounters a bold little girl in the woods who insists upon proof that he is a fox before she will be frightened.

McPhail, David. *Mole Music*. H. Holt, 1999. 32p. IL K–3, Lexile: 380
Feeling that something is missing in his simple life, Mole acquires a violin and learns to make beautiful, joyful music.

Meddaugh, Susan. *Cinderella's Rat*. Houghton Mifflin, c1997. 32p. IL K–3, Lexile: 420
One of the rats that was turned into a coachman by Cinderella's fairy godmother tells his story.

Meddaugh, Susan. *Martha Speaks*. Houghton Mifflin, c1992. 32p. IL K–3, Lexile: 420
Problems arise when Martha, the family dog, learns to speak after eating alphabet soup.

Noble, Trinka Hakes. *The Day Jimmy's Boa Ate the Wash*. Dial Press, c1980. 32p. IL K–3, Lexile: 540
Jimmy's boa constrictor wreaks havoc on the class trip to a farm.

Numeroff, Laura Joffe. *Beatrice Doesn't Want to*. Candlewick Press, 2004. 32p. IL K–3, Lexile: 140
On the third afternoon of going to the library with her brother Henry, Beatrice finally finds something she enjoys doing.

Numeroff, Laura Joffe. *If You Give a Pig a Pancake*. Laura Geringer Book, c1998. 32p. IL K–3, Lexile: 570
Shows the chaos that can happen in the house when you give a pig a pancake.

Parish, Peggy. *Amelia Bedelia*. HarperCollins, 1992. 63p. IL K–3, Lexile: 140
A literal-minded housekeeper causes a ruckus in the household when she attempts to make sense of some instructions.

Pearson, Emily. *Ordinary Mary's Extraordinary Deed*. Gibbs Smith, c2002. 32p. IL K–3
A young girl's good deed is multiplied as it is passed on by those who have been touched by the kindness of others.

Rathmann, Peggy. *10 Minutes till Bedtime*. G. P. Putnam's, c1998. 48p. IL K–3, Lexile: NP
A boy's hamster leads an increasingly large group of hamsters on a tour of the boy's house, while his father counts down the minutes to bedtime.

Sequencing

Robart, Rose. *The Cake That Mack Ate.* Little, Brown, c1986. 24p. IL K–3
A cumulative tale about the chain of events surrounding the making of a cake by a farmer's wife, eventually leading to its consumption in surprising circumstances.

Sendak, Maurice. *Where the Wild Things Are.* HarperCollins, 1963. 40p. IL K–3, Lexile: 740
After he is sent to bed without supper for behaving like a wild thing, Max dreams of a voyage to the island where the wild things are.

Seuss, Dr. *The 500 Hats of Bartholomew Cubbins.* Random House, c1965. 47p. IL K–3, Lexile: 520
Each time Bartholomew Cubbins attempts to obey the king's order to take off his hat, he finds there is another one on his head.

Shannon, David. *A Bad Case of Stripes.* Blue Sky Press, c1998. 32p. IL K–3, Lexile: 540
To ensure her popularity, Camilla Cream always does what is expected—until the day arrives when she no longer recognizes herself.

Shannon, David. *No, David!* Blue Sky Press, c1998. 32p. IL K–3, Lexile: BR
A young boy is depicted doing a variety of naughty things for which he is repeatedly admonished, but finally he gets a hug.

Sierra, Judy. *Wild about Books.* Knopf, c2004. 34p. IL K–3, Lexile: NP
A librarian named Mavis McGrew introduces the animals in the zoo to the joy of reading when she drives her bookmobile to the zoo by mistake.

Steig, William. *Brave Irene.* Farrar, Straus and Giroux, 1986. 32p. IL K–3, Lexile: 630
Plucky Irene, a dressmaker's daughter, braves a fierce snowstorm to deliver a new gown to the duchess in time for the ball.

Taback, Simms. *There Was an Old Lady Who Swallowed a Fly.* Viking, 1997. 32p. IL K–3, Lexile: NP
Ever-expanding die-cut holes show exactly what is happening in the old lady's stomach as she swallows an assortment of creatures, beginning with a small fly, and ending with a (fatal) horse.

Van Allsburg, Chris. *Two Bad Ants.* Houghton Mifflin, c1988. 31p. IL K–3, Lexile: 780
When two bad ants desert from their colony, they experience a dangerous adventure that convinces them to return to their former place of safety.

Wood, Audrey. *The Napping House.* Harcourt, c1984. 32p. IL K–3, Lexile: NP
In this cumulative tale, a wakeful flea atop a number of sleeping creatures causes a commotion, with just one bite.

Showing, Not Telling

Books for Children of All Ages

Brinckloe, Julie. *Fireflies!* Aladdin Paperbacks, 1986, c1985. 32p. IL K–3, Lexile: 630
A young boy is proud of having caught a jar full of fireflies, which seems to him like owning a piece of moonlight. As the light begins to dim, however, he realizes he must set the insects free or they will die.

Lehman, Barbara. *The Red Book.* Houghton Mifflin, c2004. 32p. IL K–3, Lexile: NP
A wordless story in which a little girl finds a red book in the snow that holds an astonishing surprise.

Palatini, Margie. *Lousy Rotten Stinkin' Grapes.* Simon & Schuster Books for Young Readers, c2009. 31p. IL K–3, Lexile: 340
In this retelling of a classic fable, a frustrated fox, after making many tries to reach a high-up bunch of grapes, decides they must be sour anyway.

Van Allsburg, Chris. *Jumanji.* Houghton Mifflin, c1981. 31p. IL K–3, Lexile: 620
Left on their own for an afternoon, two bored and restless children find more excitement than they bargained for in a mysterious and mystical jungle adventure board game.

Waddell, Martin. *The Super Hungry Dinosaur.* Dial Books for Young Readers, c2009. 32p. IL K–3
Hal must save his parents and dog, Billy, from a ravenous dinosaur. To convince the dinosaur not to eat his family, Hal must find something else for the animal to eat.

Wiesner, David. *Flotsam.* Clarion Books, c2006. 40p. IL K–3, Lexile: NP
In this colorful picture book, a young, science-minded boy goes to the beach to collect and examine anything floating that has been washed ashore and discovers an underwater camera that contains a collection of unusual pictures.

Wiesner, David. *Tuesday.* Clarion Books, c1991. 32p. IL K–3, Lexile: NP
Frogs rise on their lily pads, float through the air, and explore the nearby houses while their inhabitants sleep.

Wilson, Karma. *Bear Feels Sick.* Margaret K. McElderry Books, c2007. 34p. IL K–3
The forest friends all gather to help care for Bear when he feels sick; when they come down with the same symptoms, the newly recovered Bear returns the favor.

Yolen, Jane. *Owl Moon.* Philomel Books, c1987. 32p. IL K–3, Lexile: 630
On a winter's night under a full moon, a father and daughter trek into the woods to see the Great Horned Owl.

Books for Children Ages Eight to Twelve

MacLachlan, Patricia. *Word after Word after Word.* Katherine Tegen Books, c2010. 128p. IL 3–6, Lexile: 450
A visiting poet, Ms. Mirabel, teaches five friends in grade school about the power of words and writing.

Showing, Not Telling

Nobisso, Josephine. *Josephine Nobisso's Show; Don't Tell!: Secrets of Writing.* Gingerbread House, c2004. 44p. IL 3–6 (Non-fiction)

Presents creative writing exercises that focus on the use of adjectives and nouns. Features scratch and sniff pages, electronic sounds, comic book spreads, and Greek chorus characters.

Similes

Books for Children of All Ages

Bunting, Eve. *A Turkey for Thanksgiving.* Clarion, c1991. 31p. IL K–3, Lexile: 410
Mr. and Mrs. Moose try to invite a turkey to their Thanksgiving feast.

Cooney, Barbara. *Chanticleer and the Fox.* HarperCollins Publishers, c1986. 36p. IL K–3, Lexile: 840
A sly fox tries to outwit a proud rooster through the use of flattery.

Cronin, Doreen. *Diary of a Spider.* Joanna Cotler Books, c2005. 36p. IL K–3, Lexile: 510
A young spider discovers, day by day, that there is a lot to learn about being a spider, including how to spin webs and how to avoid vacuum cleaners.

Cronin, Doreen. *Diary of a Worm.* Joanna Cotler Books, c2003. 34p. IL K–3, Lexile: 360
A young worm discovers, day by day, that there are some very good things and some not so good things about being a worm in this great big world.

Fox, Mem. *Wilfrid Gordon McDonald Partridge.* Kane/Miller, 1985. 32p. IL K–3, Lexile: 760
A small boy tries to discover the meaning of "memory" so he can restore that of an elderly friend.

Goble, Paul. *The Girl Who Loved Wild Horses.* Atheneum Books for Young Readers, 1978. 32p. IL K–3, Lexile: 670
Although she is fond of her people, a girl prefers to live among the wild horses, where she is truly happy and free.

Igus, Toyomi. *Two Mrs. Gibsons.* Children's Book Press, c1996. 32p. IL K–3, Lexile: 530
The biracial daughter of an African American father and a Japanese mother fondly recalls growing up with her mother and her father's mother—two very different, but equally loving women.

Johnston, Tony. *Amber on the Mountain.* Puffin Books, 1994. 32p. IL K–3, Lexile: 480
Isolated on her mountain, Amber meets and befriends a girl from the city who gives her the determination to learn to read and write.

Lester, Julius. *John Henry.* Dial Books, c1994. 38p. IL K–3, Lexile: 720
Retells the legend of the African American railroad builder who raced against a steam drill to cut through a mountain.

Lester, Julius. *Sam and the Tigers: A New Telling of Little Black Sambo.* Dial Books for Young Readers, c1996. 40p. IL K–3, Lexile: 510
A little boy named Sam matches wits with several tigers that want to eat him in this retelling of the "Little Black Sambo" story.

Rylant, Cynthia. *The Ticky-Tacky Doll.* Harcourt, c2002. 32p. IL K–3
When she has to go to school without her special doll, a little girl cannot focus on learning her letters and numbers, until her grandmother realizes what the problem is.

Similes

San Souci, Robert D. *The Talking Eggs: A Folktale from the American South.* Dial Books for Young Readers, c1989. 32p. IL K–3, Lexile: 940
> In this Southern folktale, kind Blanche, who follows the instructions of an old witch, gains riches, while her greedy sister makes fun of the old woman and is duly rewarded.

Say, Allen. *The Bicycle Man.* Parnassus Press, Houghton Mifflin, c1982. 40p. IL K–3, Lexile: 500
> The amazing tricks two American soldiers do on a borrowed bicycle are a fitting finale for the school sports day festivities in a small village in occupied Japan.

Stanley, Diane. *Saving Sweetness.* Puffin, 1996. 32p. IL K–3, Lexile: 660
> The sheriff of a dusty western town rescues Sweetness, an unusually resourceful orphan, from nasty old Mrs. Sump and her terrible orphanage.

Stolz, Mary. *Storm in the Night.* HarperCollins, c1988. 32p. IL K–3, Lexile: 550
> While sitting through a fearsome thunderstorm that has put the lights out, Thomas hears a story from Grandfather's boyhood, when Grandfather was afraid of thunderstorms.

Tresselt, Alvin R. *Hide and Seek Fog.* Lothrop, Lee & Shepard, 1965. 29p. IL K–3, Lexile: 850
> When a fog comes and stays for three days at a little seaside village, children find many ways to enjoy themselves.

Turner, Ann Warren. *Dakota Dugout.* Aladdin Paperbacks, 1985. 32p. IL K–3, Lexile: 1040
> A woman describes her experiences living with her husband in a sod house on the Dakota prairie.

Van Allsburg, Chris. *The Polar Express.* Houghton Mifflin, c1985. 32p. IL K–3, Lexile: 520
> A magical train ride on Christmas Eve takes a boy to the North Pole to receive a special gift from Santa Claus.

Wood, Audrey. *I'm as Quick as a Cricket.* Child's Play, c1998. 22p. IL K–3
> A young boy describes himself using similes, comparing qualities in himself to qualities in animals.

Yashima, Taro. *Umbrella.* Viking, c1986. 30p. IL K–3, Lexile: 480
> Momo eagerly waits for a rainy day so she can use the red boots and umbrella she received on her third birthday.

Yolen, Jane. *Owl Moon.* Philomel Books, c1987. 32p. IL K–3, Lexile: 630
> On a winter's night under a full moon, a father and daughter trek into the woods to see the Great Horned Owl.

Young, Ed. *Seven Blind Mice.* Philomel Books, c1992. 40p. IL K–3, Lexile: 350
> Retells in verse the Indian fable of the blind men discovering different parts of an elephant and arguing about its appearance. The illustrations depict the blind arguers as mice.

Similes

Books for Children Ages Eight to Twelve

San Souci, Robert D. *The Faithful Friend.* Simon & Schuster Books for Young Readers, c1995. 40p. IL 3–6, Lexile: 850
   A retelling of the traditional tale from the French West Indies in which two friends, Clement and Hippolyte, encounter love, zombies, and danger on the island of Martinique.

Terban, Marvin. *Mad as a Wet Hen!: And Other Funny Idioms.* Clarion Books, 2007. 64p. IL 3–6
   Illustrates and explains more than 100 common English idioms, in categories including animals, body parts, and colors.

Van Steenwyk, Elizabeth. *When Abraham Talked to the Trees.* Eerdmans Books for Young Readers, 2000. 32p. IL 3–6, Lexile: 670 (Non-fiction)
   Picture book biography of young Abraham Lincoln, a boy who struggled against the odds to become a beloved American president.

Speech Bubbles

Books for Children of All Ages

Baker, Keith. *Potato Joe.* Harcourt, c2008. 40p. IL K–3
Potato Joe leads the other spuds from the familiar nursery rhyme, "One Potato, Two Potato," in various activities, ranging from a game of tic-tac-toe to a rodeo.

Clements, Andrew. *Double Trouble in Walla Walla.* Millbrook Press, c1997. 32p. IL K–3, Lexile: 940
It's an ordinary morning in Walla Walla until Lulu, her teacher, the school nurse, and the principal are all infected by a word warp that makes them duplicate everything they say.

Grey, Mini. *Traction Man Is Here!* Knopf, 2005. 32p. IL K–3, Lexile: 730
Traction Man, a boy's courageous action figure, has a variety of adventures with Scrubbing Brush and other objects in the house.

Griffiths, Andy. *The Big Fat Cow That Goes Kapow.* Feiwel and Friends, 2008. 123p. IL K–3, Lexile: 380
A collection of ten humorous rhyming stories for beginning readers.

Hayes, Geoffrey. *Benny and Penny in "Just Pretend": A Toon Book.* Little Lit Library, c2008. 32p. IL K–3, Lexile: 90
Annoyed with his little sister, who always wants to play pretend with him, Benny intentionally loses her, but soon feels bad after she is gone.

Krosoczka, Jarrett. *Baghead.* Dell Dragonfly Books, 2002. 32p. IL K–3, Lexile: 420
Josh hides the bad haircut he gave himself by wearing a bag on his head, until his sister has a better idea.

Lechner, John. *Sticky Burr: Adventures in Burrwood Forest.* Candlewick Press, 2008. 56p. IL 3–6
Sticky Burr is on the verge of being kicked out of his village in Burrwood Forest because he is not prickly enough to suit some of the other burrs. When the village is attacked by wild dogs, Sticky Burr and his friends come to the rescue.

Lynch, Jay. *Otto's Orange Day: A Toon Book.* Little Lit Library, c2008. 40p. IL K–3, Lexile: 230
Otto meets a magical genie who grants his wish to make the whole world orange, but Otto soon realizes orange isn't the best color for everything, especially spinach.

Meddaugh, Susan. *Martha Blah Blah.* Houghton Mifflin, c1996. 32p. IL K–3, Lexile: 390
When the current owner of the soup company breaks the founder's promise to have every letter of the alphabet in every can of soup, Martha, the talking dog, takes action.

Meddaugh, Susan. *Martha Speaks.* Houghton Mifflin, c1992. 32p. IL K–3, Lexile: 420
Problems arise when Martha, the family dog, learns to speak after eating alphabet soup.

Rostoker-Gruber, Karen. *Bandit.* Marshall Cavendish Children, c2008. 40p. IL K–3
When Bandit's family moves to a new house, the cat runs away and returns to the only home he knows. After he is brought back, Bandit understands that the new house is now home.

Speech Bubbles

Stone, Jon. *The Monster at the End of This Book.* IL K–3 Golden Books, 2004. 24p.
   Grover worries page by page about meeting the monster at the end of this book.

Thomas, Jan. *A Birthday for Cow!* Harcourt, c2008. 34p. IL K–3, Lexile: 170
   Pig and Mouse work together to make Cow the best birthday cake ever, despite Duck's unconventional cooking methods.

Willems, Mo. *Don't Let the Pigeon Drive the Bus!* Hyperion Books for Children, c2003. 34p. IL K–3, Lexile: 120
   A pigeon that longs to drive a bus sees a chance to make its dream come true when the bus driver takes a short break.

Symbolism

Books for Children of All Ages

Altman, Linda Jacobs. *Amelia's Road.* Lee & Low Books, c1993. 32p. IL K–3, Lexile: 660
Tired of moving around so much, Amelia, the daughter of migrant farm workers, dreams of a stable home.

Bradbury, Ray. *Switch on the Night.* Dell Dragonfly Books, 1955. 33p. IL K–3
A lonely little boy who is afraid of the dark is introduced to a whole new world by a little girl named Dark.

Browne, Anthony. *Piggybook.* Knopf, 1986. 32p. IL K–3, Lexile: 450
When Mrs. Piggott unexpectedly leaves one day, her demanding family begins to realize just how much she did for them.

Bunting, Eve. *Riding the Tiger.* Clarion Books, c2001. 32p. IL K–3
Ten-year-old Danny is bored and lonely, but when he hops on the back of the exciting and somewhat scary tiger that offers him a ride, he soon discovers that it's easier to get on the tiger than it is to get off.

Cherry, Lynne. *The Great Kapok Tree: A Tale of the Amazon Rain Forest.* Harcourt Brace, c1990. 33p. IL K–3, Lexile: 670
The many different animals that live in a great kapok tree in the Brazilian rain forest try to convince a man with an ax of the importance of not cutting down their home.

Connor, Leslie. *Miss Bridie Chose a Shovel.* Houghton Mifflin, c2004. 32p. IL K–3, Lexile: 1170
When Miss Bridie emigrates to America in 1856, she chooses to bring a shovel with her, which proves to be a useful tool throughout her life.

Cronin, Doreen. *Click, Clack, Moo: Cows That Type.* Simon & Schuster Books for Young Readers, c2006. 32p. IL K–3, Lexile: 160
When Farmer Brown's cows find a typewriter in the barn, they start making demands, and eventually go on strike when the farmer refuses to give them what they want.

Hopkinson, Deborah. *Sweet Clara and the Freedom Quilt.* Knopf, 1995. 35p. IL K–3, Lexile: 680
A young slave stitches a quilt with a map pattern that guides her to freedom in the North.

Levine, Ellen. *Henry's Freedom Box.* Scholastic Press, 2007. 40p. IL K–3, Lexile: 380
In this fictionalized account, a Virginia slave, Henry "Box" Brown, escapes to freedom in 1849 by shipping himself in a wooden crate from Richmond to Philadelphia.

Nolen, Jerdine. *Big Jabe.* HarperCollins, c2000. 33p. IL K–3, Lexile: 610
Momma Mary tells stories about a special young man who does wondrous things, especially for the slaves on the Plenty Plantation.

Pattou, Edith. *Mrs. Spitzer's Garden.* Harcourt, 2007. 32p. IL K–3
With her sure, loving, gardener's touch, Mrs. Spitzer nurtures the students in her classroom each year.

Symbolism

Seuss, Dr. *The Butter Battle Book*. Random House, c1984. 42p. IL K–3, Lexile: 710
Engaged in a long-running battle, the Yooks and the Zooks develop more and more sophisticated weaponry as they attempt to outdo each other.

Seuss, Dr. *The Lorax*. Random House, c1999. 64p. IL K–3, Lexile: 560
The Once-ler describes the results of the local pollution problem.

Silverstein, Shel. *The Giving Tree*. HarperCollins Publishers, c1992. 57p. IL K–3, Lexile: 530
A young boy grows to manhood and old age experiencing the love and generosity of a tree that gives to him without thought of return.

Van Allsburg, Chris. *The Stranger*. Houghton Mifflin, c1986. 31p. IL K–3, Lexile: 640
The enigmatic origins of the stranger whom Farmer Bailey hits with his truck and brings home to recuperate seem to have a mysterious relation to the changing season.

Van Allsburg, Chris. *The Sweetest Fig*. Houghton Mifflin, c1993. 30p. IL K–3, Lexile: 530
After being given two magical figs that make his dreams come true, Monsieur Bibot sees his plans for future wealth upset by his long-suffering dog.

Williams, Vera B. *A Chair for My Mother*. Greenwillow Books, c1982. 32p. IL K–3, Lexile: 640
A child, her waitress mother, and her grandmother save dimes to buy a comfortable armchair after all their furniture is lost in a fire.

Wood, Audrey. *Heckedy Peg*. Harcourt Brace, c1987. 32p. IL K–3, Lexile: 450
A mother saves her seven children from Heckedy Peg, a witch who has changed them into different kinds of food.

Woodson, Jacqueline. *The Other Side*. Putnam's, c2001. 32p. IL K–3 Lexile: 300,
Two girls, one white and one African American, gradually get to know each other as they sit on the fence that divides their town.

Woodson, Jacqueline. *Show Way*. Putnam's, c2005. 40p. IL K–3, Lexile: 720
A mother passes on the tradition of making quilts, or "show ways," that serve as secret maps for freedom-seeking slaves.

Books for Children Ages Eight to Twelve

Roy, Jennifer Rozines. *Yellow Star*. Marshall Cavendish, c2006. 227p. IL 5–8, Lexile: 710
From 1939, when Syvia is four and a half years old, to 1945, when she has just turned ten, a Jewish girl and her family struggle to survive in Poland's Lodz ghetto during the Nazi occupation.

Van Allsburg, Chris. *The Polar Express*. Houghton Mifflin, 2005. 32p. IL 3–6, Lexile: 520
A magical train ride on Christmas Eve takes a boy to the North Pole to receive a special gift from Santa Claus.

Symbolism

Van Allsburg, Chris. *The Widow's Broom.* Houghton Mifflin, c1992. 32p. IL 3–6, Lexile: 810
A witch's worn-out broom serves a widow well, until her neighbors decide the thing is wicked and dangerous.

Van Allsburg, Chris. *The Wretched Stone.* Houghton Mifflin, c1991. 31p. IL 5–8, Lexile: 580
A strange glowing stone picked up on a sea voyage captivates a ship's crew and has a terrible transforming effect on them.

Verbs

Books for Children of All Ages

Banks, Kate. *Max's Words.* Farrar, Straus and Giroux, 2006. 32p. IL K–3, Lexile: 420
When Max cuts out words from magazines and newspapers, collecting them the way his brothers collect stamps and coins, they all learn about words, sentences, and storytelling.

Buzzeo, Toni. *Dawdle Duckling.* Puffin Books, 2005, c2003. 32p. IL K–3
Mama Duck tries to keep Dawdle Duckling together with his siblings, but he wants to dawdle and dream, preen and play, splash and spin.

Dahl, Michael. *If You Were a Verb.* Picture Window Books, c2006. 24p. IL K–3, Lexile: 640
Simple text and drawings show how verbs are used to help build sentences.

Heller, Ruth. *Kites Sail High: A Book about Verbs.* Paperstar/Putnam & Grosset Group, 1998, c1988. 46p. IL K–3, Lexile: 600
Text and vivid illustrations introduce the concept of verbs and present examples of several kinds of verbs, including linking, auxiliary, helping, irregular, and regular ones, as well as the imperative, indicative, and subjunctive moods and passive and active voices.

Long, Melinda. *How I Became a Pirate.* Harcourt, c2003. 36p. IL K–3, Lexile: 470,
Jeremy Jacob joins Braid Beard and his pirate crew and finds out about pirate language, pirate manners, and other aspects of pirate life.

Pulver, Robin. *Nouns and Verbs Have a Field Day.* Holiday House, c2006. 32p. IL K–3, Lexile: 450
When the children in Mr. Wright's class have a field day, nouns and verbs in the classroom make their own fun.

Stevens, Janet. *The Great Fuzz Frenzy.* Harcourt, c2005. 48p. IL K–3, Lexile: 420
When a tennis ball lands in a prairie dog town, the residents find that their newfound frenzy for fuzz creates a fiasco.

Books for Children Ages Eight to Twelve

Cleary, Brian P. *Slide and Slurp, Scratch and Burp: More about Verbs.* Millbrook Press, c2007. 31p. IL 3–6
This illustrated rhyming text provides examples of both action and linking verbs.

Cleary, Brian P. *To Root, to Toot, to Parachute: What Is a Verb?* Carolrhoda Books, c2001. 32p. IL 3–6, Lexile: NP
Rhyming text and illustrations of comical cats present numerous examples of verbs, from "toss and tumble" and "jump and jam," to "whine and whisper" and "sleep and slam."

Lowry, Lois. *Gooney Bird Greene.* Yearling, 2004, c2002. 88p. IL 3–6, Lexile: 590
A most unusual new student who loves to be the center of attention entertains her teacher and fellow second graders by telling absolutely true stories about herself, including how she got her name.

Written in Sign Language

Books for Children of All Ages

Bornstein, Harry. *Goldilocks and the Three Bears: Told in Signed English.* Kendall Green Publications, 1996. 50p. IL K–3

The well-known tale about the little girl who wanders through the woods and disturbs the house of the three bears, accompanied by diagrams showing how to form the Signed English signs for each word of the text.

Bornstein, Harry. *Little Red Riding Hood: Told in Signed English.* Kendall Green Publications, Gallaudet University Press, c1990. 43p. IL K–3

The well-known fairy tale about a little girl who meets a wolf posing as her grandmother, accompanied by diagrams showing how to form the Signed English signs for each word of the text.

Bornstein, Harry. *The Night before Christmas: Told in Signed English: An Adaptation of the Original Poem "A Visit from St. Nicholas" by Clement C. Moore.* Kendall Green Publications, c1994. Unpaged. IL K–3

Illustrated rendition of the traditional holiday poem, including line drawings that show verses in Signed English.

Bornstein, Harry. *Nursery Rhymes from Mother Goose: Told in Signed English.* Kendall Green Publications, Gallaudet University Press, 1992. 41p.IL K–3

Presents well-known Mother Goose rhymes accompanied by diagrams showing how to form the Signed English signs for each word in the poems.

Millman, Isaac. *Moses Goes to the Circus.* Farrar, Straus and Giroux, 2003. 32p. IL K–3, Lexile: 490

Moses, who is deaf, has a good time with his family at the circus, where they communicate using sign language. The book includes illustrations of some of the signs they use.

Millman, Isaac. *Moses Goes to a Concert.* Farrar, Straus and Giroux, 1998. 40p. IL K–3, Lexile: 670

Moses and his schoolmates, who are all deaf, attend a concert where the orchestra's percussionist is also deaf. The book includes illustrations in sign language and a page showing the manual alphabet.

Millman, Isaac. *Moses Goes to School.* Frances Foster Books/Farrar, Straus and Giroux, 2000. 32p. IL K–3, Lexile: 460

Moses and his friends enjoy the first day of school at their special school for the deaf and hard of hearing, where they use sign language to talk to one another.

Millman, Isaac. *Moses Sees a Play.* Frances Foster Books/Farrar, Straus and Giroux, 2004. 32p. IL K–3

Moses and his classmates, who are deaf or hard of hearing, attend a play at their school, and Moses makes a new friend from another class.

Newby, Robert. *King Midas: With Selected Sentences in American Sign Language.* Kendall Green Publications, Gallaudet University Press, 1990. 62p. IL K–3

Presents the classic tale of the king who wished that everything he touched would turn to gold. Line drawings depict selected sentences in American Sign Language.

Part 3

Family

Absent Father

Books for Children of All Ages

Caines, Jeannette Franklin. *Just Us Women.* HarperTrophy, 1984, c1982. 32p. IL K–3, Lexile: 610
A young girl and her favorite aunt share the excitement of planning a very special car trip for just the two of them.

Waddell, Martin. *Owl Babies.* Candlewick Press, 1992. 26p. IL K–3, Lexile: 500
Three owl babies whose mother has gone out in the night try to stay calm while she is gone.

Williams, Vera B. *A Chair for My Mother.* Greenwillow Books, c1982. 32p. IL K–3, Lexile: 640
A child, her waitress mother, and her grandmother save dimes to buy a comfortable armchair after all their furniture is lost in a fire.

Williams, Vera B. *Three Days on a River in a Red Canoe.* Greenwillow Books, c1981. 32p. IL K–3, Lexile: 560
Mother, Aunt Rosie, and two children take a three-day camping trip by canoe.

Woodson, Jacqueline. *Coming on Home Soon.* Putnam's, c2004. 32p. IL K–3, Lexile: 550
After Mama takes a job in Chicago during World War II, Ada Ruth stays with Grandma, but misses her mother, who loves her more than rain and snow.

Ziefert, Harriet. *The Big Red Blanket.* Sterling, c2005. 22p. IL K–3, Lexile: 120
In this early reader geared toward children ages four to six, Kara is a little girl who finds a big red blanket to play with, and soon her family joins in the fun. The book includes a fifty-word word bank.

Books for Children Ages Eight to Twelve

Clark, Clara Gillow. *Hattie on Her Way.* Candlewick Press, 2005. 177p. IL 5–8, Lexile: 860
In the late 1800s, eleven-year-old Hattie, still grieving over the death of her mother and lonely for her absent father, moves in with her grandmother in the city of Kingston, New York, to be educated and learn about polite society. While there, she discovers the fate of her missing grandfather.

Cooper, Melrose. *Gettin' through Thursday.* Lee & Low Books, c1998. 32p. IL 3–6, Lexile: 680
Money is tight every Thursday, the day before Andre's mother gets her paycheck. As a result, Andre is upset when he realizes his report card and the promised celebration for his making the honor roll will come on a Thursday.

Fletcher, Ralph J. *Uncle Daddy.* H. Holt, 2001. 133p. IL 5–8, Lexile: 490
When his long-absent father suddenly reappears, nine-year-old Rivers struggles with conflicting feelings and reexamines his relationship with the great-uncle who had served as his surrogate father.

Kinsey-Warnock, Natalie. *Lumber Camp Library.* HarperTrophy, 2003, c2002. 87p. IL 3–6, Lexile: 730
Ruby wants to be a teacher, but after her father's death in a logging accident, she must quit school to care for her ten brothers and sisters. A chance meeting with a lonely old blind woman eventually transforms her life.

Absent Father

Ryan, Pam Muñoz. *Becoming Naomi Leon.* Scholastic, 2004. 246p. IL 5–8, Lexile: 830
When Naomi's absent mother resurfaces to claim her, Naomi runs away to Mexico with her great-grandmother and younger brother in search of her father.

Shreve, Susan Richards. *Jonah, the Whale.* Arthur A. Levine Books, c1998. 110p. IL 3–6, Lexile: 740
After moving to a new town, Jonah, an eleven-year-old with a big imagination, reinvents himself as a talk show host, hoping his new role will somehow bring his absent father back.

Stauffacher, Sue. *Donuthead.* Random House Children's Books, 2005, c2003. 144p. IL 3–6, Lexile: 850
Franklin Delano Donuthead, a fifth-grader obsessed with hygiene and safety, finds an unlikely friend and protector in Sarah Kervick, the tough new student who lives in a dirty trailer.

Voigt, Cynthia. *Homecoming.* Atheneum Books for Young Readers, c1981. 312p. IL 5–8, Lexile: 630
Abandoned by their mother, four children begin a search for a home and an identity.

Yee, Lisa. *So Totally Emily Ebers.* Arthur A. Levine Books, c2007. 280p. IL 3–6, Lexile: 660
In a series of letters to her absent father, twelve-year-old Emily Ebers deals with moving cross-country, her parents' divorce, a new friendship, and her first serious crush.

Adoption

Books for Children of All Ages

Bunting, Eve. *Jin Woo.* Clarion Books, c2001. 30p. IL K–3, Lexile: 390
  Davey is dubious about having a new adopted brother from Korea, but when he finds out that his parents still love him, he decides that having a baby brother will be fine.

Buzzeo, Toni. *The Sea Chest.* Dial Books for Young Readers, c2002. 32p. IL K–3, Lexile: 1040
  A young girl listens as her great-aunt, a lighthouse keeper's daughter, tells of her childhood living on a Maine island, and of the infant who washed ashore after a storm.

Curtis, Jamie Lee. *Tell Me Again about The Night I Was Born.* Joanna Cotler Books, c1996. 36p. IL K–3, Lexile: 1080
  A young girl asks her parents to tell her again the cherished family story of her birth and adoption.

DePaola, Tomie. *A New Barker in the House.* Putnam's, c2002. 32p. IL K–3, Lexile: 240
  Twins Moffie and Morgie are excited when they hear that their family is adopting a three-year-old Hispanic boy.

Kasza, Keiko. *A Mother for Choco.* G. P. Putnam's, c1992. 32p. IL K–3, Lexile: 390
  A lonely little bird named Choco goes in search of a mother. He tries a giraffe, a penguin and even a walrus in his pursuit of a mother.

Koehler, Phoebe. *The Day We Met You.* Aladdin Paperbacks, 1997, c1990. 40p. IL K–3, Lexile: 380
  Mom and Dad recount the exciting day when they adopted their baby.

Krishnaswami, Uma. *Bringing Asha Home.* Lee & Low Books, c2006. 32p. IL K–3, Lexile: 560
  Eight-year-old Arun waits impatiently while international adoption paperwork is completed so that he can meet his new baby sister from India.

Lewis, Rose A. *Every Year on Your Birthday.* Little, Brown, 2007. 32p. IL K–3, Lexile: 390
  Each year on the birthday of her adopted Chinese daughter, a mother recalls the moments they have shared, from the first toy to the friends left behind in China.

Lewis, Rose A. *I Love You like Crazy Cakes.* Little, Brown, c2000. 32p. IL K–3, Lexile: 550
  A woman describes how she went to China to adopt a special baby girl. The book is based on the author's own experiences.

Markle, Sandra. *Little Lost Bat.* Charlesbridge, c2006. 32p. IL K–3, Lexile: 880
  Chronicles the early life of an orphaned Mexican free-tailed bat, from its birth to its adoption by a new mother. Includes facts about bats.

McCutcheon, John. *Happy Adoption Day!* Little, Brown, c1996. 26p. IL K–3, Lexile: 350
  Parents celebrate the day on which they adopted their child and continue to reassure the new addition to their family that the child is wanted, loved, and very special. The book includes music for the song "Happy Adoption Day!"

Adoption

Okimoto, Jean Davies. *The White Swan Express: A Story about Adoption.* Clarion Books, c2002. 32p. IL K–3, Lexile: 760

Across North America, people in four different homes prepare for a special trip to China, while four baby girls in China await their new adoptive parents.

Richmond, Marianne. *I Wished for You: An Adoption Story.* Marianne Richmond Studios, c2008. 40p. IL K–3, Lexile: 200

Barley, an adopted little bear, is reassured of his mother's love after she tells him the story of how she wished for him and her wish came true.

Say, Allen. *Allison.* **Houghton Mifflin,** c1997. 32p. IL K–3, Lexile: 430

When Allison realizes that she looks more like her favorite doll than like her parents, she comes to terms with this unwelcomed discovery through the help of a stray cat.

Turner, Ann Warren. *Through Moon and Stars and Night Skies.* Charlotte Zolotow Book, c1990. 31p. IL K–3, Lexile: 250

A boy who came from far away to be adopted by an American couple remembers how unfamiliar and frightening some of the things were in his new home before he accepted the love to be found there.

Books for Children Ages Eight to Twelve

Atinsky, Steve. *Trophy Kid; Or, How I Was Adopted by the Rich and Famous.* Delacorte Press, c2008. 184p. IL 3–6, Lexile: 790

Since his much-publicized adoption at age three by American movie stars, thirteen-year-old Josef's carefully scripted public life has hidden the isolation he feels at home. Writing a book with a ghostwriter reveals much about his adoptive family and the one he lost during the war in Croatia.

Banks, Kate. *Dillon Dillon.* Farrar, Straus and Giroux, 2005, c2002. 149p. IL 3–6

During the summer in which he turns ten years old, Dillon Dillon learns the surprising story behind his name and develops a relationship with three loons, living on the lake near his family's New Hampshire cabin, that help him make sense of his life.

Cummings, Mary. *Three Names of Me.* Albert Whitman, 2006. 40p. IL 3–6, Lexile: 690

A girl adopted from China describes how her three names—one from her birth mother, one from the orphanage, and one from her American parents—are all important parts of who she is.

Diersch, Sandra. *Home Court Advantage.* James Lorimer, Distributed by Orca Book Publishers, 2001. 101p. IL 3–6

The only thing Debbie has ever wanted is a family of her own. When no one understands that having foster parents just is not the same thing, she takes out her frustrations on the basketball court.

Givner, Joan. *Ellen Fremedon: Journalist.* Groundwood Books/House of Anansi Press, Distributed by Publishers Group West, c2005. 177p. IL 3–6

Ellen and her friend Jenny decide to publish their own newspaper during summer vacation. While investigating her mysterious new neighbor for a story, Ellen learns something surprising about herself.

Adoption

Harrar, George. *Parents Wanted.* Milkweed Editions, 2001. 239p. IL 3–6
Twelve-year-old Andrew, who has attention-deficit disorder, is adopted by new parents after spending years in other foster homes; he desperately hopes that he will not mess up his new situation.

Kent, Rose. *Kimchi & Calamari.* Harper, 2010, c2007. 220p. IL 3–6, Lexile: 750
After getting caught lying on a school project about who his grandfather was, fourteen-year-old Joseph Calderno is forced to redo the assignment and learns more about his adopted Italian American family and Korean heritage than he ever thought possible.

Krementz, Jill. *How It Feels to Be Adopted.* Knopf, 1988. 107p. IL 5–8 (Non-fiction)
Interviews with adopted children and adoptive families about their experiences and feelings concerning adoption.

Lupica, Mike. *Safe at Home.* Philomel Books, c2008. 175p. IL 3–6, Lexile: 960
Nick Crandall's new foster parents are both professors who know nothing about sports, and his new teammates feel he is too young to play varsity baseball. Meanwhile, Nick is out to prove that he belongs not only on his team, but also to his parents.

McKay, Hilary. *Saffy's Angel.* Margaret K. McElderry Books, 2002. 152p. IL 3–6, Lexile: 630
After learning that she was adopted, thirteen-year-old Saffron's relationship with her eccentric, artistic family changes. Ultimately, they help her go back to Italy, where she was born, to find a special memento of her past.

Myers, Walter Dean. *Me, Mop, and the Moondance Kid.* Bantam Doubleday Dell Books for Young Readers, 1991, c1988. 154p. IL 3–6, Lexile: 640
Although adoption has taken them out of the institution where they grew up, eleven-year-old T. J. and his younger brother Moondance remain involved with their friend Mop's relentless attempts to become adopted herself and to wreak revenge on their baseball rivals, the obnoxious Eagles.

Patron, Susan. *Lucky Breaks.* Atheneum Books for Young Readers, c2009. 181p. IL 3–6, Lexile: 960
Lucky, having met a potential best friend who was visiting her uncle in Hard Pan, California, devises a plan to get the young girl back to the town.

Warren, Andrea. *Escape From Saigon: How a Vietnamese War Orphan Became an American Boy.* Farrar, Straus and Giroux, 2008. 110p. IL 5-8, Lexile: 930
Chronicles the experiences of an orphaned Amerasian boy from his birth and early childhood in Saigon through his departure from Vietnam in the 1975 Operation Babylift and his subsequent life as the adopted son of an American family in Ohio.

Weeks, Sarah. *As Simple as It Seems.* Laura Geringer Books, c2010. 181p. IL 3–6, Lexile: 910
Eleven-year-old Verbena Polter gets through a difficult summer of turbulent emotions and the revelation of a disturbing family secret with an odd new friend who believes she is the ghost of a girl who drowned many years before.

Separation and Divorce

Books for Children of All Ages

Abercrombie, Barbara. *Charlie Anderson.* Aladdin Paperbacks, 1995. 32p. IL K–3, Lexile: 480
A cat comes out of the night to steal the hearts of two sisters who look forward to his sleeping on their beds. One day, however, Charlie doesn't come home, and they learn a surprising secret about him.

Apel, Melanie Ann. *Let's Talk about Living with Your Single Dad.* PowerKids Press, 2001. 24p. IL K–3 (Non-fiction)
Discusses, in simple text, the difficulties, adjustments, and positive aspects of living with a single male parent.

Brown, Laurene Krasny. *Dinosaurs Divorce: A Guide for Changing Families.* Atlantic Monthly Press, c1986. 32p. IL K–3, Lexile: 530 (Non-fiction)
Text and illustrations of dinosaur characters introduce aspects of divorce such as its causes and effects, living with a single parent, spending holidays in two separate households, and adjusting to a step-parent.

Bunting, Eve. *My Mom's Wedding.* Sleeping Bear Press, c2006. 32p. IL K–3
Seven-year-old Pinkie has mixed feelings about her divorced mother's wedding, especially when she learns that her beloved father will be attending the ceremony as a guest.

Coffelt, Nancy. *Fred Stays with Me.* Little, Brown, 2007. 32p. IL K–3
A child describes how she lives sometimes with her mother and sometimes with her father, but her dog is her constant companion.

Crews, June Thomas. *Can Anyone Fix My Broken Heart?: Hope for Children of Divorce.* WinePress Publishing, c2000. 32p. IL K–3 (Non-fiction)
A young boy faces the pain and challenges that his parents' divorce brings by trusting in God.

Moore-Mallinos, Jennifer. *Daddy's Getting Married.* Barron's, 2006. 31p. IL K–3
A little girl explains how she feels when her dad decides to get remarried—there are so many feelings she just doesn't understand.

Ransom, Jeanie Franz. *I Don't Want to Talk about It.* Magination Press, c2000. 28p. IL K–3
After reluctantly talking with her parents about their upcoming divorce, a young girl discovers that there will be some big changes but that their love for her will remain the same. The book includes an afterword for parents on helping children through such a change.

Weitzman, Elizabeth. *Let's Talk about Living in a Blended Family.* PowerKids Press, 2004. 24p. IL K–3 (Non-fiction)
Provides advice on how to accept and deal with the challenges of living in a stepfamily, or blended family.

Weitzman, Elizabeth. *Let's Talk about Living with a Single Parent.* PowerKids Press, 1996. 24p. IL K–3, Lexile: 650 (Non-fiction)
Examines potential problems and issues that might arise in several different kinds of single-parent homes.

From *101 Great, Ready-to-Use Book Lists for Children* by Nancy J. Keane. Santa Barbara, CA: Libraries Unlimited. Copyright © 2012.

Separation and Divorce

Weninger, Brigitte. *Good-Bye, Daddy!* North-South Books, 1997, c1995. 32p. IL K–3
   A little boy's teddy bear helps him come to terms with his parents' divorce by telling him a story about a little bear in similar circumstances.

Books for Children Ages Eight to Twelve

Alvarez, Julia. *How Tia Lola Came to Visit—Stay.* A. Knopf, c2001. 147p. IL 3–6, Lexile: 740
   Ten-year-old Miguel is at first embarrassed by his colorful aunt, Tia Lola, when she comes to Vermont from the Dominican Republic to stay with his mother, his sister, and him after his parents' divorce. Eventually, he learns to love her.

Blume, Judy. *It's Not the End of the World.* Atheneum Books for Young Readers, 2001, c1972. 169p. IL 3–6, Lexile: 530
   When her parents divorce, a sixth grader struggles to understand that sometimes people are unable to live together.

Byars, Betsy Cromer. *The Pinballs.* Harper & Row, c1977. 136p. IL 3–6, Lexile: 600
   Three lonely foster children learn to care about themselves and one another.

Cleary, Beverly. *Dear Mr. Henshaw.* Morrow Junior Books, c1983. 133p. IL 3–6, Lexile: 910
   In his letters to his favorite author, ten-year-old Leigh reveals his problems in coping with his parents' divorce, being the new boy in school, and generally finding his own place in the world.

Couloumbis, Audrey. *Lexie.* Random House, c2011. 199p. IL 3–6
   When ten-year-old Lexie goes with her father to the beach for a week, she is surprised to find that he has invited his girlfriend and her two sons to join them for the entire week.

Creech, Sharon. *Walk Two Moons.* HarperCollins, c1994. 280p. IL 5–8, Lexile: 770
   After her mother leaves home suddenly, thirteen-year-old Sal and her grandparents take a car trip retracing her mother's route. Along the way, Sal recounts the story of her friend Phoebe, whose mother also left.

Danziger, Paula. *The Divorce Express.* Puffin Books, 1982. 148p. IL 5–8
   Resentful of her parents' divorce, a young girl tries to accommodate herself to their new lives and also find a place for herself.

Ferguson, Pamela. *Sunshine Picklelime.* Random House, c2010. 232p. IL 3–6
   PJ Picklelime can talk to birds, hear bells ringing in a woman's curls, and spot moonbows in the night sky, but when a close friend dies and her parents separate, she searches for understanding and a way to recover her sunshine.

Krishnaswami, Uma. *Naming Maya.* Farrar, Straus and Giroux, 2004. 178p. IL 5–8, Lexile: 770
   When Maya accompanies her mother to India to sell her grandfather's house, she uncovers family history relating to her parents' divorce and learns more about herself and her relationship with her mother.

Separation and Divorce

Park, Barbara. *Don't Make Me Smile***.** Random House, 2002. 133p. IL 3–6, Lexile: 500
Charlie Hickles' parents are getting a divorce; they don't know why Charlie can't just understand this fact and move on. With so many changes happening in his life, Charlie finds he has trouble adjusting to his parent's divorce.

Paulsen, Gary. *Hatchet***.** Atheneum Books for Young Readers, c1987. 195p. IL 5–8, Lexile: 1020
After a plane crash, thirteen-year-old Brian spends fifty-four days in the wilderness, learning to survive with only the aid of a hatchet given him by his mother, and also learning to survive his parents' divorce.

White, Ruth. *Buttermilk Hill***.** Farrar, Straus and Giroux, 2006, c2004. 167p. IL 5–8
When her parents divorce and gradually begin to make new lives for themselves, Piper finds all of the changes difficult to cope with, but in time she starts to find her own way.

Unconventional Families

Books for Children of All Ages

Byrne, Gayle. *Sometimes It's Grandmas and Grandpas, Not Mommies and Daddies.* Abbeville Kids, c2009. 32p. IL K–3

A young girl who lives with her grandparents experiences warmth, love, and closeness, even as she wonders why her parents are not raising her.

Hoffman, Mary. *The Great Big Book of Families.* Dial Books for Young Readers, 2011, c2010. 34p. IL K–3 (Non-fiction)

An illustrated overview of families, examining various aspects of families from houses to holidays to schools and pets, and discussing feelings and family trees.

Juster, Norton. *The Hello, Goodbye Window.* Michael Di Capua Books/Hyperion Books for Children, 2005. 32p. IL K–3

A little girl tells about the special kitchen window at her beloved Nanny and Poppy's house, from which a person can see anyone or anything coming and going.

Kent, Susan. *Let's Talk about Living with a Grandparent.* PowerKids Press, c2000. 24p. IL K–3 (Non-fiction)

Discusses various reasons for living with a grandparent, the benefits of such an arrangement, and ways to help out at home.

Kuklin, Susan. *Families.* Hyperion Books for Children, c2006. 36p. IL K–3, Lexile: 560 (Non-fiction)

Presents brief interviews with children from fifteen diverse American families—including large, small, mixed-race, immigrant, gay and lesbian, divorced, single-parent, religious, adoptive, and special-needs families—about their parents, siblings, lifestyles, and traditions. Includes photos of each family.

Pellegrini, Nina. *Families Are Different.* Holiday House, c1991. 32p. IL K–3, Lexile: 540

An adopted Korean girl discovers that her classmates have many different types of families.

Polacco, Patricia. *In Our Mothers' House.* Philomel Books, c2009. 48p. IL K–3, Lexile: 750

Three young children experience the joys and challenges of being raised by two mothers.

Schuette, Sarah L. *Adoptive Families.* Capstone Press, c2010. 24p. IL K–3, Lexile: 450 (Non-fiction)

Simple text and photographs provide an introduction to adoptive families and describe how family members interact with one another.

Skutch, Robert. *Who's in a Family?* Tricycle Press, c1995. 32p. IL K–3 (Non-fiction)

Shows the various combinations of individuals who can make up a family, emphasizing the positive aspects of different family structures. Uses examples from the animal kingdom to illustrate how family groupings can differ.

Weitzman, Elizabeth. *Let's Talk about Living in a Blended Family.* PowerKids Press, 2004. 24p. IL K–3 (Non-fiction)

Provides advice on how to accept and deal with the challenges of living in a stepfamily, or blended family.

Unconventional Families

Books for Children Ages Eight to Twelve

Agell, Charlotte. *The Accidental Adventures of India Mcallister.* Henry Holt, 2010. 151p. IL 3–6, Lexile: 690

India, an unusual nine-and-a-half-year-old living in small-town Maine, has a series of adventures that bring her closer to her artist-mother, strengthen her friendship with a neighbor boy, and help her to accept the man for whom her father moved away.

Byars, Betsy Cromer. *The Blossoms and the Green Phantom.* Holiday House, 2008, c1987. 163p. IL 3–6

Disasters befall the Blossom family as Pap falls into a dumpster and can't get out, Junior tries desperately to make a success of his secret invention, and Vern dreads letting a new friend meet his unusual family.

Crew, Linda. *Nekomah Creek.* Dell Yearling, 1993, c1991. 191p. IL 3–6, Lexile: 670

Nine-year-old Robby loves his noisy and somewhat unconventional family, but unwanted attention from a counselor and a bully at school make him self-conscious about just how unconventional his family might look to outsiders.

Hayter, Rhonda. *The Witchy Worries of Abbie Adams.* Dial Books for Young Readers, c2010. 242p. IL 3–6, Lexile: 1170

Fifth-grader Abbie, who is descended from a long line of witches, tries to keep her family's magic powers secret from everyone she knows—until her father brings home a kitten with some very unusual characteristics.

MacLachlan, Patricia. *Arthur, for the Very First Time.* HarperTrophy, 1989, c1980. 117p. IL 3–6, Lexile: 660

Arthur spends a summer with his unconventional aunt and uncle and begins to look at life, his family, and himself differently.

Paratore, Coleen. *The Funeral Director's Son.* Simon & Schuster Books for Young Readers, c2008. 134p. IL 3–6, Lexile: 510

The last thing twelve-year-old Christopher "Kip" Campbell wants is to take over the funeral business that has been in his family for generations, but he is the only Campbell heir and seems to have a calling to help the dead and their survivors in a most unusual way.

Raskin, Ellen. *Figgs & Phantoms.* Dutton Children's Books, 2011, c1974. 152p. IL 5–8

Chronicles the adventures of the unusual Figg family after they left show business and settled in the town of Pineapple.

Tolan, Stephanie S. *Surviving the Applewhites.* HarperTrophy, 2004, c2002. 216p. IL 5–8, Lexile: 820

Jake, a budding juvenile delinquent, is sent for home-schooling to the arty and eccentric Applewhite family's Creative Academy. There, he discovers talents and interests he never knew he had.

Death of a Grandparent

Books for Children of All Ages

DePaola, Tomie *Nana Upstairs & Nana Downstairs*. Puffin Books, 2000, c1973. 32p. IL K–3, Lexile: 530
> Four-year-old Tommy enjoys his relationship with both his grandmother and great-grandmother, but eventually learns to face their inevitable deaths.

Fox, Mem. *Sophie*. Harcourt Brace, 1997, c1989. 32p. IL K–3, Lexile: 340
> As Sophie grows bigger and her grandfather gets smaller, they continue to love each other very much.

Jukes, Mavis. *Blackberries in the Dark*. Dell Yearling, 2001, c1985. 58p. IL K–3, Lexile: 500
> Nine-year-old Austin visits his grandmother in the summer after his grandfather dies; together, they try to come to terms with their loss.

Nobisso, Josephine. *Grandma's Scrapbook*. Gingerbread House, 2000, c1990. 32p. IL K–3, Lexile: 600
> A scrapbook provides many memories of good times enjoyed with Grandma.

Nobisso, Josephine. *Grandpa Loved*. Gingerbread House, 2000. 31p. IL K–3, Lexile: 640
> Grandpa's love of life ensures that he is still present, even after his death, in the lives of all who loved him.

Shriver, Maria. *What's Heaven?* St. Martin's Press, c1999. 32p. IL K–3
> After her great-grandmother's death, a young girl learns about heaven by asking her mother all kinds of questions.

Simon, Norma. *The Saddest Time*. Whitman, 1986. 40p. IL K–3, Lexile: 520
> Explains death as the inevitable end of life and provides three situations in which children experience powerful emotions when someone close has died.

Wild, Margaret. *Old Pig*. Allen & Unwin, 2009, c1995. 32p. IL K–3
> Because Old Pig knows that her time to die is near, she puts her affairs in order and takes a slow walk with Granddaughter to savor the beauty of the world for one last time.

Woodson, Jacqueline. *Sweet, Sweet Memory*. Jump at the Sun/Hyperion Paperbacks for Children, 2007, c2000. 32p. IL K–3, Lexile: 380
> A child and her grandmother feel sad when Grandpa dies, but as time passes, funny memories of him make them laugh and feel better.

Zolotow, Charlotte. *My Grandson Lew*. HarperCollins, c2003. IL K–3
> Together Lewis and his mother remember Grandpa, who used to come in the night when Lewis called.

Death of a Grandparent

Books for Children Ages Eight to Twelve

Bredsdorff, Bodil. *The Crow-Girl: The Children of Crow Cove*. Farrar, Straus and Giroux, 2004. 155p. IL 3–6, Lexile: 810

> After the death of her grandmother, a young orphan girl leaves her house by the cove and begins a journey that leads her to people and experiences that exemplify the wisdom her grandmother had shared with her.

Buscaglia, Leo F. *The Fall of Freddie the Leaf: A Story of Life for All Ages*. Slack, 2002, c1982. 32p. IL 3–6

> As Freddie experiences the changing seasons along with his companion leaves, he learns about the delicate balance between life and death.

Fredericks, Anthony D. *The Tsunami Quilt: Grandfather's Story*. Sleeping Bear Press, c2007. 40p. IL 3–6

> Every year, Kimo and his grandfather have placed a flower lei atop a stone monument at Laupahoehoe Point. It is not until after Grandfather's death that Kimo learns of the 1946 tsunami that took the lives of twenty-four school children and teachers, including Grandfather's younger brother.

Henkes, Kevin. *Sun & Spoon*. HarperTrophy, 2007, c1997. 135p. IL 3–6, Lexile: 780

> After the death of his grandmother, ten-year-old Spoon observes the changes in his grandfather and tries to find the perfect artifact to preserve his memories of her.

Wiles, Deborah. *Love, Ruby Lavender.* Harcourt, c2001. 188p. IL 3–6, Lexile: 570

> When her quirky grandmother goes to Hawaii for the summer, nine-year-old Ruby learns to survive on her own in Mississippi by writing letters, befriending chickens as well as the new girl in town, and finally coping with her grandfather's death.

Interracial Families

Books for Children of All Ages

Ada, Alma Flor. *I Love Saturdays y Domingos*. Atheneum Books for Young Readers, c2002. 32p. IL K–3, Lexile: 510
> A young girl enjoys the similarities and the differences between her English-speaking and Spanish-speaking grandparents.

Adoff, Arnold. *Black Is Brown Is Tan*. HarperCollins, 2002, c2001. 34p. IL K–3, Lexile: NP
> Describes in verse a family with a brown-skinned mother, white-skinned father, two children, and their various relatives.

Alko, Selina. *I'm Your Peanut Butter Big Brother*. Alfred A. Knopf, c2009. 32p. IL K–3
> A child in an interracial family wonders what his yet-to-be-born sibling will look like.

Czech, Jan M. *An American Face*. Child & Family Press, c2000. 32p. IL K–3
> Adopted from Korea by American parents, Jessie excitedly waits for the day he will get his American citizenship and, he thinks, an American face.

Igus, Toyomi. *Two Mrs. Gibsons*. Children's Book Press, c1996. 32p. IL K–3, Lexile: 530
> The biracial daughter of an African American father and a Japanese mother fondly recalls growing up with her mother and her father's mother—two very different but equally loving women.

Nikola-Lisa, W. *Bein' with You This Way*. Lee & Low Books, c1994. 32p. IL K–3, Lexile: NP
> A poem about human differences and similarities, accompanied by paintings of an interracial group of children sharing a sunny day and the universal childhood joy of just being together.

Williams, Vera B. *"More More More" Said the Baby: 3 Love Stories*. Greenwillow Books, c1990. 32p. IL K–3, Lexile: 480
> Three babies are caught up in the air and given loving attention by a father, a grandmother, and a mother.

Books for Children Ages Eight to Twelve

Cheng, Andrea. *Grandfather Counts*. Lee & Low Books, c2000. 32p. IL 3–6, Lexile: 410
> When her maternal grandfather comes from China, Helen, who is biracial, develops a special bond with him despite their age and language differences.

Frazier, Sundee Tucker. *Brendan Buckley's Universe and Everything in It*. Delacorte Press, c2007. 198p. IL 3–6, Lexile: 630
> Brendan Buckley, a biracial ten-year-old, applies his scientific problem-solving ability and newfound interest in rocks and minerals to connect with his white grandfather, the president of Puyallup Rock Club, and to learn why he and Brendan's mother are estranged.

Interracial Families

Frazier, Sundee Tucker. *The Other Half of My Heart.* Delacorte Press, c2010. 296p. IL 3–6, Lexile: 750

> Twin daughters of interracial parents, eleven-year-olds Keira and Minna have very different skin tones and personalities. Even so, it is not until their African American grandmother enters them in the Miss Black Pearl Pre-Teen competition in North Carolina that red-haired, pale-skinned Minna realizes what life in their small town in the Pacific Northwest has been like for her more outgoing, darker-skinned sister.

Garcia, Cristina. *I Wanna Be Your Shoebox.* Simon & Schuster Books for Young Readers, 2009, c2008. 198p. IL 3–6, Lexile: 770

> Thirteen-year-old Southern California surfer Yumi Ruiz-Hirsch is a unique mix of Jewish, Japanese, and Cuban heritage. When her grandfather, Saul, is diagnosed with terminal cancer, she asks him to tell her his life story in an attempt to better understand her own history.

Hesse, Karen. *Aleutian Sparrow.* Aladdin Paperbacks, 2005, c2003. 156p. IL 5–8, Lexile: NP

> An Aleutian Islander recounts her suffering during World War II in American internment camps designed to "protect" the population from the invading Japanese.

Murray, Kirsty. *The Secret Life of Maeve Lee Kwong.* Allen & Unwin, 2006. 252p. IL 3–6

> When Maeve's mother dies in a car crash, she is sent to live with her strict Chinese grandparents. In her new life, she struggles to maintain relationships with her family and friends and continue her dancing as she searches for her father.

Namioka, Lensey. *Half and Half.* Dell Yearling, 2004, c2003. 136p. IL 3–6, Lexile: 800

> At Seattle's annual Folk Fest, twelve-year-old Fiona and her older brother are torn between trying to please their Chinese grandmother and making their Scottish grandparents happy.

Schwartz, Ellen. *Stealing Home.* Tundra Books of Northern New York, c2006. 217p. IL 3–6, Lexile: 630

> Nine-year-old Yankees fan and Bronx native Joey Sexton is sent to Brooklyn after his mother's death. There, he finds himself battling prejudice in his own family and trying to win the acceptance of his white, Jewish grandfather, who looks down on him because he is half African American.

From *101 Great, Ready-to-Use Book Lists for Children* by Nancy J. Keane. Santa Barbara, CA: Libraries Unlimited. Copyright © 2012.

Death of a Pet

Books for Children of All Ages

Rylant, Cynthia. *Cat Heaven*. Blue Sky Press, c1997. 34p. IL K–3, Lexile: 490
God created Cat Heaven, with fields of sweet grass where cats can play, kitty toys for them to enjoy, and angels to rub their noses and ears.

Rylant, Cynthia. *Dog Heaven*. Blue Sky Press, c1995. 34p. IL K–3, Lexile: 820
God created Dog Heaven, a place where dogs can eat ice cream biscuits, sleep on fluffy clouds, and run through unending fields.

Wilhelm, Hans. *I'll Always Love You*. Crown Publishers, c1985. 31p. IL K–3
A child's sadness at the death of a beloved dog is tempered by the remembrance of saying to it every night, "I'll always love you."

Books for Children Ages Eight to Twelve

Day, Alexandra. *Not Forgotten: A Consolation for the Loss of an Animal Friend*. Laughing Elephant, 2004. 24p. IL 3–6
A pet that has died offers comfort to its owner and hope that they will someday see each other again. The book includes illustrations by well-known artists.

Gardiner, John Reynolds. *Stone Fox*. Crowell, 1980. 85p. IL 3–6, Lexile: 550
Little Willie hopes to pay the back taxes on his grandfather's farm with the purse from a dog sled race he enters.

Grogan, John. *Marley & Me: Life and Love with the World's Worst Dog*. Morrow, c2006. 305p. IL YA (Non-fiction)
The author presents a tender story of his family's love for their yellow Labrador retriever, Marley, chronicling how he grew from a mischievous puppy into a nearly impossible adult that no amount of obedience school training could correct.

Korman, Gordon. *No More Dead Dogs*. Hyperion Paperbacks for Children, 2000. 180p. IL 3–6, Lexile: 610
Eighth-grade football hero Wallace Wallace is sentenced to detention attending rehearsals of the school play. There, in spite of himself, he becomes wrapped up in the production and begins to suggest changes that improve not only the play but his life as well.

Morehead, Debby. *A Special Place for Charlee: A Child's Companion through Pet Loss*. Partners in Publishing, c1996. 32p. IL 3–6
Mark, a young boy, learns how to handle his feelings of sadness and loss when his beloved dog Charlee gets sick and has to be euthanized.

Death of a Pet

Peck, Robert Newton. *A Day No Pigs Would Die.* Random House Sprinter Books, 1972. 150p. IL 5–8, Lexile: 690

> To a thirteen-year-old Vermont farm boy whose father slaughters pigs for a living, maturity comes early as he learns "doing what's got to be done," especially regarding his pet pig who cannot produce a litter.

Rawls, Wilson. *Where the Red Fern Grows: The Story of Two Dogs and a Boy.* Yearling, 1996, c1961. 212p. IL 5–8, Lexile: 700

> A young boy living in the Ozarks achieves his heart's desire when he becomes the owner of two redbone hounds and teaches them to be champion hunters.

Wallace, Bill. *Beauty.* Aladdin Paperbacks, 2007, c1988. 177p. IL 3–6, Lexile: 660

> Unhappy about his parents splitting up and moving with his mother to Grandpa's farm, eleven-year-old Luke finds comfort in riding and caring for a horse named Beauty.

Wallace, Bill. *A Dog Called Kitty.* Holiday House, c1980. 153p. IL 3–6, Lexile: 710

> Afraid of dogs since he was attacked by a mad one, Ricky resists taking in a homeless pup that shows up at the farm.

Part 4

Genre

Memoirs

Books for Children of All Ages

Crews, Donald. *Bigmama's.* Greenwillow Books, c1991. 32p. IL K–3, Lexile: 550
Children's author Donald Crews recalls a childhood visit to Bigmama's house in the country, where he finds his relatives full of news and the old place and its surroundings just the same as the year before.

Nikola-Lisa, W. *The Year with Grandma Moses.* H. Holt, 2000. 32p. IL K–3, Lexile: 920 (Non-fiction)
A collection of paintings and memoirs by the American folk artist describing the seasons and their related activities in rural upstate New York.

Perkins, Lynne Rae. *Pictures from Our Vacation.* Greenwillow Books, c2007. 32p. IL K–3, Lexile: 650
Given a camera that takes and prints tiny pictures just before leaving for the family farm in Canada, a young girl records a vacation that gets off to a slow start, but winds up being a family reunion filled with good memories.

Scillian, Devin. *Memoirs of a Goldfish.* Sleeping Bear Press, c2010. 28p. IL K–3
A goldfish gives a personal account of his experiences while swimming around his bowl as it slowly fills with fish and other accessories, only to realize when he is relocated for a cleaning how much he misses them.

Books for Children Ages Eight to Twelve

Byars, Betsy Cromer. *The Moon and I.* Beech Tree Books, 1991. 96p. IL 5–8, Lexile: 870
While describing her humorous adventures with a blacksnake, Betsy Byars recounts childhood anecdotes and explains how she writes a book.

DePaola, Tomie. *26 Fairmount Avenue.* G. P. Putnam's Sons, c1999. 56p. IL 3–6, Lexile: 760
Children's author-illustrator Tomie De Paola describes his experiences at home and in school when he was a boy.

DePaola, Tomie. *I'm Still Scared.* G. P. Putnam's Sons, c2006. 83p. IL 3–6
The author recalls his fears as a first grader during the initial days of World War II, the attack on Pearl Harbor, air raid drills, and blackouts, and the reassurance he received from his parents.

DePaola, Tomie. *On My Way.* Puffin Books, 2002, c2001. 73p. IL 3–6, Lexile: 590
A memoir in which children's author Tomie De Paola recalls his baby sister's frightening bout with pneumonia, and the exciting events of the summer between kindergarten and first grade.

Jansson, Tove. *Moominpappa's Memoirs.* Farrar, Straus and Giroux, 2010, c1994. 167p. IL 3–6
When stricken with a severe cold, Moominpappa decides to set down an account of his eventful youth, which he shares chapter by chapter with Moomintroll, Sniff, and Snufkin.

Memoirs

Lu, Chi Fa. ***Double Luck: Memoirs of a Chinese Orphan.*** Holiday House, c2001. 212p. IL 5–8, Lexile: 740

Tells the story of the author's struggles after being orphaned at the age of three and how he held on to his dream of coming to the United States as he passed from one relative to another and was even sold to a Communist couple.

Biography

Books for Children of All Ages

Corey, Shana. *Mermaid Queen: The Spectacular True Story of Annette Kellerman, Who Swam Her Way to Fame, Fortune, & Swimsuit History!* Scholastic Press, 2009. 42p. IL K–3, Lexile: 650 (Non-fiction)

An illustrated biography of Annette Kellerman, an early feminist who overcame a childhood illness to become internationally recognized for her swimming, invention of water ballet, and introduction of the modern swimsuit for women.

Gerstein, Mordicai. *The Man Who Walked between the Towers.* Roaring Brook Press, c2003. 40p. IL K–3, Lexile: 480 (Non-fiction)

A lyrical evocation of Philippe Petit's 1974 tightrope walk between the World Trade Center towers.

Kerley, Barbara. *What to Do about Alice?: How Alice Roosevelt Broke the Rules, Charmed the World, and Drove Her Father Teddy Crazy!* Scholastic Press, 2008. 44p. IL K–3, Lexile: 800 (Non-fiction)

An illustrated biography of Alice Roosevelt Longworth that focuses on her experiences while her father was president of the United States.

Krull, Kathleen. *Harvesting Hope: The Story of Cesar Chavez.* Harcourt, c2003. 48p. IL K–3, Lexile: 800 (Non-fiction)

A biography of Cesar Chavez, from age ten, when he and his family lived happily on their Arizona ranch, to age thirty-eight, when he led a peaceful protest against California migrant workers' miserable working conditions.

Levine, Ellen. *Henry's Freedom Box.* Scholastic Press, 2007. 40p. IL K–3, Lexile: 380

A fictionalized account of how a Virginia slave, Henry "Box" Brown, escapes to freedom in 1849 by shipping himself in a wooden crate from Richmond to Philadelphia.

Matthews, Elizabeth. *Different like Coco.* Candlewick Press, 2007. 36p. IL K–3, Lexile: 990 (Non-fiction)

An illustrated look at the life of fashion designer Coco Chanel, discussing her youth in France and the development of her own particular style, which eventually caught on around the world.

Medina, Tony. *Love to Langston.* Lee & Low Books, c2002. 34p. IL K–3. Lexile: NP (Non-fiction)

A series of poems written from the point of view of the poet Langston Hughes, offering an overview of key events and themes in his life.

Moss, Marissa. *Mighty Jackie: The Strike-Out Queen.* Simon & Schuster Books for Young Readers, c2004. 32p. IL K–3, Lexile: 770 (Non-fiction)

In 1931, seventeen-year-old Jackie Mitchell pitches against Babe Ruth and Lou Gehrig in an exhibition game, becoming the first professional female pitcher in baseball history.

Pena, Matt de la. *A Nation's Hope: The Story of Boxing Legend Joe Louis.* Dial Books for Young Readers, c2011. 40p. IL K–3 (Non-fiction)

An illustrated introduction to the life and accomplishments of professional boxer Joe Louis.

Biography

Rabin, Staton. *Mr. Lincoln's Boys: Being the Mostly True Adventures of Abraham Lincoln's Trouble-Making Sons, Tad and Willie.* Viking, 2008. 36p. IL K–3, Lexile: 710 (Non-fiction)

An illustrated story recounting the adventures of Abraham Lincoln and his two sons, which focuses on the years during which Lincoln was U.S. President.

Stone, Tanya Lee. *Elizabeth Leads the Way: Elizabeth Cady Stanton and the Right to Vote.* Henry Holt, 2008. 32p. IL K–3, Lexile: 700 (Non-fiction)

A brief description of the life and achievements of Elizabeth Cady Stanton, a nineteenth-century women's rights activist who fought for women's right to vote.

Weatherford, Carole Boston. *Moses: When Harriet Tubman Led Her People to Freedom.* Jump at the Sun/Hyperion Books for Children, c2006. 41p. IL K–3, Lexile: 660

A fictionalized account of Harriet Tubman's escape from slavery to freedom in Philadelphia, where she turned her talents to leading others along the Underground Railroad.

White, Linda Arms. *I Could Do That!: Esther Morris Gets Women the Vote.* Farrar, Straus, Giroux, 2005. 38p. IL K–3, Lexile: 780 (Non-fiction)

In 1869, Esther Morris, whose "can-do" attitude had shaped her life, was instrumental in making Wyoming the first state to allow women to vote. Subsequently, she became the first woman to hold public office in the United States.

Winter, Jonah. *Roberto Clemente: Pride of the Pittsburgh Pirates.* Atheneum Books for Young Readers, c2005. 36p. IL K–3, Lexile: 800 (Non-fiction)

An illustrated biography of baseball great Roberto Clemente, who played for the Pittsburgh Pirates from 1955 until his untimely death in an airplane crash in 1972.

Yaccarino, Dan. *The Fantastic Undersea Life of Jacques Cousteau.* Knopf, 2009. 33p. IL K–3, Lexile: 840 (Non-fiction)

A pictorial biography of Jacques Cousteau, covering his adventures aboard the ship *Calypso* with his team of scientists, diving equipment, and waterproof cameras, and his work to protect the oceans from pollution.

Yolen, Jane. *All Star!: Honus Wagner and the Most Famous Baseball Card Ever.* Philomel Books, c2010. 34p. IL K–3, Lexile: 880 (Non-fiction)

A biography of the personal and professional life of American shortstop Honus Wagner, a baseball star who played mostly for the Pittsburgh Pirates from 1897 to 1917.

Yolen, Jane. *Lost Boy: The Story of the Man Who Created Peter Pan.* Dutton Children's Books, c2010. 40p. IL K–3, Lexile: 970 (Non-fiction)

An illustrated exploration of the childhood and adult life of J. M. Barrie, the author of *Peter Pan.*

Biography

Books for Children Ages Eight to Twelve

Barton, Chris. *The Day-Glo Brothers: The True Story of Bob and Joe Switzer's Bright Ideas and Brand-New Colors.* Charlesbridge, c2009. 42p, IL 3–6, Lexile: 990 (Non-fiction)
Illustrations and easy-to-follow text describe how brothers Bob and Joe Switzer invented fluorescent paint and colors. The book also explains how fluorescence works.

Bryant, Jennifer. *A River of Words: The Story of William Carlos Williams.* Eerdmans Books for Young Readers, 2008. 34p. IL 3–6, Lexile: 820
An illustrated biography of American poet William Carlos Williams, who studied to become a doctor but still found time to write poetry.

Grimes, Nikki. *Talkin' about Bessie: The Story of Aviator Elizabeth Coleman.* Orchard Books, 2002. 48p. IL 3–6, Lexile: 970 (Non-fiction)
A biography of the woman who became the first licensed African American pilot.

Halfmann, Janet. *Seven Miles to Freedom: The Robert Smalls Story.* Lee & Low Books, c2008. 40p. IL 3–6, Lexile: 870 (Non-fiction)
A biography of Robert Smalls who, during the Civil War, commandeered the Confederate ship *Planter* to carry his family and twelve other slaves to freedom. Smalls went on to become a member of the U.S. House of Representatives working toward African American advancement.

Jackson Issa, Kai. *Howard Thurman's Great Hope.* Lee & Low Books, c2008. 32p. IL 3–6, Lexile: 840 (Non-fiction)
A biography of Howard Thurman that describes how he obtained a scholarship to attend an out-of-town high school, went on to graduate college, and became a civil rights leader for the African American community.

Johnson, Jen Cullerton. *Seeds of Change: Planting a Path to Peace.* Lee & Low Books, c2010. 40p. IL 3–6, Lexile: 820 (Non-fiction)
Examines the life of Nobel Peace Prize winner and environmentalist Wangari Maathai, who made a stand in the face of opposition to women's rights in her native Kenya and started an effort to restore the country's ecosystem.

Kerley, Barbara. *Walt Whitman: Words for America.* Scholastic Press, 2004. 42p. IL 3–6, Lexile: 970 (Non-fiction)
A biography of the American poet whose compassion led him to nurse soldiers during the Civil War, to give voice to the nation's grief at President Abraham Lincoln's assassination, and to capture the true American spirit in verse.

Krull, Kathleen. *Wilma Unlimited: How Wilma Rudolph Became the World's Fastest Woman.* Harcourt Brace, c1996. 44p. IL 3–6, Lexile: 730 (Non-fiction)
A biography of the African American woman who overcame crippling polio as a child to become the first woman to win three gold medals in track in a single Olympic Games.

Biography

Lasky, Kathryn. *One Beetle Too Many: The Extraordinary Adventures of Charles Darwin.* Candlewick Press, 2009. 40p. IL 3–6, Lexile: 1050 (Non-fiction)
> Describes the life and work of the renowned nineteenth-century biologist who transformed conventional Western thought with his theory of natural evolution.

Novesky, Amy. *Me, Frida.* Abrams Books for Young Readers, 2010. 32p. IL 3–6
> Artist Frida Kahlo finds her own voice and style when her famous husband, Diego Rivera, is commissioned to paint a mural in San Francisco, California, in the 1930s and she finds herself exploring the city on her own.

Rappaport, Doreen. *Martin's Big Words: The Life of Dr. Martin Luther King, Jr.* Jump at the Sun/ Hyperion Books for Children, c2001. 34p. IL 3–6, Lexile: 410 (Non-fiction)
> Looks at the life of Dr. Martin Luther King, Jr., explaining his work to bring about a peaceful end to segregation.

Rockwell, Anne F. *Only Passing through: The Story of Sojourner Truth.* Dell Dragonfly Books, 2002, c2000. 38p. IL 3–6, Lexile: 790 (Non-fiction)
> An illustrated biography of nineteenth-century abolitionist Sojourner Truth, who was born into slavery and fought for the rights of African Americans and women.

Weatherford, Carole Boston. *Jesse Owens: Fastest Man Alive.* Walker, Distributed by Holtzbrinck, 2007. 32p. IL 3–6, Lexile: 880 (Non-fiction)
> A biography of Jesse Owens, the African American track and field athlete who won four gold medals at the 1936 Berlin Olympic Games.

Yoo, Paula. *Sixteen Years in Sixteen Seconds: The Sammy Lee Story.* Lee & Low Books, c2005. 32p. IL 3–6, Lexile: 880 (Non-fiction)
> Presents the true story of Dr. Sammy Lee and his desire to become an Olympic diver in an age when racism and prejudice ruled in America, and describes how he honored his father's wishes to become a doctor as well.

Graphic Novels

Books for Children Ages Eight To Twelve: Series

Cibos, Lindsay. *Peach Fuzz.* Tokyopop, c2005– . IL 3–6
Nine-year-old Amanda and her new pet, a ferret she names "Peach," embark on a battle of wills as Amanda struggles to teach Peach not to bite, while Peach struggles to vanquish her new enemy, Handra the five-headed monster—also known as Amanda's hand.

Denton, Shannon Eric. *Boxcar Children Graphic Novels.* A. Whitman, c2008– . IL 3–6
Everyone's favorite easy-to-read mysteries are now graphic novels! The original Boxcar Children stories you know and love have been adapted by world-class authors and illustrators to appeal to a whole new generation.

Gownley, Jimmy. *Amelia Rules!* Atheneum Books for Young Readers, c2009– . IL 3–6
Amelia and the gang take on everything from gym class to ninjas, first kisses to becoming superheroes.

Holm, Jennifer. *Babymouse.* Random House, c2005– . IL 3–6
Features comical and adventurous stories about the hopes and expectations of a very imaginative mouse.

Kibuishi, Kazu. *Amulet.* Graphix, c2008– . IL 3–6
After Emily and Navin's family moves to their ancestral home, their mother is kidnapped by a tentacled creature in the basement that leads the children on a deadly chase into the magical world beneath their home.

Konomi, Takeshi. *Prince of Tennis.* VIZ Media, 2004– . IL 5–8
Ryoma Echizen is the Prince of Tennis. He may be ready for the Seishun Gakuen tennis team, but are they ready for him?

Krosoczka, Jarrett. *Lunch Lady.* Alfred A. Knopf, c2009. IL 3–6
She's the lunch lady and a secret crime fighter! When not at school, she may be found in her secret lair. Armed with her assortment of lunch-themed gadgets, there is no stopping her.

Runton, Andy. *Owly.* Top Shelf, c2004– . IL 3–6
Owly is a kind, yet lonely, little owl who's always on the lookout for new friends and adventure. He befriends Wormy and they live together in a friendly forest. The series follows the two friends as they share adventures.

Smith, Jeff. *Bone Series.* Graphix, 2005– . IL 3–6
Three cousins from Boneville—Fone Bone, Phoney Bone, and Smiley Bone—leave home and are swept up in a series of epic adventures.

Stanley, John. *Little Lulu.* Dark Horse, c2004– . IL 3–6
Lulu Moppet, her best friend/worst nemesis Tubby, and the rest of the Main Street gang never run out of new ways into and out of (but mostly into) trouble.

Telgemeier, Raina. *The Baby-sitter's Club.* Graphix, 2006– . IL 3–6
Each title in this popular series is now presented as a graphic novel. They're sure to bring those reluctant readers back for more!

Gross Books

Books for Children of All Ages

Beaumont, Karen. *I Ain't Gonna Paint No More!* Harcourt, c2005. 32p. IL K–3
In the rhythm of the folk song *It Ain't Gonna Rain No More,* a child who loves to paint the walls and everything else he sees cannot resist adding one more dab of paint to some surprising places.

Brown, Marc Tolon. *Monster's Lunchbox.* Little, Brown, c1995. 17p. IL K–3
An interactive picture book that details the gruesome contents of a monster's lunchbox.

Facklam, Margery. *Bugs for Lunch.* Charlesbridge, c1999. 32p. IL K–3, Lexile: NP
Rhyming text introduces bug-eating animals such as geckos, trout, and even people. The book includes additional facts about each creature.

Gomi, Taro. *Everyone Poops.* Kane/Miller, 1993. 27p. IL K–3
Colorful illustrations and text show and describe how different animals and humans perform excretory functions.

Grossman, Bill. *My Little Sister Ate One Hare.* Dragonfly Books, 1996. 24p. IL K–3, Lexile: 380
Little sister has no problem eating one hare, two snakes, and three ants, but when she gets to ten peas, she throws up quite a mess.

Kotzwinkle, William. *Walter, the Farting Dog.* Frog, Ltd., c2001. 33p. IL K–3, Lexile: 490
Walter the dog creates problems with his farts but becomes a hero when burglars enter the house.

Levine, Martha Peaslee. *Stop That Nose!* Marshall Cavendish Children, c2006. 32p. IL K–3
When young David's father loses his nose after a particularly hearty sneeze, it takes a chase and an airplane ride before the naughty nose can be returned to its rightful face.

McKy, Katie. *It All Began with a Bean.* Tanglewood Press, 2004. 32p. IL K–3
A series of incidents and eating choices lead to an entire town passing gas at the same time—with interesting consequences.

Munsch, Robert N. *Smelly Socks.* Scholastic, c2004. 28p. IL K–3, Lexile: 680
Tina buys what she believes to be the perfect pair of socks and vows never to take them off, but they get so smelly her friends at school decide to take action.

O'Keefe, Susan Heyboer. *One Hungry Monster: A Counting Book in Rhyme.* Little, Brown, c1989. 20p. IL K–3
Insatiable monsters demanding food increase in number from one to ten, until a small boy finally orders them all out of his house.

Palatini, Margie. *Stinky Smelly Feet: A Love Story.* Dutton Children's Books, c2004. 32p. IL K–3, Lexile: 550
When stinky feet threaten the romance between Douglas and Dolores, they must find a solution.

Ross, Tony. *Don't Do That!* Andersen Press, 1991. 26p. IL K–3
Nellie discovers why people say "Don't do that!" when her finger gets stuck in her nose and all kinds of people try to help her get it out.

Gross Books

Scieszka, Jon. *The Stinky Cheese Man and Other Fairly Stupid Tales.* Viking, 1992. 51p. IL K–3, Lexile: 520
Madcap revisions of familiar fairy tales.

Sierra, Judy. *Thelonius Monster's Sky-High Fly Pie: A Revolting Rhyme.* Dragonfly Books, c2006.
34p. IL K–3
A good-natured monster thinks a pie made out of flies would be a good dessert, and invites all his
friends and relatives over to try it.

Books for Children Ages Eight to Twelve

Barnhill, Kelly Regan. *The Sweaty Book of Sweat.* Capstone Press, c2010. 32p. IL 3–6, Lexile: 790
(Non-fiction)
Describes the gross qualities of sweat, and explains how sweating works to benefit a person's health.

Brown, Jordan. *Micro Mania: A Really Close-up Look at Bacteria, Bedbugs & the Zillions of Other Gross
Little Creatures That Live in, on & All Around You!* Imagine!, c2009. 80p. IL 3–6, Lexile: 1010 (Non-fiction)
Introduces microorganisms through text and magnified images of virus cells, molds, bacteria,
fungus, creatures, and more; describes how these organisms affect human life.

Lew, Kristi. *Clot & Scab: Gross Stuff about Your Scrapes, Bumps, and Bruises.* Millbrook Press,
c2010. 48p.IL 3–6, Lexile: 760 (Non-fiction)
Explores some repulsive aspects of the human body with a focus on the body's healing processes,
and provides facts and information on bleeding, clots, scabs, scars, and other related topics.

Masoff, Joy. *Oh, Yikes!: History's Grossest, Wackiest Moments.* Workman Publishing, c2006. 308p. IL
3–6, Lexile: 990 (Non-fiction)
Provides facts about some of the grossest, messiest, and strangest moments in history, relating
information about the disgusting habits of Attila and the Huns, the Aztecs, cavemen, circus
performers, cowboys, gladiators, the Vikings, and many others.

Masoff, Joy. *Oh, Yuck!: The Encyclopedia of Everything Nasty.* Workman Publishing, c2000. 212p. IL
3–6, Lexile: 950 (Non-fiction)
An alphabetically organized collection of articles about disgusting things, from acne, ants, and bacteria to worms, x-periments, and zits.

Miller, Connie Colwell. *The Pukey Book of Vomit.* Capstone Press, c2010. 32p. IL 3–6, Lexile: 780
(Non-fiction)
Describes what vomit consists of, how the human body manufactures vomit, and why most people
think it is gross.

Murphy, Glenn. *How Loud Can You Burp?: More Extremely Important Questions (and Answers!)*
Flash Point/Roaring Brook Press, 2009, c2007. 284p. IL 3–6, Lexile: 1020 (Non-fiction)
Contains answers to a selection of frequently silly, sometimes scientific, often gross questions,
many submitted by real-life ten-year-olds, providing information such as how loud an average
middle schooler can burp.

Gross Books

Owen, Ruth. *Creepy Backyard Invaders.* Bearport Publishing, c2011. 24p. IL 3–6 (Non-fiction)
A microscopic study of creatures that live in backyards, such as earwigs, honeybees, ants, and jumping spiders.

Reeves, Diane Lindsey. *Gross Jobs.* Ferguson, c2009. 47p. IL 3–6 (Non-fiction)
Profiles ten messy careers, including exterminator, forensic anthropologist, janitor, landfill manager, and mortician, describing their responsibilities, daily tasks, and training.

Rosenberg, Pam. *Blecch! Icky, Sticky, Gross Stuff in Your School.* Child's World, c2008. 24p. IL 3–6 (Non-fiction)
Describes distasteful things that can be found in schools, such as sweat, mucus, vomit, and lice, among other topics.

Rosenberg, Pam. *Eek! Icky, Sticky, Gross Stuff in Your Food.* Child's World, c2008. 24p. IL 3–6 (Non-fiction)
Describes surprising foods around the world, including the poisonous puffer fish, deep-fried tarantula, and rat, as well as the contents of hot dogs.

Rosenberg, Pam. *Eew! Icky, Sticky, Gross Stuff in Your Body.* Child's World, c2008. 24p. IL 3–6 (Non-fiction)
Provides facts about some of the grosser aspects of the human body, discussing head lice, dandruff, mucus, bad breath, vomit, and similar topics.

Royston, Angela. *Ooze and Goo.* Raintree, c2010. 32p. IL 3–6 (Non-fiction)
Text, photographs, and illustrations discuss gross aspects of the human body, focusing on body fluids, and discussing nasal mucus, phlegm, saliva, earwax, conjunctivitis, bleeding, scabs, boils, sweat, and smelly feet.

Royston, Angela. *Puke and Poo.* Raintree, c2010. 31p. IL 3–6 (Non-fiction)
Text, photographs, and illustrations discuss gross aspects of the human body, focusing on digestion, and discussing vomit, gas, feces, diarrhea, and constipation.

Stewart, Melissa. *Blasts of Gas: The Secrets of Breathing, Burping, and Passing Gas.* Marshall Cavendish Benchmark, c2010. 48p. IL 3–6 (Non-fiction)
Provides comprehensive information on the role gas plays in the body science of humans and animals.

Szpirglas, Jeff. *Gross Universe: Your Guide to All Disgusting Things under the Sun.* Maple Tree Press, Distributed by Publishers Group West, c2004. 64p. IL 3–6 (Non-fiction)
Presents a scientific look at some of the more disgusting organisms and behaviors found in the natural world.

LOL: Humor for Upper Elementary School Children

List by: Jessica Gilcreast, McDonough Elementary School, New Hampshire

Books for Children Ages Eight to Twelve

Prelutsky, Jack. *Pizza, Pigs, and Poetry: How to Write a Poem.* Greenwillow Books, c2008. 208p. IL 3–6, Lexile: 870.

> Explains how to write poems about everyday subjects from children's lives, such as experiences with their family, friends, and pets, providing tips, example poems, and exercises.

Scieszka, Jon. *Knucklehead: Tall Tales & Mostly True Stories about Growing Up Scieszka.* Viking, c2008. 106p. IL 3–6, Lexile: 750

> A memoir of what it was like to grow up in the 1950s and other almost true stories by American children's author Jon Scieszka.

Series

Benton, Jim. *Franny K. Stein, Mad Scientist.* Simon & Schuster Children's Publishing, 2005. IL 3–6.

> Meet Franny—a pint-sized mad scientist with enough pluck to face down any challenge!

Myers, Bill. *Incredible Worlds of Wally McDoogle.* Thomas Nelson, 1993– . IL 3–6

> This hilarious collection features the boy blunder—lovable, but nerdy Wally McDoogle, who blunders his way through life in these exciting and imaginative adventures.

Oliver, Lin. *Who Shrunk Daniel Funk?* Simon & Schuster Books for Young Readers, 2009– . IL 3–6.

> Daniel Funk, who lives with his three sisters, mother, grandmother, and great-grandmother, has always wanted a brother. When he suddenly shrinks to the size of a toe, he discovers that he has a twin brother who is the same size.

Thorpe, Kiki. *Meet the Kreeps.* Scholastic, 2008– . IL 3–6

> Ten-year-old Polly Winkler just wants to be normal, but it looks like her goal will remain out of reach when her dad decides to marry Veronica Kreep, the mother of the weirdest family in town.

Mother Goose Take-off

Books for Children of All Ages

Bell, Krista. *If the Shoe Fits.* Charlesbridge, 2008. 60p. IL K–3, Lexile: 450
Cassie wants to be a dancer when she grows up but is afraid to dance in front of anyone outside her family, until the day of her first jazz performance arrives and her mother and a new friend help her to gain confidence.

Edwards, Pamela Duncan. *The Neat Line: Scribbling through Mother Goose.* Katherine Tegen Books, c2005. 32p. IL K–3
A young scribble matures into a neat line, then wriggles into a book of nursery rhymes where it transforms itself into different objects to assist the characters it meets there.

Ernst, Lisa Campbell. *This Is the Van That Dad Cleaned.* Simon & Schuster Books for Young Readers, c2005. 32p. IL K–3
In the style of a classic cumulative rhyme, the children undo all of Dad's hard work in cleaning the family car.

Grey, Mini. *The Adventures of the Dish and the Spoon.* Knopf, 2006. 32p. IL K–3, Lexile: 410
Having run away together, the Dish and the Spoon from the nursery rhyme "The Cat and the Fiddle" become vaudeville stars before turning to a life of crime.

Scieszka, Jon. *The Book That Jack Wrote.* Puffin, 1994. 32p. IL K–3
A madcap variation of the cumulative nursery rhyme, this time beginning when Jack writes a book.

Shulevitz, Uri. *Snow.* Farrar, Straus and Giroux, 1998. 32p. IL K–3, Lexile: 220
As snowflakes slowly come down, one by one, people in the city ignore them. Only a boy and his dog think that the snowfall will amount to anything.

Stanley, Diane. *The Giant and the Beanstalk.* HarperCollins, c2004. 32p. IL K–3, Lexile: 670
In this version of the traditional tale, a young giant chases Jack down the beanstalk to rescue his beloved hen and meets other Jacks from various nursery rhymes along the way.

Stevens, Janet. *And the Dish Ran Away with the Spoon.* Harcourt, c2001. 50p. IL K–3, Lexile: 200
When Dish and Spoon run away, their nursery rhyme friends Cat, Cow, and Dog set out to rescue them in time for the next evening's reading of their rhyme.

Ziefert, Harriet. *Ode to Humpty Dumpty.* Houghton Mifflin, 2001. 30p. IL K–3, Lexile: NP
After the King fails to save Humpty Dumpty, his friends find different ways to help him deal with his grief.

Books for Children Ages Eight to Twelve

Becker, Helaine. *Mother Goose Unplucked: Crazy Comics, Zany Activities, Nutty Facts & Other Twisted Takes on Childhood Favorites.* Maple Tree Press, c2007. 160p. IL 3–6
An illustrated collection of Mother Goose–themed activities, comics, puzzles, facts, stories, and recipes.

Mother Goose Take-off

Bradman, Tony. *Jack and the Bean Snacks.* Stone Arch Books, 2009, c2006. 49p. IL 3–6, Lexile: 600
    After besting the giant and stealing the golden goose, Jack is determined to help out his mother. When a trip to the grocery store goes awry, he realizes he will have to try harder to understand what makes his mother happy.

Seibold, J. Otto. *Other Goose: Re-Nurseried, Re-Rhymed, Re-Mothered, and Re-Goosed.* Chronicle Books, c2010. 69p. IL 3–6
    Contains more than thirty illustrated nursery rhymes featuring classic Mother Goose characters with a modern twist, such as Humpty Dumpty, Jack and Jill, and Jack Splat.

Mystery Books

Books for Children of All Ages

Base, Graeme. *The Eleventh Hour: A Curious Mystery.* Abrams Books for Young Readers, 1993. 32p. IL 3–6

> An elephant's eleventh birthday party is marked by eleven games preceding the banquet to be eaten at the eleventh hour. When the time to eat arrives, however, the birthday feast has disappeared. The reader is invited to guess the thief.

Base, Graeme. *Enigma: A Magical Mystery.* Abrams Books for Young Readers, c2008. 36p. IL K–3

> When Bertie the badger visits his grandfather at a retirement home for magicians, he learns that his grandfather's rabbit, Enigma, has disappeared, along with everyone else's magical things. The reader is invited to help break a code to find the items hidden throughout the book. The book includes a built-in decoder.

Biedrzycki, David. *Ace Lacewing, Bug Detective.* Charlesbridge, c2005. 44p. IL K–3, Lexile: 560

> Aided by his friends, Ace Lacewing, bug detective, sets out on the trail of the kidnappers who took Queenie Bee.

Biedrzycki, David. *Ace Lacewing, Bug Detective: Bad Bugs Are My Business.* Charlesbridge, c2009. 40p. IL K–3, Lexile: 570

> After being mugged, Scratch Murphy the flea asks Ace Lacewing, bug detective, for help in finding the culprit who stole money from his Six Legs Amusement Park.

Christelow, Eileen. *The Robbery at the Diamond Dog Diner.* Clarion Books, c1986. 32p. IL K–3, Lexile: 460

> Lola Dog doesn't wear her usual diamonds to the Diamond Dog Diner when she hears that jewel thieves are prowling around town, but she doesn't take into account Glenda Feathers' loud talk about where Lola should hide her jewels.

Clement, Rod. *Grandpa's Teeth.* HarperCollins, 1998, c1997. 28p. IL K–3, Lexile: 530

> Soon after Grandpa's teeth disappear from a glass of water near his bed, Inspector Rate has the whole town under investigation.

Jacobson, Jennifer. *Andy Shane and the Barn Sale Mystery.* Candlewick Press, 2009. 50p. IL K–3, Lexile: 540

> Andy Shane holds a barn sale to earn enough money to buy Granny Webb a case for her favorite binoculars. Once he has the cash, he cannot find the binoculars and must enlist his friend Dolores Starbuckle in a quest to locate them.

Kelly, David A. *The Fenway Foul-up.* Random House, c2011. 101p. IL K–3

> Cousins Mike Walsh and Kate Hopkins are watching batting practice at Fenway Park when Red Sox slugger Big D's lucky bat is stolen. Knowing that Big D is in a slump, Mike and Kate rush to find the bat before the Sox lose the game.

Koontz, Robin Michal. *The Case of the Missing Goldfish.* Magic Wagon, c2010. 32p. IL K–3

> Furry detectives Furlock and Muttson are on the case when Mrs. Bumblebear calls to report her goldfish is missing.

Mystery Books

Quackenbush, Robert M. *Miss Mallard's Case Book.* Robert Quackenbush Studios, c2000. 48p. IL 3–6

Contains ten mysteries featuring the duck detectives Miss Mallard and her nephew Willard Widgeon. The solutions to the mysteries appears at the end of the book.

Ransom, Jeanie Franz. *What Really Happened to Humpty?: (From the Files of a Hard-Boiled Detective).* Charlesbridge, 2009. 32p. IL K–3, Lexile: 550

Detective Joe Dumpty rushes to investigate the mysterious circumstances under which his older brother, Humpty, fell from a wall on his first day as captain of the new Neighborhood Watch program.

Skofield, James. *Detective Dinosaur Undercover.* Harper, c2010. 46p. IL K–3

In three brief mysteries, Detective Dinosaur learns about doing undercover work, gets chased by strange blobs, and finds rain on a sunny day.

Wood, Audrey. *Alphabet Mystery.* Blue Sky Press, c2003. 32p. IL K–3, Lexile: 430

Little x is missing from Charley's Alphabet, and the other lowercase letters go off to solve the mystery of his disappearance, learning in the end how valuable a little x can be.

Yolen, Jane. *Piggins.* Harcourt, c1987. 32p. IL K–3, Lexile: 450

During a dinner party, the lights go out and Mrs. Reynard's beautiful diamond necklace is stolen, but Piggins the butler quickly discovers the real thief.

Series

Teague, Mark. *Detective LaRue.* Scholastic Press, 2002– . IL K–3

Hilarious stories about Mrs. LaRue's lovable pet dog, Ike LaRue, the obedience school dropout.

Page Turners for Reluctant Readers

List by: Jessica Gilcreast, McDonough Elementary School, New Hampshire

Avi. *The Seer of Shadows.* Harper Collins, c2008. 202p. IL 3–6, Lexile: 720
In 1872, Horace, who is apprenticed to a shady photographer in New York City, is placed in an awkward position when his employer decides to take advantage of a wealthy lady who tells them that her daughter has recently died.

Gaiman, Neil. *The Graveyard Book.* HarperCollins, c2008. 312p. IL 5–8, Lexile: 820
After escaping the murder of his family, a toddler is taken in by the ghosts of a graveyard. Growing up in this strange setting leads to many adventures, including a final showdown with the murderer.

Greenwald, Sheila. *Rosy Cole's Memoir Explosion: A Heartbreaking Story about Losing Friends, Annoying Family, and Ruining Romance.* Farrar, Straus and Giroux, c2006. 103p. IL 3–6, Lexile: 720
When Rosy writes a memoir about herself and her friends for a school assignment, she is surprised when they are not thrilled with the result.

Hahnke, Julie. *The Grey Ghost (Wolf's Apprentice).* Publishing Works, 2009. 180p. IL 3–6
When Black Duncan Campbell starts murdering his neighbors in sixteenth-century Scotland, eleven-year-old Angus suddenly finds himself the sole survivor of Clan Macnab. Aided by a goshawk and a pine marten, and urged forward by a mysterious luna moth, Angus must uncover his clan's heritage, reveal ancient secrets, and try to end the Campbell's bloody rampage.

Park, Barbara. *Mick Harte Was Here.* Yearling, c1996. 96p. IL 3–6, Lexile: 730
Phoebe, an eighth grader, loses her brother Mick in a tragic accident, in which Mick was not wearing his bicycle helmet. In the course of the book, Phoebe and her family learn how to live with the loss of a family member.

Paulsen, Gary. *Captive!* Dell Yearling, c1995. 56p. IL 3–6, Lexile: 600
Roman Sanchez, still suffering from the death of his father, must use all his skills and knowledge to save himself and three classmates when they are kidnapped from school and held for ransom.

Petersen, P. J. *Wild River.* Delacorte Press, c2009. 120p. IL 3–6, Lexile: 420
Considered lazy and unathletic, twelve-year-old Ryan discovers a heroic side of himself when a kayak trip with his older brother goes horribly awry.

Salisbury, Graham. *Lord of the Deep.* Delacorte Press, c2001. 182p. IL YA, Lexile: 540
Working for his stepfather on a charter fishing boat in Hawaii teaches thirteen-year-old Mikey about fishing, and about taking risks, making sacrifices, and facing some of life's difficult choices.

Temple, Bob. *The Golden Age of Pirates: An Interactive History Adventure.* Capstone Press, c2008. 112p. IL 5–8, Lexile: 660
This is only one volume of many in this adventure series filled with historical facts. Readers decide which way the story will progress. In *Pirates,* options include joining the dreaded Blackbeard or being marooned on a desert island.

Books for English Language Learners

Books for Children of All Ages

Aliki. *Marianthe's Story.* Greenwillow Books, c1998. 32p. IL K–3, Lexile: 550
  Two separate stories, the first telling of Mari's starting school in a new land, and the second describing village life in her country before she and her family left in search of a better life.

Bunting, Eve. *One Green Apple.* Clarion Books, c2006. 32p. IL K–3, Lexile: 450
  While on a school field trip to an orchard to make cider, a young Muslim immigrant named Farah gains self-confidence when the green apple she picks perfectly complements the other students' red apples.

Levine, Ellen. *I Hate English!* Scholastic, c1989. 32p. IL K–3, Lexile: 390
  When her family moves to New York from Hong Kong, Mei Mei finds it difficult to adjust to school and learn the alien sounds of English.

Mora, Pat. *Tomas and the Library Lady.* Knopf, c1997. 32p. IL K–3, Lexile: 440
  While helping his family in their work as migrant laborers far from their home, Tomas finds an entire world to explore in the books at the local public library.

Books for Children Ages Eight to Twelve

Fleming, Candace. *Lowji Discovers America.* Aladdin Paperbacks, 2008, c2005. 152p. IL 3–6, Lexile: 510
  A nine-year-old East Indian boy tries to adjust to his new life in suburban America.

Knight, Margy Burns. *Who Belongs Here?: An American Story.* Tilbury House, c1993. 40p. IL 3–6, Lexile: 900
  Describes the new life of Nary, a Cambodian refugee, in America, and discusses his encounters with prejudice. The book also includes some general facts on the history of U.S. immigration.

Montes, Marisa. *A Crazy Mixed-up Spanglish Day.* Scholastic Press, c2003. 120p. IL 3–6, Lexile: 420
  In Northern California, Maritza Gabriela Morales Mercado struggles to deal with the third-grade bully, to control her temper, and to remember to speak Spanish at home and English at school.

Tan, Shaun. *The Arrival.* A. A. Levine, 2006. IL 5–8
  In this wordless graphic novel, a man leaves his homeland and sets off for a new country, where he must build a new life for himself and his family.

Wong, Li Keng. *Good Fortune: My Journey to Gold Mountain.* Peachtree, c2006. 136p. IL 5–8, Lexile: 630
  The author describes her journey in 1933, at the age of seven, with her mother and two sisters from their village in southern China to the United States; she also recalls important moments from their first eight years in America.

Poems for Two Voices

Books for Children of All Ages

Franco, Betsy. *Messing around on the Monkey Bars: and Other School Poems for Two Voices.* Candlewick Press, 2009. 45p. IL K–3
> A collection of nineteen poems for children about what happens on a normal school day.

Hall, Donald. *I Am the Dog, I Am the Cat.* Dial Books, c1994. 32p. IL K–3, Lexile: NP
> A dog and a cat take turns explaining what is wonderful about being who they are.

Harrison, David L. *Farmer's Dog Goes to the Forest: Rhymes for Two Voices.* Wordsong/Boyds Mills Press, 2005. 32p. IL K–3
> A collection of illustrated rhymes to be read aloud in two voices, in which a curious dog interviews all the animals on a farm.

Harrison, David L. *Farmer's Garden: Rhymes for Two Voices.* Wordsong, 2003, c2000. 32p. IL K–3
> A curious dog asks various animals what they are doing in the garden in this picture book featuring verse with questions and answers.

Hoberman, Mary Ann. *You Read to Me, I'll Read to You: Very Short Mother Goose Tales to Read Together.* Little, Brown, c2005. 32p. IL K–3, Lexile: NP
> Presents a collection of short retellings of familiar Mother Goose fairy tales, each told in two voices, designed especially for young children and adults to read together.

Books for Children Ages Eight to Twelve

Ciardi, John. *You Read to Me, I'll Read to You.* HarperTrophy, 1987, c1962. 64p. IL 3–6, Lexile: NP
> Contains poetry for parents to read to their children and simpler poems for children to read to their parents.

Fleischman, Paul. *I Am Phoenix: Poems for Two Voices.* HarperTrophy, 1989, c1985. 51p. IL 5–8, Lexile: NP
> A collection of poems about birds to be read aloud by two voices.

Fleischman, Paul. *Joyful Noise: Poems for Two Voices.* HarperCollins, c1988. 44p. IL 5–8, Lexile: NP
> A collection of poems describing the characteristics and activities of a variety of insects.

Scary Books

Biro, Val. *The Hobyahs.* Star Bright Books, 1998. 32p. IL K–3
  Little Dog Turpie saves his master's family from the Hobyahs.

Brown, Ruth. *A Dark Dark Tale.* Puffin, 1984. 32p. IL K–3, Lexile: 400
  Journeying through a dark, dark house, a black cat surprises the only inhabitant of the abandoned residence.

Bunting, Eve. *Night of the Gargoyles.* Clarion Books, c1994. 30p. IL K–3, Lexile: 1090
  In the middle of the night, the gargoyles that adorn the walls of a museum come to life and frighten the night watchman.

Cole, Joanna. *Bony-Legs.* Scholastic, c1983. 47p. IL K–3, Lexile: 370
  When a terrible witch vows to eat her for supper, a little girl escapes with the help of a mirror and comb given to her by the witch's cat and dog.

Crum, Shutta. *Who Took My Hairy Toe?* Albert Whitman, 2001. 32p. IL K–3, Lexile: 550
  An old man known for taking what isn't his picks up the wrong thing one Halloween night, and its owner wants it back.

Galdone, Joanna. *The Tailypo: A Ghost Story.* Clarion, c1977. 32p. IL K–3, Lexile: 880
  A strange varmint haunts the woodsman who lopped off its tail.

Galdone, Paul. *The Teeny-Tiny Woman: A Ghost Story.* Clarion Books, c1984. 32p. IL K–3, Lexile: 880
  A teeny-tiny woman finds a teeny-tiny bone in a churchyard and puts it away in her cupboard before she goes to sleep.

Hoffmann, Heinrich. *The English Struwwelpeter, or, Pretty Stories and Funny Pictures.* Pavilion Children's Books, 2010. 48p. IL K–3
  Classic tales in verse about naughty boys and girls and the fates that befall them when they misbehave.

Mayer, Mercer. *There's a Nightmare in My Closet.* Dial Books for Young Readers, c1968. 31p. IL K–3, Lexile: 670
  A little boy decides to get rid of the nightmare in his closet.

Mayer, Mercer. *There's an Alligator under My Bed.* Dial Books for Young Readers, c1987. 32p. IL K–3, Lexile: 490
  The alligator under his bed makes a boy's bedtime a hazardous operation, until he lures it out of the house and into the garage.

McKissack, Pat. *Precious and the Boo Hag.* Atheneum Books for Young Readers, c2005. 32p. IL K–3, Lexile: 710
  Home alone with a stomachache while the family works in the fields, a young girl faces up to the horrifying Boo Hag that her brother warned her about.

Scary Books

Mosel, Arlene. *The Funny Little Woman.* Puffin, 1986, c1972. 40p. IL K–3, Lexile: 570
While chasing a dumpling, a little lady is captured by wicked creatures, from which she eventually escapes with the means of becoming the richest woman in Japan.

Peet, Bill. *Cowardly Clyde.* Houghton Mifflin, c1979. 38p. IL K–3, Lexile: 730
For a war horse, Clyde is an abysmal coward. He finally decides that even if he isn't really brave, he can at least act brave.

Schwartz, Alvin. *In a Dark, Dark Room, and Other Scary Stories.* Harper & Row, c1984. 63p. IL K–3, Lexile: 430
Seven scary stories to tell at night based on traditional stories and folktales from various countries.

Seeger, Pete. *Abiyoyo: Based on a South African Lullaby and Folk Story.* Aladdin Paperbacks, 1994, c1963. 48p. IL K–3, Lexile: 610
Banished from the town for making mischief, a little boy and his father are welcomed back when they find a way to make the dreaded giant Abiyoyo disappear.

Sendak, Maurice. *Where the Wild Things Are.* HarperCollins, 1963. 40p. IL K–3, Lexile: 740
After he is sent to bed without supper for behaving like a wild thing, Max dreams of a voyage to the island where the wild things are.

Wood, Audrey. *Heckedy Peg.* Harcourt Brace, c1987. 32p. IL K–3, Lexile: 450
A mother saves her seven children from Heckedy Peg, a witch who has changed them into different kinds of food.

Books for Children Ages Eight to Twelve

Bruchac, Joseph. *Skeleton Man.* HarperTrophy, 2003. IL 5–8, Lexile: 730
After her parents disappear and she is turned over to the care of a strange "great-uncle," Molly must rely on her dreams about an old Mohawk story for her safety—and maybe even for her life.

Gaiman, Neil. *The Wolves in the Walls.* HarperCollins, c2003. 56p. IL 3–6, Lexile: 500
Lucy is sure there are wolves living in the walls of her house, although others in her family disagree. When the wolves come out, the real adventure begins.

Nixon, Joan Lowery. *The House on Hackman's Hill.* Scholastic, 1990. IL 3–6, Lexile: 780
Jeff and Debbie make their way through the snow to the old Hackman mansion to look for a stolen Egyptian mummy. Soon they are trapped in the house by the snow.

Prelutsky, Jack. *Nightmares: Poems to Trouble Your Sleep.* Greenwillow Books, c1976. 38p. IL 3–6, Lexile: NP
Twelve poems featuring a vampire, werewolf, ghoul, and other monsters.

Personal Narrative

Books for Children of All Ages

Bottner, Barbara. *Miss Brooks Loves Books! (and I Don't).* Alfred A. Knopf, c2010. 26p. IL K–3, Lexile: 470
> A first-grade girl—who does not like to read—stubbornly resists her school librarian's efforts to convince her to love books, until she finds one that might change her mind.

Brinckloe, Julie. *Fireflies!* Aladdin Paperbacks, 1986, c1985. 32p. IL K–3, Lexile: 630
> A young boy is proud of having caught a jar full of fireflies, which seems to him like owning a piece of moonlight. As the light begins to dim, however, he realizes that he must set the insects free or they will die.

Broach, Elise. *When Dinosaurs Came with Everything.* Atheneum Books for Young Readers, c2007. 40p. IL K–3, Lexile: 380
> Although his mother is a little worried, a young boy is delighted to discover that every shop in town is giving away real dinosaurs to their customers.

Bunting, Eve. *Flower Garden.* Harcourt Brace, c1994. 32p. IL K–3, Lexile: NP
> Helped by her father, a young girl prepares a flower garden as a birthday surprise for her mother.

Caines, Jeannette Franklin. *Just Us Women.* HarperTrophy, 1982. 32p. IL K–3, Lexile: 610
> A young girl and her favorite aunt share the excitement of planning a very special car trip for just the two of them.

Coffelt, Nancy. *Fred Stays with Me.* Little, Brown, 2007. 32p. IL K–3
> A child describes how she lives sometimes with her mother and sometimes with her father, but her dog is her constant companion.

Creech, Sharon. *Fishing in the Air.* Joanna Cotler Books, c2000. 32p. IL K–3, Lexile: 570
> A young boy and his father go on a fishing trip and discover the power of imagination.

Crews, Donald. *Shortcut.* Greenwillow Books, c1992. 32p. IL K–3, Lexile: 210
> Children who take a shortcut by walking along a railroad track find excitement and danger when a train approaches.

Curtis, Jamie Lee. *Today I Feel Silly & Other Moods That Make My Day.* Joanna Cotler Books, c1998. 34p. IL K–3, Lexile: 250
> A child's emotions range from silliness to anger to excitement, coloring and changing each day.

Fletcher, Ralph J. *Grandpa Never Lies.* Clarion Books, c2000. 32p. IL K–3
> A poetic description of the special relationship between a grandfather and a young child.

Hoberman, Mary Ann. *I'm Going to Grandma's.* Harcourt, c2007. 32p. IL K–3,
> A special quilt keeps a little girl from feeling homesick when she sleeps over with her grandparents.

Igus, Toyomi. *Two Mrs. Gibsons.* Children's Book Press, c1996. 32p. IL K–3, Lexile: 530
> The biracial daughter of an African American father and a Japanese mother fondly recalls growing up with her mother and her father's mother—two very different but equally loving women.

Personal Narrative

Juster, Norton. *The Hello, Goodbye Window.* Michael Di Capua Books/Hyperion Books for Children, 2005. 32p. IL K–3
 A little girl tells about the special kitchen window at her beloved Nanny and Poppy's house, from which a person can see anyone or anything coming and going.

Keats, Ezra Jack. *The Snowy Day.* Viking Press, 1962. 32p. IL K–3, Lexile: 500
 The adventures of a little boy in the city on a very snowy day.

Laminack, Lester L. *Saturdays and Teacakes.* Peachtree, c2004. 32p. IL K–3, Lexile: 840
 A young boy remembers the Saturdays when he was nine or ten and he would ride his bicycle to his Ma'am-maw's house, where they spent the day together mowing the lawn, picking vegetables, eating lunch, and making delicious, sweet teacakes.

Lin, Grace. *Dim Sum for Everyone!* Dell Dragonfly Books, 2003, c2001. 31p. IL K–3
 A child describes the various little dishes of dim sum that she and her family enjoy on a visit to a restaurant in Chinatown.

Lipson, Eden Ross. *Applesauce Season.* Roaring Brook Press, 2009. 32p. IL K–3. Lexile: 940
 A family works together to buy, peel, cook, and stir apples for the homemade applesauce they make every year.

Long, Melinda. *How I Became a Pirate.* Harcourt, c2003. 36p. IL K–3, Lexile: 470
 Jeremy Jacob joins Braid Beard and his pirate crew and finds out about pirate language, pirate manners, and other aspects of pirate life.

Maccarone, Grace. *My Tooth Is about to Fall Out.* Scholastic, c1995. 32p. IL K–3, Lexile: 410
 A little girl with a wiggly, jiggly tooth worries about where it might fall out. Once she has that hole in her mouth, she feels like a big kid.

MacLachlan, Patricia. *All the Places to Love.* HarperCollins, c1994. 32p. IL K–3, Lexile: 920
 A young boy describes the favorite places that he shares with his family on his grandparent's farm and in the nearby countryside.

Mills, Lauren A. *The Rag Coat.* Little Brown, c1991. 32p. IL K–3, Lexile: 630
 Minna proudly wears her new coat made of clothing scraps to school, where the other children laugh at her until she tells them the stories behind the scraps.

O'Connor, Jane. *Fancy Nancy.* HarperCollins, c2006. 32p. IL K–3, Lexile: 420
 A young girl who loves fancy things helps her family to be fancy for one special night.

Paulsen, Gary. *Canoe Days.* Dragonfly Books, 2001, c1999. 32p. IL K–3, Lexile: 840
 A canoe ride on a northern lake during a summer day reveals the quiet beauty and wonder of nature in and around the peaceful water.

Penn, Audrey. *The Kissing Hand.* Tanglewood Press, 2006. 16p. IL K–3
 When Chester the raccoon is reluctant to go to kindergarten for the first time, his mother teaches him a secret way to carry her love with him.

Personal Narrative

Polacco, Patricia. *Some Birthday!* Aladdin Paperbacks, c1991. 32p. IL K–3, Lexile: 590
On a young girl's birthday, her father takes her and her brother to see the Monster at Clay Pit Bottom.

Pomerantz, Charlotte. *The Chalk Doll.* HarperCollins, c1989. 30p. IL K–3, Lexile: NP
Rosy's mother remembers the pleasures of her childhood in Jamaica and the very special dolls she used to play with.

Ryder, Joanne. *My Father's Hands.* Morrow Junior Books, c1994. 32p. IL K–3, Lexile: 730
A child's father digs in the garden, finding and presenting for inspection such wonders as a round gold beetle and a leaf-green mantis.

Rylant, Cynthia. *The Relatives Came.* Atheneum Books for Young Readers, 2001. 32p. IL K–3, Lexile: 940
The relatives come to visit from Virginia and everyone has a wonderful time.

Rylant, Cynthia. *Tulip Sees America.* Scholastic, 1998. 32p. IL K–3, Lexile: 530
A young man and his dog drive west from Ohio and marvel at the farms of Iowa, the skies of Nebraska, the wind in Wyoming, the mountains of Colorado, the desert in Nevada, and the ocean in Oregon.

Rylant, Cynthia. *When I Was Young in the Mountains.* Dutton Children's Books, c1982. 32p. IL K–3, Lexile: 980
A young girl recalls her childhood days living with her younger brother and her loving grandparents in the rural Southern mountains.

Viorst, Judith. *Alexander and the Terrible, Horrible, No Good, Very Bad Day.* Atheneum, c1972. 32p. IL K–3, Lexile: 970
On a day when everything goes wrong for him, Alexander is consoled by the thought that other people have bad days, too.

Williams, Vera B. *A Chair for My Mother.* Greenwillow Books, c1982. 32p. IL K–3, Lexile: 640
A child, her waitress mother, and her grandmother save dimes to buy a comfortable armchair after all their furniture is lost in a fire.

Wong, Janet S. *The Trip Back Home.* Harcourt, c2000. 31p. IL K–3, Lexile: 1190
A young girl and her mother travel to Korea to visit their extended family. Along with the gifts and hugs, the young girl learns about her family's traditions.

Woodson, Jacqueline. *Sweet, Sweet Memory.* Jump at the Sun/Hyperion Paperbacks for Children, 2007, c2000. 32p. IL K–3, Lexile: 380
A child and her grandmother feel sad when Grandpa dies. As time passes, funny memories of him make them laugh and feel better.

Woodson, Jacqueline. *We Had a Picnic This Sunday Past.* Hyperion Paperbacks for Children, 2007, c1997. 32p. IL K–3, Lexile: 710
A young girl describes her various relatives and the foods they bring to the annual family picnic.

Personal Narrative

Books for Children Ages Eight to Twelve

Byars, Betsy Cromer. *The Moon and I.* Beech Tree Books, 1991. 96p. IL 5–8, Lexile: 870
While describing her humorous adventures with a blacksnake, Betsy Byars recounts childhood anecdotes and explains how she writes a book.

MacLachlan, Patricia. *What You Know First.* Joanna Cotler Books, c1995. 32p. IL 3–6, Lexile: NP
As a family prepares to move away from their farm, the daughter reflects on all the things she loves there so that, when her baby brother is older, she can tell him what it was like.

Van Allsburg, Chris. *The Polar Express.* Houghton Mifflin, 2005. 32p. IL 3–6, Lexile: 520
A magical train ride on Christmas Eve takes a boy to the North Pole to receive a special gift from Santa Claus.

From *101 Great, Ready-to-Use Book Lists for Children* by Nancy J. Keane. Santa Barbara, CA: Libraries Unlimited. Copyright © 2012.

Persuasive Writing

Books for Children of All Ages

Child, Lauren. *I Will Never Not Ever Eat a Tomato.* Candlewick Press, 2000. 32p. IL K–3, Lexile: 370
A fussy eater decides to sample the carrots after her brother convinces her that they are really orange twiglets from Jupiter.

Cronin, Doreen. *Duck for President.* Simon & Schuster Books for Young Readers, c2004. 40p. IL K–3, Lexile: 680
When Duck gets tired of working for Farmer Brown, his political ambition eventually leads to his being elected president.

Hoose, Phillip M. *Hey, Little Ant.* Tricycle Press, c1998. 26p. IL K–3, Lexile: NP
A song in which an ant pleads with the kid who is tempted to squish it.

Kasza, Keiko. *My Lucky Day.* G. P. Putnam's Sons, c2003. 32p. IL K–3, Lexile: 270
When a young pig knocks on a fox's door, the fox thinks dinner has arrived, but the pig has other plans.

Kellogg, Steven. *Can I Keep Him?* Puffin, 1976, c1971. 32p. IL K–3, Lexile: 510
Mother objects to every pet Arnold asks to keep except one—a person.

Khalsa, Dayal Kaur. *I Want a Dog.* Tundra, 2002, c1987. 24p. IL K–3, Lexile: 610
When her parents refuse to get her a dog, May creates an imaginary dog out of a roller skate.

LaRochelle, David. *The Best Pet of All.* Dutton Children's Books, c2004. 32p. IL K–3
A young boy enlists the help of a dragon to persuade his mother to let him have a dog as a pet.

Orloff, Karen Kaufman. *I Wanna Iguana.* Putnam, c2004. 32p. IL K–3, Lexile: 460
Alex and his mother write notes back and forth in which Alex tries to persuade her to let him have a baby iguana for a pet.

Pomerantz, Charlotte. *The Piggy in the Puddle.* Aladdin Paperbacks, 1989, c1974. 32p. IL K–3, Lexile: NP
Unable to persuade a young pig from frolicking in the mud, her family finally joins her for a mud party.

Scieszka, Jon. *The True Story of the 3 Little Pigs.* Viking, 1989. 32p. IL K–3, Lexile: 570
The wolf gives his own outlandish version of what really happened when he tangled with the three little pigs.

Teague, Mark. *Dear Mrs. Larue: Letters from Obedience School.* Scholastic Press, 2002. 32p. IL K–3, Lexile: 500
Gertrude LaRue receives typewritten and paw-written letters from her dog Ike, entreating her to let him leave the Igor Brotweiler Canine Academy and come back home.

Viorst, Judith. *Earrings!* Atheneum Books for Young Readers, c1990. 32p. IL K–3, Lexile: 470
A young girl uses a variety of arguments to convince her parents to let her have her ears pierced.

Persuasive Writing

Willems, Mo. *Don't Let the Pigeon Drive the Bus!* Hyperion Books for Children, c2003. 34p. IL K–3, Lexile: 120

A pigeon that longs to drive a bus sees a chance to make its dream come true when the bus driver takes a short break.

Wilson, Karma. *Bear's New Friend.* Margaret K. McElderry Books, c2006. 32p. IL K–3, Lexile: NP

Bear and his friends persuade a bashful owl to play with them.

Tear Jerkers: Characters Whom Kids Can Relate to

List by: Jessica Gilcreast, McDonough Elementary School, New Hampshire

Books for Children Ages Eight to Twelve

Erskine, Kathy. *Mockingbird.* Puffin Press, c2011. 256p. IL 5–8, Lexile: 630
"Tear jerker" does not begin to cover the way in which this powerful story about how a family recovers from school violence can reduce a reader to a slobbering mess. This book was the deserving winner of a National Book Award.

Gorman, Carol. *Stumptown Kid.* Peachtree, c2005. 284p. IL 3–6, Lexile: 620
In a small Iowa town in 1952, eleven-year-old Charlie Nebraska, whose father died in the Korean War, learns the meanings of both racism and heroism when he befriends a black man who has played baseball in the Negro Leagues.

Graff, Lisa. *Umbrella Summer.* Laura Geringer Books, c2009. 235p. IL 3–6, Lexile: 820
After her brother Jared dies, ten-year-old Annie worries about the hidden dangers of everything, from bug bites to bicycle riding, until she is befriended by a new neighbor who is grieving her own loss.

Mazer, Harry. *A Boy at War: A Novel of Pearl Harbor.* Aladdin Paperback, c2002. 104p. IL 3–6
While fishing with his friends off Honolulu on December 7, 1941, teenaged Adam is caught in the midst of the Japanese attack. Through the chaos of the subsequent days, he tries to find his father, a naval officer who was serving on the U.S.S. *Arizona* when the bombs fell.

Park, Barbara. *Mick Harte Was Here.* Yearling, c1996. 96p. IL 3–6, Lexile: 730
Phoebe, an eighth grader, loses her brother Mick in a tragic accident, in which Mick was not wearing his bicycle helmet. During the course of the book, Phoebe and her family learn how to live with the loss of a family member.

Paterson, Katherine. *The Great Gilly Hopkins.* Harper Collins, c1978. 148p. IL 5–8, Lexile: 800
Gilly Hopkins is a determined-to-be-unpleasant eleven-year-old foster kid whom the reader can't help but like by the end of this book. Gilly has been in the foster system all her life, and she dreams of getting back to her (as she imagines) wonderful mother. (The mother makes these longings worse by writing the occasional letter.) Gilly is all the more determined to leave after she's placed in a new foster home with a "gross guardian and a freaky kid." She soon learns about the false promise of her illusions—the hard way.

Tsuchiya, Yukio. *Faithful Elephants: A True Story of Animals, People, and War.* Houghton Mifflin, c1988, 32p. IL 3–6, Lexile 640
Recounts how three elephants in a Tokyo zoo were put to death in a time of war, focusing on the pain shared by the elephants and the keepers who had to starve them.

From *101 Great, Ready-to-Use Book Lists for Children* by Nancy J. Keane. Santa Barbara, CA: Libraries Unlimited. Copyright © 2012.

Part 5

Subjects

Estimation

Books for Children of All Ages

Cobb, Annie. *The Long Wait.* Kane Press, 2000. 32p. IL K–3, Lexile: 140
Two friends try to estimate how long they will have to wait in line to get on the fantastic new ride.

Dalton, Julie. *Farmer's Market Rounding.* Children's Press, c2007. 31p. IL K–3 (Non-fiction)
Teaches how to round numbers to the nearest ten, following a little boy and his father as they buy food at a farmer's market.

Franco, Betsy. *Time to Estimate.* Yellow Umbrella Books, c2002. 17p. IL K–3 (Non-fiction)
Text and photographs introduce everyday uses for estimation.

Goldstone, Bruce. *Greater Estimations.* Henry Holt, c2008. 31p. IL K–3 (Non-fiction)
Presents techniques for making reasonably accurate estimations of high quantities of items or vast ranges of measurement, with creative examples for building skill in guessing lengths, volumes, and area.

Hirschmann, Kris. *The Dog: Is a Paw a Foot?: All about Measurement.* Scholastic, c2005. 32p. IL K–3 (Non-fiction)
Teaches about aspects of measurement, including units such as inches and feet, estimation of length and distance, and use of a ruler. The book also includes photos of and facts on different kinds of dogs.

Matzke, Ann H. *Can You Guess?* Rourke Publishing, c2011. 24p. IL K–3 (Non-fiction)
Introduces mathematical notation by asking readers to make guesses about different objects and consider the concepts of "more" and "less."

Murphy, Stuart J. *Betcha!* HarperCollins, c1997. 33p. IL 3–6, Lexile: 290 (Non-fiction)
Readers learn how to estimate as two friends guess how many passengers are on a bus, how many cars are in a traffic jam, and how many jelly beans are in a jar. The book also includes extension activities.

Murphy, Stuart J. *Coyotes All Around.* HarperCollins, c2003. 31p. IL K–3 (Non-fiction)
A pack of coyotes tries to determine how many roadrunners and other creatures are in their vicinity. While some count different groups and add their totals together, Clever Coyote rounds off and estimates their numbers.

Noonan, Diana. *People Who Predict: Estimating.* Teacher Created Materials, c2009. 32p. IL K–3, Lexile: 670 (Non-fiction)
Introduces young readers to people who predict and prepare for natural disasters, such as volcanologists, seismologists, and meteorologists.

Sargent, Brian. *Can You Guess?* Children's Press, c2004. 31p. IL K–3 Lexile: 380, (Non-fiction)
A counting book about some of the things seen in a zoo, such as elephants, giraffes, peanuts, and peacocks.

VanVoorst, Jennifer. *Can You Guess?* Yellow Umbrella, c2004. 17p. IL K–3 (Non-fiction)
Simple text and photographs introduce the concept of estimation, providing examples of ways one can estimate time and amounts.

Civil Rights

Books for Children of All Ages

Coleman, Evelyn. *White Socks Only.* Whitman, 1996. 32p. IL K–3
Grandma tells the story about her first trip alone into town during the days when segregation still existed in Mississippi.

Farris, Christine King. *My Brother Martin: A Sister Remembers Growing up with the Rev. Dr. Martin Luther King Jr.* Simon & Schuster Books for Young Readers, c2003. 35p. IL K–3, Lexile: 970 (Non-fiction)
Looks at the early life of Martin Luther King, Jr., as seen through the eyes of his older sister.

Morrison, Toni. *Remember: The Journey to School Integration.* Houghton Mifflin, c2004. 78p. IL 3–6, Lexile: 660 (Non-fiction)
Presents a selection of archival photographs that document events surrounding the integration of U.S. schools following the 1954 Supreme Court decision in *Brown v. Board of Education*, and includes captions in which the author imagines what the people in the pictures must have been thinking and feeling.

Pinkney, Andrea Davis. *Boycott Blues: How Rosa Parks Inspired a Nation.* Greenwillow Books, c2008. 40p. IL K–3, Lexile: 560 (Non-fiction)
Uses the form of a blues song to share the story of the year-long bus boycott in Montgomery, Alabama, sparked by seamstress Rosa Parks's refusal to give up her seat on a city bus to a white passenger in 1955, which resulted in a repeal of the Jim Crow segregation laws.

Reynolds, Aaron. *Back of the Bus.* Philomel Books, c2010. 32p. IL K–3, Lexile: 720
From the back of the bus, an African American child watches the arrest of Rosa Parks when she defies the law and takes a seat at the front of the bus.

Robinson, Sharon. *Testing the Ice: A True Story about Jackie Robinson.* Scholastic Press, 2009. 40p. IL K–3, Lexile: 800
As a testament to his courage, Jackie Robinson's daughter shares memories of him, from his baseball career to the day he tests the ice for her, her brothers, and their friends.

Ryan, Pam Muñoz. *When Marian Sang: The True Recital of Marian Anderson, the Voice of a Century.* Scholastic Press, 2002. 37p. IL K–3, Lexile: 780 (Non-fiction)
An introduction to the life of Marian Anderson, extraordinary singer and civil rights activist, who was the first African American to perform at the Metropolitan Opera, and whose life and career encouraged social change.

Shelton, Paula Young. *Child of the Civil Rights Movement.* Schwartz & Wade Books, c2010. 42p. IL K–3, Lexile: 960 (Non-fiction)
Paula Young Shelton shares her memories of the civil rights movement and her involvement in the historic march from Selma to Montgomery.

Stauffacher, Sue. *Bessie Smith and the Night Riders.* Putnam's, c2006. 32p. IL K–3
African American blues singer Bessie Smith single-handedly scares off Ku Klux Klan members who are trying to disrupt her show one hot July night in Concord, North Carolina.

Civil Rights

Weatherford, Carole Boston. *Freedom on the Menu: The Greensboro Sit-ins.* Dial Books for Young Readers, c2005. 32p. IL K–3, Lexile: 660 (Non-fiction)

> The 1960 civil rights sit-ins at the Woolworth's lunch counter in Greensboro, North Carolina, are seen through the eyes of a young Southern black girl.

Wiles, Deborah. *Freedom Summer.* Atheneum Books for Young Readers, c2001. 31p. IL K–3, Lexile: 460

> In 1964, Joe is pleased that a new law will allow his best friend John Henry, who is African American, to share the town pool and other public places with him, but he is dismayed to find that prejudice still exists.

Books for Children Ages Eight to Twelve

Freedman, Russell. *Freedom Walkers: The Story of the Montgomery Bus Boycott.* Holiday House, c2006. 114p. IL 3–6, Lexile: 1110 ((Non-fiction)

> Presents the story of the Montgomery bus boycott in 1955 and the major events and people who contributed to the year-long struggle for equal rights on Montgomery's city buses.

Giovanni, Nikki. *Rosa.* Holt, 2005. 34p. IL 3–6, Lexile: 900 (Non-fiction)

> An illustrated account of Rosa Parks's refusal to give up her seat on a bus in Montgomery, Alabama, in 1955, and the subsequent bus boycott by the black community.

Golenbock, Peter. *Teammates.* Harcourt Brace, c1990. 32p. IL 3–6, Lexile: 930 (Non-fiction)

> Describes the racial prejudice experienced by Jackie Robinson when he joined the Brooklyn Dodgers to become the first African American player in Major League Baseball, and depicts the acceptance and support he received from his white teammate Pee Wee Reese.

Rappaport, Doreen. *Martin's Big Words: The Life of Dr. Martin Luther King, Jr.* Jump at the Sun/ Hyperion Books for Children, c2001. 34p. IL 3–6, Lexile: 410

> Looks at the life of Dr. Martin Luther King, Jr., explaining his work to bring about a peaceful end to segregation.

Endangered Species

Base, Graeme. *The Water Hole*. Harry N. Abrams, 2001. 32p. IL K–3, Lexile: 230
> As ever-growing numbers of animals visit a watering hole, introducing the numbers from one to ten, the water dwindles.

Cherry, Lynne. *The Great Kapok Tree: A Tale of the Amazon Rain Forest*. Harcourt, c1990. 33p. IL K–3, Lexile: 670
> The many different animals that live in a great kapok tree in the Brazilian rain forest try to convince a man with an ax of the importance of not cutting down their home.

Cowcher, Helen. *Antarctica*. Square Fish, c1990. 36p. IL K–3, Lexile: 700
> Emperor penguins, Weddell seals, Adelie penguins, and other creatures of Antarctica wonder if the new visitors, who arrive in noisy helicopters and metal ships, will be friends or harbingers of destruction.

Cowcher, Helen. *Desert Elephants*. Farrar, Straus and Giroux, c2011. IL K–3 (Non-fiction)
> Describes the migration of the desert elephants of Mali, West Africa, and discusses how the Tuareg, Dogon, and Fulani peoples work together to protect the balance of life in the desert.

Jenkins, Steve. *Almost Gone: The World's Rarest Animals*. HarperCollins, c2006. 33p. IL K–3 (Non-fiction)
> Profiles animal species around the world that have gone extinct during the course of human history, or that are currently at risk for extinction.

Martin, Bill. *Panda Bear, Panda Bear, What Do You See?* Holt, 2003. 28p. IL K–3, Lexile: NP
> Illustrations and rhyming text present ten different endangered animals.

Books for Children Ages Eight to Twelve

Bow, James. *Saving Endangered Plants and Animals*. Crabtree Publishing, 2009. 32p. IL 3–6, Lexile: 930 (Non-fiction)
> Explores the scientific methods being used to protect rare and endangered animal species around the world and profiles scientists involved in wildlife conservation.

Hirsch, Rebecca E. *Helping Endangered Animals*. Cherry Lake Publishing, c2010. 32p. IL 3–6 (Non-fiction)
> Discusses the importance of helping endangered animals, including pandas in China, elephants in Chad, and right whales, and covers the importance of sea ice to polar bears and other topics related to recovery and conservation.

Parker, Steve. *100 Things You Should Know about Endangered Animals*. Mason Crest, 2009. 48p. IL 3–6 (Non-fiction)
> Collects one hundred facts about endangered animals, covering threats, pollution problems, captive breeding, and more. The book also includes illustrations, cartoons, quizzes, and activities.

Endangered Species

Turner, Pamela S. *Gorilla Doctors: Saving Endangered Great Apes.* Houghton Mifflin, 2005. 64p. IL 3–6, Lexile: 910 (Non-fiction)

This full-color, illustrated examination of the mountain gorillas of Rwanda describes the effects of human exposure on the gorillas, the delivery of emergency medical care to the animals in the wild, and ways to protect their species from poachers and common human diseases.

Wright, Alexandra. *Will We Miss Them?: Endangered Species.* Charlesbridge, c1992. 31p. IL 3–6, Lexile: 860 (Non-fiction)

Introduces children to the lives and challenges of endangered species from the perspective of an eleven-year-old author.

Mapping

Books for Children of All Ages

Berenstain, Stan. *The Berenstain Bears and the Spooky Old Tree.* Random House, c1978. 40p. IL K–3, Lexile: 100
> One by one, three brave little bears have second thoughts about exploring the interior of a spooky old tree.

Buzzeo, Toni. *Adventure Annie Goes to Work.* Dial Books for Young Readers, c2009. 30p. IL K–3
> When she goes to work with her mother on a Saturday, Adventure Girl uses her own special methods to help find a missing report.

Caseley, Judith. *On the Town: A Community Adventure.* Greenwillow Books, c2002. 32p. IL K–3
> Charlie and his mother walk around the neighborhood doing errands so that Charlie can write in his notebook about the people and places that make up his community.

Ernst, Lisa Campbell. *Stella Louella's Runaway Book.* Simon & Schuster Books for Young Readers, c1998. 34p. IL K–3, Lexile: 640
> As she tries to find the book that she must return to the library that day, Stella gathers a growing group of people who have all enjoyed reading the book.

Larson, Kirby. *Two Bobbies: A True Story of Hurricane Katrina, Friendship, and Survival.* Walker, c2008. 32p. IL K–3, Lexile: 810 (Non-fiction)
> Tells the true story of Bobbie the dog and Bob Cat, two pets who bonded together and were able to survive the devastation of Hurricane Katrina.

Ljungkvist, Laura. *Follow the Line.* Viking, 2006. 28p. IL K–3
> Invites the reader to visit a wide variety of places and count different objects found in each, from fire hydrants in a big city in the morning, to starfish in the ocean during the day, to babies sleeping in a country village at night.

McCloskey, Robert. *Make Way for Ducklings.* Viking, c1969. 65p. IL K–3, Lexile: 630
> Mr. and Mrs. Mallard proudly return to their home in the Boston Public Garden with their eight offspring.

Pattison, Darcy. *The Journey of Oliver K. Woodman.* Harcourt, c2003. 48p. IL K–3, Lexile: 640
> Oliver K. Woodman, a man made of wood, takes a remarkable journey across America, as told through the postcards and letters of those he meets along the way.

Pattison, Darcy. *Searching for Oliver K. Woodman.* Harcourt, c2005. 48p. IL K–3, Lexile: 690
> Imogene Poplar, a private investigator made of wood, is sent by a reporter and Tameka's Uncle Ray in search of the missing Oliver K. Woodman. Her journey is related through the letters and postcards of those she meets along the way.

Priceman, Marjorie. *How to Make an Apple Pie and See the World.* Knopf, 1994. 32p. IL K–3, Lexile: 590
> Since the market is closed, the reader is led around the world to gather the ingredients for making an apple pie. The book includes a recipe.

Mapping

Shulevitz, Uri. *How I Learned Geography.* Farrar, Straus and Giroux, 2008. 32p. IL K–3, Lexile: 660
By spending hours studying his father's world map, a young boy escapes from the hunger and misery of refugee life. Based on the author's childhood in Kazakhstan, where he lived as a Polish refugee.

Sis, Peter. *Madlenka.* Square Fish/Farrar, Straus and Giroux, 2010, c2000. 48p. IL K–3, Lexile: 110
Madlenka, whose New York City neighbors include the French baker, the Indian news vendor, the Italian ice cream man, the South American grocer, and the Chinese shopkeeper, goes around the block to show her friends her loose tooth and finds that it is like taking a trip around the world.

Stevens, Janet. *And the Dish Ran Away with the Spoon.* Harcourt, c2001. 50p. IL K–3, Lexile: 200
When Dish and Spoon run away, their nursery rhyme friends Cat, Cow, and Dog set out to rescue them in time for the next evening's reading of their rhyme.

Williams, Linda. *The Little Old Lady Who Was Not Afraid of Anything.* HarperCollins, c1986. 32p. IL K–3, Lexile: 710
A little old lady who is not afraid of anything must deal with a pumpkin head, a tall black hat, and other spooky objects that follow her through the dark woods trying to scare her.

Refugees

Books for Children of All Ages

Bunting, Eve. *How Many Days to America?: A Thanksgiving Story.* Clarion Books, c1988. 32p. IL K–3, Lexile: 460

Refugees from a Caribbean island embark on a dangerous boat trip to America, where they have a special reason to celebrate Thanksgiving.

Cha, Dia. *Dia's Story Cloth.* Lee & Low Books, c1996. IL K–3

The story cloth made for her by her aunt and uncle chronicles the life of the author and her family in their native Laos and their eventual emigration to the United States.

Graber, Janet. *Muktar and the Camels.* Henry Holt, 2009. 32p. IL K–3, Lexile: 670

Muktar, an eleven-year-old refugee living in a Kenyan orphanage, dreams of tending camels again, as he did with his nomadic family in Somalia. He has a chance to prove himself when a traveling librarian with an injured camel arrives at his school.

Lee-Tai, Amy. *A Place Where Sunflowers Grow.* Children's Book Press, c2006. 31p. IL K–3, Lexile: 790

While she and her family are interned at Topaz Relocation Center during World War II, Mari gradually adjusts as she enrolls in an art class, makes a friend, and plants sunflowers and waits for them to grow.

Lofthouse, Liz. *Ziba Came on a Boat.* Kane/Miller, 2007. 33p. IL K–3

Tells the story of a young girl's family and their long journey to make a better life for themselves far away from their home.

Shea, Pegi Deitz. *The Whispering Cloth: A Refugee's Story.* Boyds Mills Press, 1996. 32p. IL K–3, Lexile: 780

A young girl in a Thai refugee camp finds the story within herself needed to create her own pa'ndau.

Surat, Michele Maria. *Angel Child, Dragon Child.* Scholastic, 1989, c1983. 35p. IL K–3, Lexile: 420

Ut, a Vietnamese girl attending school in the United States, is lonely for her mother left behind in Vietnam. Over time, she makes a new friend, who presents her with a wonderful gift.

Uchida, Yoshiko. *The Bracelet.* Philomel Books, c1993. 32p. IL K–3, Lexile: 710

Emi, a Japanese American girl in the second grade, is sent with her family to an internment camp during World War II. The loss of the bracelet her best friend has given her proves that she does not need a physical reminder of that friendship.

Williams, Karen Lynn. *Four Feet, Two Sandals.* Eerdmans Books for Young Readers, 2007. 32p. IL K–3, Lexile: 620

Two young Afghani girls living in a refugee camp in Pakistan share a precious pair of sandals brought by relief workers.

Refugees

Books for Children Ages Eight to Twelve

Applegate, Katherine. *Home of the Brave.* Feiwel and Friends, 2007. 249p. IL 5–8, Lexile: NP
Kek, an African refugee, is confronted by many strange things at the Minneapolis home of his aunt and cousin, as well as in his fifth-grade classroom. He longs for his missing mother, but finds comfort in the company of a cow and her owner.

Burg, Ann E. *All the Broken Pieces: A Novel in Verse.* Scholastic Press, 2009. 218p. IL 5–8, Lexile: 680
Two years after being airlifted out of Vietnam in 1975, Matt Pin is haunted by the terrible secret he left behind. Now, while is living in a loving adoptive home in the United States, a series of profound events forces him to confront his past.

Burg, Ann E. *Rebekkah's Journey: A World War II Refugee Story.* Sleeping Bear Press, Thomson/Gale, c2006. 48p. IL 3–6
After eluding capture by the Nazis, seven-year-old Rebekkah and her mother are brought from Italy to the United States to begin a new life.

Flood, Bo. *Warriors in the Crossfire.* Front Street, c2010. 142p. IL 5–8, Lexile: 560
Joseph, living on the island of Saipan during World War II, learns what it means to be a warrior as he and his family struggle to survive in the face of impending invasion.

Hesse, Karen. *Aleutian Sparrow.* Aladdin Paperbacks, 2005, c2003. 156p. IL 5–8, Lexile: NP
An Aleutian Islander recounts her suffering during World War II in American internment camps designed to "protect" the population from the invading Japanese.

Kadohata, Cynthia. *A Million Shades of Gray.* Atheneum Books for Young Readers, c2010. 216p. IL 5–8, Lexile: 700
A boy takes refuge in the jungle with his elephant when the Viet Cong launch an attack on his village in the aftermath of the Vietnam War.

Kurtz, Jane. *The Storyteller's Beads.* Harcourt Brace, c1998. 154p. IL 3–6, Lexile: 750
During the political strife and famine of the 1980s, two Ethiopian girls—one Christian and the other Jewish and blind—struggle to overcome many difficulties, including their prejudices about each other, as they make the dangerous journey out of Ethiopia.

Levitin, Sonia. *The Return.* Fawcett Juniper, c1987. 181p. IL 5–8, Lexile: 720
Desta and the other members of her Falasha family, who are Jews suffering from discrimination in Ethiopia, finally flee the country and attempt the dangerous journey to Israel.

Lieurance, Suzanne. *The Lucky Baseball: My Story in a Japanese-American Internment Camp.* Enslow Publishers, c2010. 160p. IL 3–6
In 1942, after the Japanese troops bomb Pearl Harbor, twelve-year-old Harry Yakamoto and his family are forced to move to an internment camp, where they must learn to survive in the desert of California under the watch of armed guards. The book includes a section about the treatment of Japanese Americans during World War II.

Refugees

Lobel, Anita. *No Pretty Pictures: A Child of War.* Collins, 2008, c1998. 239p. IL 5–8, Lexile: 750 (Non-fiction)

> The author, known as an illustrator of children's books, describes her experiences as a Polish Jew during World War II and her years in Sweden after the war.

Magorian, Michelle. *Good Night, Mr. Tom.* HarperTrophy, 1986, c1981. 318p. IL 5–8, Lexile: 760

> A battered child learns to embrace life when he is adopted by an old man in the English countryside during World War II.

Mazer, Norma Fox. *Good Night, Maman.* Houghton Mifflin Harcourt, c1999. 185p. IL 5–8, Lexile: 510

> After spending years fleeing from the Nazis in war-torn Europe, twelve-year-old Karin Levi and her older brother Marc find a new home in a refugee camp in Oswego, New York.

Paterson, Katherine. *The Day of the Pelican.* Clarion Books, 2009. 145p. IL 5–8, Lexile: 770

> In 1998, when the Kosovo hostilities escalate, thirteen-year-old Meli's life as an ethnic Albanian changes forever after her brother escapes his Serbian captors. The entire family is forced to flee from one refugee camp to another, until they are finally able to immigrate to America.

Pellegrino, Marge. *Journey of Dreams.* Frances Lincoln Children's Books, 2009. 250p. IL 5–8, Lexile: 740

> Tomasa and her family struggle during a time of war in Guatemala before setting out on a journey to find Mama and Carlos, who have gone into hiding. They must brave many dangers before eventually making their way to the United States.

Robinson, Anthony. *Hamzat's Journey: A Refugee Diary.* Frances Lincoln Children's Books, 2010, c2009. 29p. IL 3–6 (Non-fiction)

> Hamzat, a boy born in Chechnya in 1993, tells about his life in a time of war, and explains how he and his family came to live in England after he stepped on a landmine and had to have his leg amputated.

Shea, Pegi Deitz. *Tangled Threads: A Hmong Girl's Story.* Clarion Books, c2003. 236p. IL 5–8, Lexile: 630

> After spending ten years in a refugee camp in Thailand, thirteen-year-old Mai Yang travels to Providence, Rhode Island. There, her Americanized cousins introduce her to pizza, shopping, and beer, while her grandmother and new friends keep her connected to her Hmong heritage.

Williams, Mary. *Brothers in Hope: The Story of the Lost Boys of Sudan.* Lee & Low, c200538p. IL 3–6, Lexile: 670

> Eight-year-old Garang, orphaned by a civil war in Sudan, finds the inner strength to help lead other boys as they trek hundreds of miles seeking safety in Ethiopia, and then Kenya, before being offered sanctuary in the United States many years later.

Part 6

Themes

Abandonment

Books for Children of All Ages

Atwood, Margaret Eleanor. *Bashful Bob and Doleful Dorinda.* Bloomsbury Children's Books, Distributed by Holtzbrinck Publishers, 2006. 31p. IL K–3
> A story told mainly with words that begin with the letters "b" and "d," in which bashful Bob, who has been abandoned and raised by dogs, meets doleful Dorinda, who deals with dirty dishes, and the two become friends and eventually heroes.

Furstinger, Nancy. *Maggie's Second Chance: A Gentle Dog's Rescue.* Gryphon Press, c2011. 26p. IL K–3
> A group of school children, disturbed by the plight of Maggie, a dog abandoned by her family and slated to be euthanized at the local pound, raise money and volunteers to build and run a no-kill shelter.

Goble, Paul. *Mystic Horse.* HarperCollins, c2003. 34p. IL K–3, Lexile: 580
> After caring for an old abandoned horse, a poor young Pawnee boy is rewarded by the horse's mystic powers.

Hodgkins, Fran. *The Orphan Seal.* Down East Books, c2000. 32p. IL K–3 (Non-fiction)
> Recounts the story of Howler, an abandoned harbor seal pup, from his rescue and recovery in early spring at the New England Aquarium until he is released in the fall.

Jackson, Emma. *A Home for Dixie: The True Story of a Rescued Puppy.* Collins, c2008. 32p. IL K–3, Lexile: 750 (Non-fiction)
> Tells the true story of Emma, who desperately wanted a dog, and an abandoned puppy, which wanted a home.

Oelschlager, Vanita. *Porcupette Finds a Family.* Vanita Books, c2010. 34p. IL K–3
> A baby porcupine that has lost its mother is adopted by a bear family, but worries the mother bear will abandon it when she realizes the porcupine is very different from her own cubs.

Slate, Joseph. *I Want to Be Free.* G. P. Putnam's Sons, c2009. 32p. IL K–3, Lexile: 150
> A children's story based on a sacred Buddhist tale that recounts the story of an escaped slave who rescues an abandoned baby from slave hunters.

Teckentrup, Britta. *Grumpy Cat.* Boxer Books, 2008. 28p. IL K–3, Lexile: 530
> A street cat, increasingly grumpy in its loneliness, changes its attitude when a small, abandoned kitten decides to be its friend.

Books for Children Ages Eight to Twelve

Brown, Susan Taylor. *Hugging the Rock.* Tricycle Press, c2006. 170p. IL 3–6, Lexile: NP
> Through a series of poems, Rachel expresses her feelings about her parents' divorce, living without her mother, and her changing attitude toward her father.

Abandonment

Bunting, Eve. *Some Frog!* Harcourt, c1998. 48p. IL 3–6, Lexile: 390
  Billy is disappointed when his father doesn't show up to help him catch a frog for the frog-jumping competition at school. The one he and his mother catch wins the championship, however, and Billy begins to accept his father's absence.

Byars, Betsy Cromer. *The Pinballs.* Harper & Row, c1977. 136p. IL 3–6, Lexile: 600
  Three lonely foster children learn to care about themselves and one another.

DiCamillo, Kate. *Because of Winn-Dixie.* Candlewick Press, c2000. 185p. IL 3–6, Lexile: 610
  Ten-year-old India Opal Buloni describes her first summer in the town of Naomi, Florida, and all the good things that happen to her because of her big ugly dog Winn-Dixie.

Gantos, Jack. *Joey Pigza Swallowed the Key.* Farrar, Straus and Giroux, 1998. 153p. IL 5–8, Lexile: 970
  To the constant disappointment of his mother and his teachers, Joey has trouble paying attention or controlling his mood swings when his prescription medications wear off and he starts getting worked up and acting wired.

Patron, Susan. *The Higher Power of Lucky.* Atheneum Books for Young Readers, 2006. 134 p. IL 3–6, Lexile: 1010
  Fearing that her legal guardian plans to abandon her to return to France, ten-year-old aspiring scientist Lucky Trimble determines to run away while also continuing to seek the Higher Power that will bring stability to her life.

Smith, Hope Anita. *The Way a Door Closes.* Henry Holt, 2003. 52p. IL 3–6, Lexile: NP
  A collection of poems about a thirteen-year-old boy whose father abandoned him and his family. When Daddy loses his job and does not come back, the poems go from loving to angry as the young boy confronts his feelings of abandonment.

Accident or on Purpose

Books for Children of All Ages

Buehner, Caralyn. *I Did It, I'm Sorry.* Puffin, 1998. 38p. IL K–3, Lexile: 460
Ollie Octopus, Bucky Beaver, Howie Hogg, and other animal characters encounter moral dilemmas involving such virtues as honesty, thoughtfulness, and trustworthiness. The reader is invited to select the appropriate behavior from a series of choices.

Cooper, Helen. *Little Monster Did It!* Doubleday/Picture Corgi Books, 1995. 32p. IL K–3, Lexile: 350
A small girl's favorite plush toy seems to be responsible for the mischievous "accidents" that begin occurring when a new baby brother joins the household.

Fox, Mem. *Harriet, You'll Drive Me Wild!* Harcourt, c2000. 32p. IL K–3, Lexile: 280
When a young girl has a series of mishaps at home one day, her mother tries not to lose her temper—and does not quite succeed.

Geisert, Arthur. *Oops.* Houghton Mifflin, 2006. 32p. IL K–3, Lexile: 380
Depicts, in wordless illustrations, how a little spilled milk led to the destruction of the pig family's house.

Lester, Helen. *It Wasn't My Fault.* Houghton Mifflin, 1985. 30p. IL K–3, Lexile: 420
When accidents happen to Murdley Gurdson, they are usually his own fault. When a bird lays an egg on Murdley's head one day, however, he tries hard to find someone else to blame.

Offill, Jenny. *17 Things I'm Not Allowed to Do Anymore.* Schwartz & Wade Books, c2007. 32p. IL K–3, Lexile: 750
A young girl lists seventeen things she is not allowed to do, including not being able use the stapler after attaching a pillow case to her brother's head.

Shannon, David. *David Gets in Trouble.* Blue Sky Press, c2002. 32p. IL K–3, Lexile: BR
When David gets in trouble, he has excuses right up until bedtime, when he realizes he really is sorry.

Szpirglas, Jeff. *Something's Fishy.* Orca Book Publishers, 2011. 55p. IL K–3, Lexile: 200
When Jamie has an accident while feeding the new classroom pet and upsets the rest of the class, he needs to find a way to make things right.

Willis, Jeanne. *That's Not Funny!* Andersen Press USA, 2010. 25p. IL K–3, Lexile: AD870
When Hyena puts a banana skin in Giraffe's path, causing a chain reaction of accidents that Hyena finds hilarious, he soon learns what it is like to be the butt of a joke.

Williams, Suzanne. *Ten Naughty Little Monkeys.* HarperCollins, c2007. 32p. IL K–3, Lexile: 200
A version of the counting rhyme featuring monkeys engaging in a variety of activities and getting hurt.

Autism and Asperger Syndrome

Books for Children of All Ages

Amenta, Charles A. *Russell's World: A Story for Kids about Autism.* Magination Press, c2011. 38p. IL K–3

Describes the daily life, likes and dislikes, and habits of Russell Amenta, who is a happy boy despite being severely autistic.

Larson, Elaine Marie. *I Am Utterly Unique: Celebrating the Strengths of Children with Asperger Syndrome and High-Functioning Autism.* Autism Asperger Publishing Co., c2006. 52p. IL K–3

Presents the unique talents and abilities of children with autism and Asperger syndrome, listing the positive characteristics from A to Z, with illustrations of each.

Niekerk, Clarabelle van. *Understanding Sam and Asperger Syndrome.* Skeezel Press, c2006. 26p. IL K–3

Helps readers to understand Asperger syndrome through a story about Sam, who has been diagnosed with the disorder. The book also offers advice for parents, teachers, and children on being with other children who have Asperger syndrome.

Thompson, Mary. *Andy and His Yellow Frisbee.* Woodbine House, 1996. 22p. IL K–3

The new girl at school tries to befriend Andy, an autistic boy who spends every recess by himself, spinning a yellow Frisbee under the watchful eye of his older sister.

Books for Children Ages Eight to Twelve

Ely, Lesley. *Looking after Louis.* Albert Whitman, 2004. 28p. IL 3–6

When a new boy with autism joins their classroom, the children try to understand his world and to include him in theirs.

Hoopmann, Kathy. *Blue Bottle Mystery: An Asperger Adventure.* Jessica Kingsley Publishers, 2001. 96p. IL 3–6

A boy named Ben, frustrated by his problems in school, hopes for adventure with his friend Andy when they find what looks like a genie's bottle—but Ben's life changes when he learns he has Asperger syndrome.

Hoopmann, Kathy. *Lisa and the Lacemaker: An Asperger Adventure.* Jessica Kingsley Publishers, 2002. 116p. IL 3–6

Lisa, a girl with Asperger syndrome, discovers a series of basement rooms under her friend Ben's house and spends hours exploring the remnants of a past era.

Keating-Velasco, Joanna L. *A Is for Autism, F Is for Friend: A Kid's Book on Making Friends with a Child Who Has Autism.* Autism Asperger Publishing, c2007. 54p. IL 3–6

Helps middle school students better understand what autism is and encourages them to try to make friends with autistic students in the class.

Autism and Asperger Syndrome

Lancelet, Matthew. *Sundays with Matthew: A Young Boy with Autism and an Artist Share Their Sketchbooks.* Autism Asperger Publishing, c2006. 37p. IL 3–6
> Matthew Lancelet, an eleven-year-old boy with autism, and Jeanette Lead, his art therapist, describe their time together and explore such topics as the sea, grandmothers, and friendship in words and pictures.

Leers, Laurie. *Ian's Walk: A Story about Autism.* Albert Whitman, 1998. 32p. IL 3–6
> Ian, who is autistic, takes a walk with his sisters and demonstrates how he sees, hears, smells, and tastes things differently.

Ogaz, Nancy. *Buster and the Amazing Daisy.* Jessica Kingsley, 2002. 125p. IL 3–6
> When Daisy, who is autistic, joins a mainstreamed class and trains Buster the rabbit for a pet show, she faces new challenges and makes new friends.

Birdwatching

Books for Children of All Ages

Freeman, Marcia S. *Let's Look for Birds*. Rourke Classroom Resources, c2004. 8p. IL K–3 (Non-fiction)
> Describes some of the places where birds can be found and the types of birds that might be there.

Malnor, Carol. *The Blues Go Birding across America: Meet the Blues*. Dawn Publications, c2010. 36p. IL K–3, Lexile: 600
> Looking for a new song to sing, five little birds go on a birdwatching trip and see species from the bald eagle in Alaska to mallard ducks in Boston.

Malnor, Carol. *The Blues Go Extreme Birding*. Dawn Publications, c2011. 36p. IL K–3, Lexile: 600
> Five little bluebirds go on a birdwatching trip to find and admire the world's record-setting birds, such as the fastest diving (peregrine falcon), longest migrating (arctic tern), and best mimic (superb lyrebird).

McCarthy, Meghan. *City Hawk: The Story of Pale Male*. Simon & Schuster Books for Young Readers, c2007. 34p. IL K–3, Lexile: 880
> Pale Male and his mate Lola, a pair of red-tailed hawks, build a nest on the ledge of an apartment building and raise their chicks in downtown New York City.

Books for Children Ages Eight to Twelve

Auch, Mary Jane. *Wing Nut*. H. Holt, 2005. 231p. IL 5–8, Lexile: 740
> Twelve-year-old Grady and his mother relocate yet again, this time finding work taking care of an elderly man, who teaches Grady about cars, birds, and what it means to have a home.

Avi. *Blue Heron*. Avon, 1993, c1992. 186p. IL 5–8, Lexile: 590
> While spending the month of August on the Massachusetts shore with her father, her stepmother, and their new baby, almost thirteen-year-old Maggie finds beauty in and draws strength from a great blue heron, even as the family around her unravels.

Banerjee, Anjali. *Looking for Bapu*. Yearling, 2008, c2006. 162p. IL 3–6, Lexile: 590
> When his beloved grandfather dies, eight-year-old Anu feels that his spirit is near and will stop at nothing to bring him back, including trying to become a Hindu holy man.

Estes, Eleanor. *Pinky Pye*. Harcourt, c1979. 258p. IL 3–6, Lexile: 890
> While spending a birdwatching summer on Fire Island, the Pye family acquires a small black kitten that can use a typewriter.

Loizeaux, William. *Wings*. Farrar, Straus and Giroux, 2006. 138p. IL 3–6, Lexile: 890
> Ten-year-old Nick, missing his father who died in the Korean War, finds companionship after rescuing an injured baby mockingbird in the summer of 1960.

Birdwatching

Prosek, James. *The Day My Mother Left.* Aladdin Paperbacks, 2007. 290p. IL YA, Lexile: 790
When his mother leaves to live with another man, nine-year-old Jeremy faces his own pain and loss, his father's depression and sister's distance, the pity of friends and strangers, and his father's remarriage two years later. He finds solace from his troubles in fishing and his artwork.

Whelan, Gloria. *Listening for Lions.* HarperCollins Publishers, c2005. 194p. IL 5–8, Lexile: 900
Left an orphan after the influenza epidemic in British East Africa in 1919, thirteen-year-old Rachel is tricked into assuming a deceased neighbor's identity to travel to England, where her only dream is to return to Africa and rebuild her parents' mission hospital.

Boats

Books for Children of All Ages

Allen, Pamela. *Who Sank the Boat?* Putnam & Grosset Group, 1996, c1982. 32p. IL K–3, Lexile: 470
The reader is invited to guess who causes the boat to sink when five animal friends of varying sizes decide to go for a row.

Barton, Byron. *Boats.* Crowell, c1986. 32p. IL K–3, Lexile: BR
Depicts several kinds of boats and ships.

Brett, Jan. *On Noah's Ark.* Putnam's, c2003. 32p. IL K–3, Lexile: 420
Noah's granddaughter helps him bring the animals onto the ark, calm them down, and get them to sleep.

Buffett, Jimmy. *The Jolly Mon.* Harcourt, c1988. 32p. IL K–3, Lexile: 510
Relates the adventures of a fisherman who finds a magic guitar floating in the Caribbean Sea. The book includes the music for the song *Jolly Mon Sing.*

Burningham, John. *Mr. Gumpy's Outing.* H. Holt, c1970. 32p. IL K–3, Lexile: 390
Mr. Gumpy accepts more and more riders on his boat, until the inevitable occurs.

Casanova, Mary. *One-Dog Canoe.* Farrar, Straus and Giroux, 2003. 32p. IL K–3, Lexile: 190
A girl and her dog set out in their canoe one morning, only to be insistently joined by a series of animals, large and small.

Crews, Donald. *Harbor.* Mulberry Books, 1987, c1982. 32p. IL K–3, Lexile: 220
Presents various kinds of boats that come and go in a busy harbor.

Crews, Donald. *Sail Away.* Greenwillow Books, c1995. 40p. IL K–3, Lexile: 330
A family takes an enjoyable trip in their sailboat and watches the weather change throughout the day.

Haas, Irene. *The* Maggie B. Atheneum, 1975. 32p. IL K–3, Lexile: 710
A little girl's wish to sail for a day on a boat named for her, "with someone nice for company," comes true.

Kellogg, Steven. *The Island of the Skog.* Dial Books for Young Readers, c1973. 32p. IL K–3, Lexile: 530
To escape the dangers of urban life, Jenny and her friends sail away to an island, only to be faced with a new problem—its single inhabitant, the Skog.

Lewis, Kevin. *Tugga-Tugga Tugboat.* Hyperion Books for Children, c2006. 27p. IL K–3, Lexile: 500
Colorful illustrations and simple text tell the story of a little tugboat.

McMullan, Kate. *I'm Mighty!* Joanna Cotler Books, 2003. 34p IL K–3, Lexile: 250
A little tugboat shows how he can bring big ships into the harbor even though he is small.

Pallotta, Jerry. *Dory Story.* Talewinds/Charlesbridge, c2000. 32p. IL K–3, Lexile: 500
While taking a bath with his new red toy dory, a boy imagines himself to be alone on the ocean, getting a first-hand look at the ocean's food chain.

Boats

Rockwell, Anne F. *Boats.* Puffin Books, 1985, c1982. 24p. IL K–3, Lexile: BR
Depicts boats and ships of varying sizes and uses.

Shaw, Nancy. *Sheep on a Ship.* Houghton Mifflin, 1989. 32p. IL K–3, Lexile: 160
Sheep on a deep-sea voyage run into trouble when it storms and are glad to come paddling into port.

Van Allsburg, Chris. *The Wreck of the* Zephyr. Houghton Mifflin, c1983. 34p. IL K–3, Lexile: 500
A boy's ambition to be the greatest sailor in the world brings him to ruin when he misuses his new ability to sail his boat in the air.

Books for Children Ages Eight to Twelve

Clark, Willow. *Boats on the Move.* PowerKids Press, 2010. 24p. IL 3–6 (Non-fiction)
An exploration of boats that discusses their history, parts, and various uses, and describes a number of different types.

Graham, Ian. *Superboats.* Heinemann Library, c2003. 32p. IL 3–6 (Non-fiction)
Describes the specifications, safety equipment, and uses of a variety of fast, powerful, and luxurious powerboats, including ski-boats, motor yachts, one-person hydroplanes, and 2,000-horsepower offshore racing powerboats.

Hughes, Susan. *Off to Class: Incredible and Unusual Schools around the World.* Owlkids, c2011. 64p. IL 3–6 (Non-fiction)
Introduces readers to children from around the world who attend unique schools in strange locations, such as caves, boats, and train platforms, and describes what it is like to attend those schools.

Kline, Suzy. *Horrible Harry Goes to Sea.* Puffin, 2003, c2001. 58p. IL 3–6, Lexile: 420
The students in Miss Mackle's third-grade class enjoy a boat trip on the Connecticut River after a class discussion of ancestors reveals that Sidney and Ida both have connections to the sea.

Wilkinson, Philip. *Ships.* Kingfisher, 2000. 63p. IL 3–6 (Non-fiction)
Text and illustrations describe how ships and boats have been used throughout history, from the earliest trading vessels to modern luxury liners.

Books That Travel

Books for Children of All Ages

Coy, John. *Around the World.* Lee & Low Books, c2005. 32p. IL K–3, Lexile: NP
Describes a game of street basketball being played literally around the world, in ten locations from New York to Australia to China and elsewhere, and then back to New York.

Hopkinson, Deborah. *Apples to Oregon: Being the (Slightly) True Narrative of How a Brave Pioneer Father Brought Apples, Peaches, Pears, Plums, Grapes, and Cherries (and Children) across the Plains.* Atheneum Books for Young Readers, c2004. 34p. IL K–3, Lexile: 840
A pioneer father transports his beloved fruit trees and his family to Oregon in the mid-nineteenth century. The book is based loosely on the life of Henderson Luelling.

McClintock, Barbara. *Adele & Simon.* Farrar, Straus and Giroux, 2006. 33p. IL K–3, Lexile: 550
When Adele walks her little brother Simon home from school, he loses one thing at every stop: his drawing of a cat at the grocer's shop, his books at the park, his crayons at the art museum, and more.

Pattison, Darcy. *The Journey of Oliver K. Woodman.* Harcourt, c2003. 48p. IL K–3, Lexile: 640
Oliver K. Woodman, a man made of wood, takes a remarkable journey across America, as told through the postcards and letters of those he meets along the way.

Rylant, Cynthia. *The Relatives Came.* Atheneum Books for Young Readers, 2001. 32p. IL K–3, Lexile: 940
The relatives come to visit from Virginia and everyone has a wonderful time.

Rylant, Cynthia. *Tulip Sees America.* Scholastic, 2002, c1998. 32p. IL K–3, Lexile: 530
A young man and his dog drive west from Ohio and marvel at the farms of Iowa, the skies of Nebraska, the wind in Wyoming, the mountains of Colorado, the desert in Nevada, and the ocean in Oregon.

Schuett, Stacey. *Somewhere in the World Right Now.* Knopf, 1997, c1995. 32p. IL K–3, Lexile: 550
Describes what is happening in different places around the world at a particular time throughout a day.

Sis, Peter. *Madlenka.* Square Fish/Farrar, Straus and Giroux, c2000. 48p. IL K–3, Lexile: 110
Madlenka, whose New York City neighbors include the French baker, the Indian news vendor, the Italian ice cream man, the South American grocer, and the Chinese shopkeeper, goes around the block to show her friends her loose tooth and finds that it is like taking a trip around the world.

Spinelli, Eileen. *Something to Tell the Grandcows.* Eerdmans Books for Young Readers, 2004. 32p. IL K–3, Lexile: 610
Hoping to have an adventure to impress her grandcows, Emmadine Cow joins Admiral Richard E. Byrd on his 1933 expedition to the South Pole.

Van Allsburg, Chris. *Ben's Dream.* Houghton Mifflin, c1982. 31p. IL K–3, Lexile: 370
On a terrifically rainy day, Ben has a dream in which he and his house float by the monuments of the world, which are half-submerged in flood waters.

Boys Reading

Books for Children of All Ages

Banks, Kate. *Max's Words*. Farrar, Straus and Giroux, 2006. 32p. IL K–3, Lexile: 420
When Max cuts out words from magazines and newspapers, collecting them the way his brothers collect stamps and coins, they all learn about words, sentences, and storytelling.

Bradby, Marie. *More Than Anything Else*. Orchard Books, c1995. 32p. IL K–3, Lexile: 660
Nine-year-old Booker works with his father and brother at the saltworks but dreams of the day when he'll be able to read.

Cazet, Denys. *Will You Read to Me?* Atheneum Books for Young Readers, c2007. 30p. IL K–3, Lexile: 400
Hamlet enjoys reading books and writing poetry, not playing in the mud and fighting over supper like the other pigs, but he finally finds someone who appreciates him just as he is.

Crimi, Carolyn. *Henry & the Buccaneer Bunnies*. Candlewick Press, 2005. 34p. IL K–3, Lexile: 910
Captain Barnacle Black Ear, baddest of the Buccaneer Bunnies, is ashamed of his book-loving son, Henry—until the day a great storm approaches.

Donaldson, Julia. *Charlie Cook's Favorite Book*. Dial Books for Young Readers, 2006. 26p. IL K–3, Lexile: NP
A circular tale in which each new book character is reading about the next, beginning and ending with Charlie Cook.

Jeffers, Oliver. *The Incredible Book Eating Boy.* Philomel Books, c2006. 32p. IL K–3, Lexile: 440
Henry loves to eat books, until he begins to feel quite ill and decides that maybe he could do something else with the books he has been devouring.

McPhail, David. *Edward and the Pirates*. Little, Brown, c1997. 32p. IL K–3, Lexile: 550
Once Edward has learned to read, books and his vivid imagination provide him with great adventures.

Mora, Pat. *Tomas and the Library Lady*. Knopf, c1997. 32p. IL K–3. Lexile: 440
While helping his family in their work as migrant laborers far from their home, Tomas finds an entire world to explore in the books at the local public library.

Morris, Carla. *The Boy Who Was Raised by Librarians*. Peachtree, c2007. 32p. IL K–3, Lexile: 720
Melvin discovers that the public library is the place where he can find just about anything—including three librarians who help in his quest for knowledge.

Plourde, Lynn. *Book Fair Day*. Dutton Children's Books, c2006. 32p. IL K–3, Lexile: 550
Upon learning that his class will not be going to the school book sale until the last half-hour of the day, Dewey worries that all the best books will already be taken.

Rahaman, Vashanti. *Read for Me, Mama*. Boyds Mills Press, 1997. 32p. IL K–3, Lexile: 540
A young boy who loves to read helps his mother on the road to literacy.

Boys Reading

Schotter, Roni. *The Boy Who Loved Words.* Schwartz & Wade Books, c2006. 33p. IL K–3, Lexile: 780
Selig, who loves words and copies them on pieces of paper that he carries with him, goes on a trip to discover his purpose.

Williams, Suzanne. *Library Lil.* Puffin Books, c1997. 32p. IL K–3, Lexile: 570
A formidable librarian makes readers out of not only the once-resistant residents of her small town, but also a tough-talking, television-watching motorcycle gang.

Books for Children Ages Eight to Twelve

Borden, Louise. *The Day Eddie Met the Author.* Aladdin Paperbacks, c2001. 32p. IL 3–6, Lexile: 660
Eddie is very excited when a real author comes to his school, because he has a very important question to ask her.

Miller, William. *Richard Wright and the Library Card.* Lee & Low Books, c1997. 32p. IL 3–6, Lexile: 700
Based on a scene from Wright's autobiography, *Black Boy*, in which the seventeen-year-old African American borrows a white man's library card and devours every book as a ticket to freedom.

Scieszka, Jon. *Summer Reading Is Killing Me!* Viking, 1998. 73p. IL 3–6, Lexile: 610
At the beginning of summer vacation Joe, Sam, and Fred find themselves trapped inside their summer reading list, involved in a battle between good and evil characters from well-known children's books.

Bullying

List by: Catherine Cowette, Smyth Road School, New Hampshire

Books for Children of All Ages

Alexander, Martha. *Move Over, Twerp.* Dial Press, c1981. 32p. IL K–3
Jeffrey shows his classmates that his being younger and smaller doesn't mean that he can be pushed around.

Binkow, Howard. *Howard B. Wigglebottom Learns about Bullies.* Thunderbolt Publishing, 2008. 32p. IL K–3
Howard tries several strategies to stop from being bullied by the Snorton twins, until at last he learns that telling a teacher is both "brave and bold" and the right thing to do.

Bottner, Barbara. *Bootsie Barker Bites.* Putnam, c1992. 32p. IL K–3, Lexile: 530
Bootsie Barker only wants to play games in which she bites, until one day her friend comes up with a better game.

Hazen, Barbara Shook. *The New Dog.* Dial Books for Young Readers, c1997. 32p. IL K–3
When Tootsie, a small, pampered dog, joins Danny Dougle's Dogwalking Group, he is teased and tormented by the other dogs—until he wins their respect by foiling a robbery.

Henkes, Kevin. *Chester's Way.* Greenwillow Books, c1988. 32p. IL K–3, Lexile: 570
Chester and Wilson share the same exact way of doing things, until Lilly moves into the neighborhood and shows them that new ways can be just as good.

Henkes, Kevin. *Chrysanthemum.* Greenwillow Books, c1991. 32p. IL K–3, Lexile: 460
Chrysanthemum loves her name, until she starts going to school and the other children make fun of it.

Henkes, Kevin. *A Weekend with Wendell.* Greenwillow Books, c1986. 32p. IL K–3, Lexile: 510
Sophie does not enjoy energetic, assertive Wendell's weekend visit until the very end, when she learns to assert herself and finds out Wendell can be fun to play with after all.

Isenberg, Barbara, and Susan Wolf. *Albert the Running Bear Gets the Jitters.* Clarion Books, c1987. 40p. IL K–3
Albert the Running Bear is challenged to a race by a new bully at the zoo and has to deal with all sorts of stress systems. The book includes relaxation techniques.

Kasza, Keiko. *The Rat and the Tiger.* G. P. Putnam's Sons, c1993. 32. IL K–3
In his friendship with Rat, Tiger takes advantage and plays the bully because of his greater size, but one day Rat stands up for his rights.

Keats, Ezra Jack. *Goggles.* Puffin Books, c1998. 40p. IL K–3, Lexile: 340
Two boys must outsmart the neighborhood bullies before they can enjoy their new treasure, a pair of lens-less motorcycle goggles.

Bullying

Lovell, Patty. *Stand Tall, Molly Lou Melon.* G. P. Putnam's Sons, c2001. 32p. IL K–3, Lexile: 560
Even when the class bully at her new school makes fun of her, Molly remembers what her grandmother told her and she feels good about herself.

McCain, Becky Ray. *Nobody Knew What to Do: A Story about Bullying.* Albert Whitman & Company, c2001. 32p. IL K–3
When bullies pick on a boy at school, a classmate is afraid, but decides that he must do something.

Pfeffer, Susan Beth. *Awful Evelina.* A. Whitman, c1979. 32p. IL K–3
Meredith, dreading an encounter with her cousin, who always hits her and steps on her toes, fantasizes about some imaginative disasters that might prevent their visit.

Sommer, Carl. *King of the Pond.* Advance Publishing, c2000. 48p. IL K–3, Lexile: 440
Tombo, the biggest, fastest, and strongest tadpole in the pond, teases and chases all the other tadpoles. Eventually, he comes to regret his bullying when he turns into the smallest, slowest, and weakest frog.

Staunton, Ted. *Taking Care of Crumley.* Kids Can Press, c1984. 31p. IL K–3
Maggie, the Greenapple Street genius, comes up with a plan to help Cyril get rid of a bully.

Swope, Sam. *The Araboolies of Liberty Street.* Farrar, Straus and Giroux, c2001. 32p. IL K–3
The kids of Liberty Street join forces to help the Araboolies when mean General Pinch orders them to move because they look different.

Taylor, Scott. *Dinosaur James.* Morrow Junior Books, c1990. 32p. K–3
People doubt the value of James's dinosaur obsession, until it helps him deal with the playground bully.

Wells, Rosemary. *Hazel's Amazing Mother.* Dial Books for Young Readers, c1985. 32p. IL K–3, Lexile: 570
When Hazel and her beloved doll Eleanor are set upon by bullies, Hazel's mother comes to the rescue in a surprising way.

Books for Children Ages Eight to Twelve

Blume, Judy. *Blubber.* Bradbury Press, 1974. 153p. IL 3–6, Lexile: 660
Jill goes along with the rest of the fifth-grade class in tormenting a classmate and then finds out what it is like when she, too, becomes a target.

Clements, Andrew. *Jake Drake, Bully Buster.* Simon & Schuster Books for Young Readers, c2001. 73 p. IL 3–6, Lexile: 570
Fourth grader Jake Drake relates how he comes to terms with SuperBully Link Baxter, especially after they are assigned to be partners on a class project.

Codell, Esme Raji. *Vive la Paris.* Hyperion Books for Children, 2006. 210 p. IL 3–6, Lexile: 860
Fifth-grader Paris learns some lessons about dealing with bullies of all kinds as she wonders how to stop a classmate from beating up her brother at school, and as she learns about the Holocaust from her piano teacher, Mrs. Rosen.

Bullying

Cox, Judy. *Mean, Mean Maureen Green.* Holiday House, 2000. 89 p. IL 3–6
With help from Adam, a boy in her third-grade class, Lilley gains enough confidence to stand up to the school bus bully, Mean Maureen Green.

DeBell, Susan. *Miranda Peabody and the Case of the Lunchroom Spy.* YouthLight, c2009. 36p. IL 3–6
Miranda Peabody and her classmates discover the consequences of group bullying and gossip when they wrongly target a fellow student for being a "spy."

DePino, Catherine. *Blue Cheese Breath and Stinky Feet: How to Deal with Bullies.* Magination Press, c2001. 48p. IL 3–6
With the help of his teacher and his parents, Steve devises "The Plan"—strategies for avoiding, defending against, and disarming a bully who has been tormenting him at school.

Estes, Eleanor. *The Hundred Dresses.* Harcourt, 2004. 80p. IL 3–6, Lexile: 870
In winning a medal she is no longer there to receive, a tight-lipped little Polish girl teaches her classmates a lesson. The book includes a note from the author's daughter, Helena Estes.

Gervay, Susanne. *I Am Jack.* Tricycle Press, c2000, 2009. 126p. IL 3–6, Lexile: 550
Eleven-year-old Jack suffers terrible headaches as he worries that his grandmother will soon die, his mother's boyfriend will move in (or leave), and especially that the school bully will get revenge for Jack's ill-timed joke at his expense.

Hahn, Mary Downing. *Stepping on the Cracks.* Clarion, c1991. 216p. IL 3–6, Lexile: 780
In 1944, while her brother is overseas fighting in World War II, eleven-year-old Margaret gets a new view of the school bully Gordy when she finds him hiding his own brother, an army deserter, and decides to help him.

Hiser, Constance. *Ghosts in Fourth Grade.* Holiday House, c1991. 68p. IL 3–6
James and his friends turn the old Hathaway house into a haunted house to scare Mean Mitchell, the class bully, on Halloween night.

Ludwig, Trudy. *Confessions of a Former Bully.* Tricycle Press, c2010. 48p. IL 3–6, Lexile: 810
Nine-year-old Katie's punishment for bullying classmates includes making up for the hurt she has caused. She decides to write a book about bullying, why it is not okay, and how to start being a better friend.

Polacco, Patricia. *Thank You, Mr. Falker.* Philomel Books, c1998. 40p. IL K–3, Lexile: 650
At first, Trisha loves school, but her difficulty learning to read makes her feel dumb until, in the fifth grade, a new teacher helps her understand and overcome her problem.

Sachar, Louis. *Marvin Redpost: Why Pick on Me?* Random House, c1993. 64p. IL 3–6, Lexile: 410
A small incident during recess threatens to turn nine-year-old Marvin into the outcast of his third-grade class.

Shapiro, Ouisie. *Bullying and Me: Schoolyard Stories.* Albert Whitman & Company, c2010. 32p. IL 3–6, Lexile: 740
Thirteen true stories, told by children and adults, about their experiences of being bullied. Each story has an afterword by Dr. Dorothy Espelage, a specialist in adolescent bullying, to help the reader better understand how to deal with bullying problems.

Bullying

Voigt, Cynthia. *Bad Girls*. Scholastic, c1996. 277p. IL 3–6

After meeting on the first day in Mrs. Chemsky's fifth-grade class, Margalo and Mikey help each other in and out of trouble, as they try to maintain a friendship while each asserts her own independence.

Warnock-Kinsey, Natalie. *The Night the Bells Rang*. Cobblehill Books, c1991. 79p. IL 3–6, Lexile: 790

The last year of World War I is an eventful one for Vermont farm boy Mason, as he helps with the chores, tries to get along with his little brother, and sees an older bully go off to the war.

Zindel, Paul. *Attack of the Killer Fishsticks*. Bantam Books, c1993. 117p. IL 3–6

When Dave and the other members of the Wacky Facts Lunch Bunch decide to help a new kid named Max run in the fifth-grade class election, they face off with the Nasty Blobs, two of the most rotten, creepy goons in their class. Will the Lunch Bunch win?

Character Analysis

Books for Children of All Ages

Buzzeo, Toni. *Adventure Annie Goes to Kindergarten.* Dial Books for Young Readers, c2010. 32p. IL K–3

Even though there are rules to follow, a little girl who loves adventure has an exciting first day of kindergarten.

Buzzeo, Toni. *Adventure Annie Goes to Work.* Dial Books for Young Readers, c2009. 30p. IL K–3

When she goes to work with her mother on a Saturday, Adventure Girl uses her own special methods to help find a missing report.

Henkes, Kevin. *Lilly's Purple Plastic Purse.* Greenwillow Books, c1996. 32p. IL K–3, Lexile: 540

Lilly loves everything about school, especially her teacher. When he asks her to wait a while before showing the class her new purse, however, she does something for which she is very sorry later.

McKissack, Pat. *Goin' Someplace Special.* Atheneum Books for Young Readers, c2001. 34p. IL K–3, Lexile: 550

In segregated 1950s Nashville, a young African American girl braves a series of indignities and obstacles to get to one of the few integrated places in town: the public library.

O'Connor, Jane. *Fancy Nancy.* HarperCollins, c2006. 32p. IL K–3, Lexile: 420

A young girl loves being fancy. From her tiara down to her sparkly shoes, she thrives on fancy. And now she helps her family to be fancy for one special night.

Pilkey, Dav. *The Hallo-Wiener.* Blue Sky Press, c1995. 32p. IL K–3, Lexile: 580

All of the other dogs make fun of Oscar the dachshund until one Halloween when Oscar, who is dressed as a hot dog, bravely rescues the others.

Polacco, Patricia. *My Rotten Redheaded Older Brother.* Aladdin Paperbacks, 1998, c1994. 32p. IL K–3, Lexile: 480

After losing running, climbing, throwing, and burping competitions to her obnoxious older brother, a young girl makes a wish on a falling star.

Polacco, Patricia. *Welcome Comfort.* Philomel Books, c1999. 32p. IL K–3, Lexile: 520

Welcome Comfort, a lonely foster child, is assured by his friend the school custodian that there is a Santa Claus, but he does not discover the truth until one wondrous and surprising Christmas Eve.

Sierra, Judy. *Tell the Truth, B. B. Wolf.* Alfred A. Knopf, c2010. 32p. IL K–3, Lexile: 500

When Big Bad Wolf, who now lives at the Villain Villa Retirement Residence, is invited to tell his story at the library, he faces the truth about what he did to the three little pigs and decides to make amends.

Character Analysis

Willems, Mo. *Don't Let the Pigeon Drive the Bus!* Hyperion Books for Children, c2003. 34p. IL K–3, Lexile: 120

> A pigeon that longs to drive a bus sees a chance to make its dream come true when the bus driver takes a short break.

Willems, Mo. *Knuffle Bunny: A Cautionary Tale.* Hyperion Books for Children, c2004. 34p. IL K–3, Lexile: 120

> Trixie becomes very unhappy when she accompanies her daddy to the laundromat and realizes she has lost her stuffed bunny.

Crossing the Border

Books for Children of All Ages

Bunting, Eve. *Going Home*. HarperCollins Publishers, c1996. 32p. IL K–3, Lexile: 480
Although a Mexican family comes to the United States to work as farm laborers so that their children will have more opportunities in life, the parents still consider Mexico to be their real home.

Mora, Pat. *The Rainbow Tulip*. Puffin Books, 2003, c1999. 31p. IL K–3, Lexile: 310
A Mexican American first grader experiences the difficulties and pleasures of being different when she wears a tulip costume with all the colors of the rainbow for the school May Day parade.

Mora, Pat. *Tomas and the Library Lady*. Knopf, c1997. 32p. IL K–3, Lexile: 440
While helping his family in their work as migrant laborers far from their home, Tomas finds an entire world to explore in the books at the local public library.

Books for Children Ages Eight to Twelve

Alvarez, Julia. *Return to Sender*. Knopf, c2009. 325p. IL 3–6, Lexile: 890
After his family hires migrant Mexican workers to help save their Vermont farm from foreclosure, eleven-year-old Tyler befriends the oldest daughter. When he discovers that the family may not be in the country legally, however, he realizes that real friendship knows no borders.

Beatty, Patricia. *Lupita Manana*. HarperTrophy, 2000, c1981. 190p. IL 5–8, Lexile: 760
To help her poverty-stricken family, thirteen-year-old Lupita enters California as an illegal alien and starts to work while constantly on the lookout for "la migra."

Buss, Fran Leeper. *Journey of the Sparrows*. Puffin, 2002. 155p. IL 5–8, Lexile: 760
Maria and her brother and sister, all of whom are Salvadoran refugees, are smuggled into the United States in crates and try to eke out a living in Chicago with the help of a sympathetic family.

Fullerton, Alma. *Libertad*. Fitzhenry & Whiteside, c2008. 215p. IL 5–8
After their mother dies, Libertad and his younger brother Julio leave their home near the Guatemala City dump and perform as street musicians along the Rio Grande River while hoping to cross the border into the United States and locate their father.

Mikaelsen, Ben. *Red Midnight*. HarperTrophy/Rayo, 2003, c2002. 212p. IL 5–8, Lexile: 690
After soldiers kill his family, twelve-year-old Santiago and his four-year-old sister flee Guatemala in a kayak and try to reach the United States.

Mikaelsen, Ben. *Sparrow Hawk Red*. Hyperion Books for Children, c1993. 185p. IL 5–8, Lexile: 620
Thirteen-year-old Ricky, the Mexican American son of a former Drug Enforcement Agency official, tries to avenge his mother's murder by crossing over into Mexico to steal a high-tech radar plane from drug smugglers.

Crossing the Border

Paulsen, Gary. *The Crossing.* Scholastic, 2006, c1987. 114p. IL 3–6, Lexile: 1150
Thirteen-year-old Manny, a street kid fighting for survival in a Mexican border town, develops a strange friendship with an emotionally disturbed American soldier who decides to help him get across the border.

Resau, Laura. *Red Glass.* Delacorte Press, c2007. 275p. IL 5–8, Lexile: 800
Sixteen-year-old Sophie has been frail and delicate since her premature birth. She discovers her true strength during a journey through Mexico, where the six-year-old orphan her family hopes to adopt was born, and to Guatemala, where her would-be boyfriend hopes to find his mother and plans to remain.

Ryan, Pam Muñoz. *Becoming Naomi Leon.* Scholastic, 2004. 246p. IL 5–8, Lexile: 830
When Naomi's absent mother resurfaces to claim her, Naomi runs away to Mexico with her great-grandmother and younger brother in search of her father.

Ryan, Pam Muñoz. *Esperanza Rising.* Scholastic, 2000. 262p. IL 5–8, Lexile: 750
Esperanza and her mother are forced to leave their life of wealth and privilege in Mexico to work in the labor camps of Southern California, where they must adapt to the harsh circumstances facing Mexican farm workers on the eve of the Great Depression.

Saldana, Rene. *The Jumping Tree: A Novel.* Dell Laurel-Leaf, 2002, c2001. 181p. IL 5–8, Lexile: 770
Rey, a Mexican American living with his close-knit family in a Texas town near the Mexican border, describes his transition from boy to young man.

Taylor, Theodore. *The Maldonado Miracle.* Harcourt, 2003. 167p. IL 5–8, Lexile: 710
For twelve-year-old Jose Maldonado, dreams of a life as an artist are yet that – dreams. His day-to-day life revolves around survival. When he crosses the border illegally to join his father in California, things do not go as planned.

Villareal, Ray. *Alamo Wars.* Pinata Books, c2008. 187p. IL 5–8, Lexile: 650
When a Texas school puts on an original play about the Alamo, the students and teachers confront modern conflicts about history, identity, and the meaning of courage.

Cryptids

Books for Children of All Ages

Johnston, Tony. *Bigfoot Cinderrrrrella.* Puffin Books, 2000, c1998. 32p. IL K–3, Lexile: 570
This version of the familiar story in which a mistreated stepchild finds happiness with the "man" of her dreams is set in the old-growth forest and features Bigfoot characters.

Kent, Jack. *There's No Such Thing as a Dragon.* Dragonfly Books, 2009, c1975. 32p. IL K–3
Billy Bixbee's mother will not admit that dragons exist—until it is nearly too late.

Pilkey, Dav. *Ricky Ricotta's Mighty Robot: An Adventure Novel.* Scholastic, c2000. 111p. IL K–3, Lexile: 340
Ricky Ricotta, a small mouse, saves a giant robot from his evil creator, Dr. Stinky. In turn, the robot protects Ricky from the bullies at school and saves the city from Dr. Stinky's plan to destroy it.

Robertson, M. P. *Hieronymus Betts and His Unusual Pets.* Frances Lincoln Children's Books, Distributed by Publishers Group West, 2005. 26p. IL K–3
A book for early readers about all the strange pets owned by Hieronymus Betts.

Yorke, Malcolm. *Beastly Tales: Yeti, Bigfoot, and the Loch Ness Monster.* DK Publishing, 1998. 48p, IL K–3 Lexile: 850, (Non-fiction)
Contains information on mysterious monsters, such as Bigfoot, Yeti, and the Loch Ness monster, and includes real-life stories of people who claim to have seen these beasts, in simple text with illustrations.

Book for Children Ages Eight to Twelve

Coleman, Loren. *Cryptozoology A to Z: The Encyclopedia of Loch Monsters, Sasquatch, Chupacabras, and Other Authentic Mysteries of Nature.* Fireside, c1999. 270p. IL YA (Non-fiction)
Contains two hundred entries that profile unusual beasts, new animal finds, and the explorers and scientists who search for them.

Cox, Judy. *Weird Stories from the Lonesome Café.* Harcourt, c2000. 72p. IL 3–6, Lexile: 350
Sam moves to Nevada with his uncle to run a cafe in the middle of nowhere. Although Uncle Clem insists that nothing ever happens there, his clientele consists of a number of strange characters, including Dorothy and Toto, Elvis, and Bigfoot.

Duey, Kathleen. *Castle Avamir.* Aladdin Paperbacks, 2003. 73p. IL 3–6, Lexile: 460
Heart must solve the riddle of Castle Avamir, which is, among other things, "deep in a valley" and "over the moon," to find a safe haven for the unicorns as the Gypsies leave Lord Levin's mountains for Lord Kaybale's plains.

Duey, Kathleen. *True Heart.* Aladdin Paperbacks, 2003. 75p. IL 3–6, Lexile: 420
With Moonsilver the unicorn disguised in armor, young Heart Avamir, searching for her Gypsy friends, attempts to travel unnoticed through the crowds gathered for the crowning of a new lord.

From 101 Great, Ready-to-Use Book Lists for Children by Nancy J. Keane. Santa Barbara, CA: Libraries Unlimited. Copyright © 2012.

Cryptids

Emmer, Rick. *Giant Anaconda and Other Cryptids: Fact or Fiction?* Chelsea House, c2010. 109p. IL 5–8 (Non-fiction)
> Examines evidence for the existence of giant animals that remain hidden from humans, such as the Tasmanian thylacine and a mermaid-like creature in the waters around a Pacific Ocean island.

Greenburg, Dan. *The Boy Who Cried Bigfoot.* Grosset & Dunlap, c2000. 58p. IL 3–6, Lexile: 440
> After hearing stories that a Bigfoot-like monster is haunting Camp Weno-wanna-getta-wedgee, ten-year-old Zack begins to find evidence that the legend may be true.

Halls, Kelly Milner. *Tales of the Cryptids: Mysterious Creatures That May or May Not Exist.* Darby Creek Publishing, c2006. 72p. IL 3–6, Lexile: 1160 (Non-fiction)
> Introduces young readers to the animals studied in cryptozoology—that is, the study of animals that may or may not be real.

Halls, Kelly Milner. *In Search of Sasquatch.* Houghton Mifflin, c2011. IL 3–6 (Non-fiction)
> Draws on interviews with cryptozoologists, linguistics experts, anthropologists, biologists, and others to examine evidence related to the existence of Sasquatch.

Myers, Bill. *My Life as a Bigfoot Breath Mint.* Tommy Nelson, c1997. 113p. IL 3–6, Lexile: 690
> Wally's visit to the Fantasmo World amusement park, where his Uncle Max works as a stuntman, turns into a disaster involving computer errors, runaway rides, and other outrageous mistakes.

Osborne, Mary Pope. *Blizzard of the Blue Moon.* Random House, c2006. 110p. IL 3–6, Lexile: 570
> A magic tree house carries Jack and Annie to New York City in 1938 on a mission to rescue the last unicorn.

Roberts, Rachel. *Song of the Unicorns.* Seven Seas, c2008. 223p. IL 3–6
> Emily, Adriane, and Kara—three friends who have learned they are destined to be magic masters—travel to New Mexico to visit Emily's father. There, the trio becomes involved in a quest to save a herd of baby unicorns from an evil hunter.

Rodda, Emily. *The Unicorn.* HarperCollins, c2004. 106p. IL 3–6, Lexile: 530
> When wicked Queen Valda of the Outlands threatens both the Fairy Realm and the human world, Jessie seeks the help of the unicorns to protect them.

Smith, Roland. *Cryptid Hunters.* Hyperion Paperbacks for Children, 2006, c2005. 348p. IL 5–8, Lexile: 750
> Grace and Marty, along with their mysterious uncle, are dropped into the middle of the Congolese jungle in search of the twins' missing photojournalist parents.

Smith, Roland. *Sasquatch.* Hyperion Paperbacks for Children, 1999, c1998. 188p. IL 5–8, Lexile: 680
> Thirteen-year-old Dylan follows his father into the woods on the slopes of Mount St. Helens, which is on the brink of another eruption, in an attempt to protect the resident Sasquatch from ruthless hunters.

Yomtov, Nelson. *Tracking Sea Monsters, Bigfoot, and Other Legendary Beasts.* IL 5–8 Capstone Press, c2011. 48p.
> Covers the search for animals that may or may not exist, including evidence for and against the existence of cryptids.

Earth Day

Books for Children of All Ages

Cherry, Lynne. *The Great Kapok Tree: A Tale of the Amazon Rain Forest.* Harcourt, c1990. 33p. IL K–3, Lexile: 670

The many different animals that live in a great kapok tree in the Brazilian rain forest try to convince a man with an ax of the importance of not cutting down their home.

Child, Lauren. *Clarice Bean, What Planet Are You from?* Candlewick Press, c2001. 32p. IL K–3

When Clarice has to do a school project on the environment, she and her family become eco-warriors in an attempt to save a tree on their street.

Fleming, Denise. *Where Once There Was a Wood.* H. Holt, 1996. 34p. IL K–3, Lexile: NP (Non-fiction)

Examines the many forms of wildlife that can be displaced if their environment is destroyed by development, and discusses how communities and schools can provide spaces for them to live.

Leedy, Loreen. *The Great Trash Bash.* Holiday House, c1991. 32p. IL K–3, Lexile: 400

The animal citizens of Beaston discover better ways to recycle and control their trash.

Madden, Don. *The Wartville Wizard.* Aladdin Paperbacks, 1993, c1986. 32p. IL K–3

An old man fights a town of litterbugs by magically sending each piece of trash back to the person who dropped it.

Matsen, Bradford. *Go Wild in New York City.* National Geographic, c2005. 79p. IL K–3 (Non-fiction)

An illustrated guide to the natural plant and animal life in New York City, including descriptions of the butterflies, squirrels, trees, flowers, bugs, waterways, and geology of the city.

Murphy, Stuart J. *Earth Day—Hooray!* HarperCollins, c2004. 32p. IL K–3 (Non-fiction)

A drive to recycle cans on Earth Day teaches the children of the Maple Street School Save-the-Planet Club about place value.

Peet, Bill. *Farewell to Shady Glade.* Houghton Mifflin, c1994. 38p. IL K–3, Lexile: 760

When building machinery moves into their woodland home, the animal inhabitants of Shady Glade must search for a new place to live.

Peet, Bill. *The Wump World.* Houghton Mifflin, c1970. 44p. IL K–3, Lexile: 930

The Pollutians, having made their own planet unlivable, arrive on Wump World and proceed to destroy the small planet, forcing the peaceful Wumps to take refuge underground.

Schnetzler, Pattie L. *Earth Day Birthday.* Dawn Publications, c2003. 32p. IL K–3 (Non-fiction)

Set to the familiar music of *The Twelve Days of Christmas*, verses describe different animals that illustrate the wonders of the wild world.

Seuss, Dr. *The Lorax.* Random House, c1999. 64p. IL K–3, Lexile: 560

The Once-ler describes the results of the local pollution problem.

Silverstein, Shel. *The Giving Tree.* HarperCollins Publishers, c1992. 57p. IL K–3, Lexile: 530

A young boy grows to manhood and old age experiencing the love and generosity of a tree that gives to him without thought of return.

Earth Day

Taback, Simms. *Joseph Had a Little Overcoat.* Viking, 1999. 36p. IL K–3, Lexile: BR
An ingenious man named Joseph finds numerous ways to make use of his overcoat as it wears away over time.

Van Allsburg, Chris. *Ben's Dream.* Houghton Mifflin, c1982. 31p. IL K–3, Lexile: 370
On a terrifically rainy day, Ben has a dream in which he and his house float by the monuments of the world, which are half-submerged in flood waters.

Van Allsburg, Chris. *Just a Dream.* Houghton Mifflin, c1990. 48p. IL K–3, Lexile: 550
When he has a dream about a future Earth devastated by pollution, Walter begins to understand the importance of taking care of the environment.

Books for Children Ages Eight to Twelve

Cherry, Lynne. *A River Ran Wild: An Environmental History.* Harcourt, c1992. 34p. IL 3–6, Lexile: 670 (Non-fiction)
An environmental history of the Nashua River, from its discovery by Indians through the polluting years of the Industrial Revolution to the ambitious clean-up that revitalized it.

Paton Walsh, Jill. *The Green Book.* Farrar, Straus and Giroux, 1986, c1982. 69p. IL 5–8. Lexile: 980
As their small stock of essential supplies dwindles, a group of refugees from Earth struggle to make their strange new planet provide life's necessities.

Earthquakes

Books for Children of All Ages

Bauer, Marion Dane. *Earthquake!* Aladdin, 2009. 32p. IL K–3 (Non-fiction)
Illustrations and simple text introduce young readers to earthquakes and their causes.

Danticat, Edwidge. *Eight Days: A Story of Haiti.* Orchard Books, 2010. 24p. IL K–3, Lexile: 820
Junior, a seven-year-old boy, is trapped under his house after the Port-au-Prince earthquake, and his vivid imagination helps him find the strength to survive.

Kroll, Virginia L. *Selvakumar Knew Better.* Shen's Books, 2006. 32p. IL K–3
When a giant tsunami approaches his village, seven-year-old Dinakaran is saved by the family dog. Based on a true story, the book includes facts about the 2004 Indian Ocean tsunami.

Levy, Janey. *World's Worst Earthquakes.* PowerKids Press, 2009. 24p. IL K–3 (Non-fiction)
Examines what happens during an earthquake, why earthquakes occur, and how to keep safe during such an event; and describes disastrous earthquakes throughout history.

Lewis, Thomas P. *Hill of Fire.* HarperCollins, c1971. 63p. IL K–3, Lexile: 350
An easy-to-read account of the birth of Paricutin volcano in the field of a poor Mexican farmer.

Napoli, Donna Jo. *The Earth Shook: A Persian Tale.* Disney/Hyperion Books, c2009. 40p. IL K–3, Lexile: 450
A little girl awakens to an earthquake in her town in Iran and is left alone and confused, but in her despair, she begins to laugh and dance.

Perry, Phyllis Jean. *Pandas' Earthquake Escape.* Sylvan Dell Publishing, c2010. 32p. IL K–3, Lexile: 580
A mother panda, Liling, and her one-year-old cub, Tengfei, struggle to survive when an earthquake destroys their nature reserve home.

Schuh, Mari C. *Earthquakes.* Capstone Press, c2010. 24p. IL K–3, Lexile: 350
Describes earthquakes, how they occur, and what kinds of damage they cause.

Books for Children Ages Eight to Twelve

Duey, Kathleen. *Earthquake.* Aladdin Paperbacks, 1998. 174p. IL 3–6, Lexile: 630
When two young strangers meet by chance on the day of the 1906 San Francisco earthquake, they struggle to survive the terror of crumbling buildings, fire, looting, and chaos.

Karwoski, Gail. *Quake!: Disaster in San Francisco, 1906.* Peachtree, c2004. 153p. IL 3–6, Lexile: 770
Tells the story of the 1906 San Francisco earthquake as seen through the eyes of Jacob, a thirteen-year-old Jewish boy who lives in a boarding house with his father and younger sister.

Kehret, Peg. *Earthquake Terror.* Puffin Books, 1998, c1996. 132p. IL 5–8, Lexile: 690
When an earthquake hits the isolated island in northern California where his family had been camping, twelve-year-old Jonathan Palmer must find a way to keep himself, his partially paralyzed younger sister, and their dog alive until help arrives.

Earthquakes

Kehret, Peg. *Escaping the Giant Wave.* Aladdin Paperbacks, 2003. 151p. IL 3–6, Lexile: 750
When an earthquake creates a tsunami while thirteen-year-old Kyle is babysitting his sister during a family vacation at a Pacific Coast resort, he tries to save himself, his sister, and a boy who has bullied him for years. The book includes an author's note that provides factual information on tsunamis.

Salisbury, Graham. *Night of the Howling Dogs.* Wendy Lamb Books, c2007. 191p. IL 3–6, Lexile: 530
In 1975, eleven Boy Scouts, their leaders, and some new friends who are camping at Halape, Hawaii, find their survival skills put to the test when a massive earthquake strikes, followed by a tsunami.

Yep, Laurence. *Dragonwings.* HarperTrophy, 2001, c1975. 317p. IL 5–8, Lexile: 870
In the early twentieth century, a young Chinese boy joins his father in San Francisco and helps him realize his dream of making a flying machine.

Yep, Laurence. *The Earth Dragon Awakes: The San Francisco Earthquake of 1906.* HarperTrophy, 2006. 117p. IL 3–6, Lexile: 510
Eight-year-old Henry and nine-year-old Chin love to read about heroes in popular "penny dreadful" novels, until both witness real courage while trying to survive the 1906 San Francisco earthquake.

Global Action

Books for Children of All Ages

Andrews, Andy. *The Boy Who Changed the World.* Tommy Nelson, c2010. 42p. IL K–3
Beginning with Norman Borlaug and going back to those who influenced him directly or indirectly, shows how one ordinary boy came to develop "super plants" that helped save billions of people from starvation.

Blessing, Charlotte. *New Old Shoes.* Pleasant St. Press, c2009. 28p. IL K–3
A pair of red sneakers describes the journey from the store window, onto a young boy's feet, across the Atlantic to Africa, and then onto the feet of others.

Cooney, Barbara. *Miss Rumphius.* Viking Press, 1982. 32p. IL K–3, Lexile: 680
After making her girlhood dreams of world travel and living by the sea come true, a retired librarian follows her grandfather's old advice of doing something to make the world more beautiful, and then passes that wisdom on to her grandniece.

Onyefulu, Ifeoma. *My Grandfather Is a Magician: Work and Wisdom in an African Village.* Frances Lincoln, 2000, c1998. 32p. IL K–3
A child in Africa tells about the different jobs performed by his relatives, but has a special feeling for the work done by his grandfather, an expert in the traditional healing arts.

Proimos, James. *Paulie Pastrami Achieves World Peace.* Little, Brown Books for Young Readers, 2009. 40p. IL K–3, Lexile: 390
Seven-year-old Paulie, an ordinary boy, brings peace to his home and school through small acts of kindness, but needs help to achieve his goal of world peace.

Rumford, James. *Rain School.* Houghton Mifflin Books for Children, 2010. 32p. IL K–3, Lexile: 420
When children arrive on the first day of school, they build a mud structure to be their classroom for the next nine months until the rainy season comes and washes it all away.

Books for Children Ages Eight to Twelve

Cherry, Lynne. *A River Ran Wild: An Environmental History.* Harcourt, c1992. 34p. IL 3–6, Lexile: 670 (Non-fiction)
An environmental history of the Nashua River, from its discovery by Indians through the polluting years of the Industrial Revolution to the ambitious clean-up that revitalized it.

Shoveller, Herb. *Ryan and Jimmy: And the Well in Africa That Brought Them Together.* Kids Can Press, c2006. 55p. IL 3–6, Lexile: 810 (Non-fiction)
Chronicles the friendship of Ryan Hreljac and Akana Jimmy, who became pen pals after Ryan, a Canadian boy, raised money to build a well in Jimmy's village in Uganda, and explains how they became brothers.

Global Action

Smith, David J. *If the World Were a Village: A Book about the World's People.* Kids Can Press, 2011, c2002. 32p. IL 3–6 (Non-fiction)

Breaks down the population of the world into a collection of one hundred representative people and describes what one would find in this global village, covering languages, ages, religions, food, air and water, schooling, and possessions. The text is accompanied by vivid color illustrations.

Winter, Jeanette. *Nasreen's Secret School: A True Story from Afghanistan.* Beach Lane Books, c2009. 40p. IL 3–6, Lexile: 630 (Non-fiction)

Nasreen stops speaking and tries to isolate herself after the Taliban take her parents. Eventually, with the help of a good friend and a secret school, Nasreen slowly begins to break out of her shell.

Healthy Eating

Books for Children of All Ages

Barron, Rex. *Showdown at the Food Pyramid.* G. P. Putnam's Sons, c2004. 27p. IL K–3
When snack foods take over the food pyramid and make it collapse, members of the various food groups have to work together using the Great Food Guide to rebuild it.

Brunhoff, Laurent de. *Babar's Yoga for Elephants.* Abrams Image, 2006. 48p. IL K–3 (Non-fiction)
Babar the elephant describes and demonstrates various yoga techniques and positions and shows how he and Celeste use them to relax.

Child, Lauren. *I Will Never Not Ever Eat a Tomato.* Candlewick Press, 2000. 32p. IL K–3, Lexile: 370
A fussy eater decides to sample the carrots after her brother convinces her that they are really orange twiglets from Jupiter.

Freymann, Saxton. *Food for Thought: The Complete Book of Concepts for Growing Minds.* Arthur A. Levine Books, 2005. 61p. IL K–3 (Non-fiction)
Uses bright photographs of fruits and vegetables shaped like animals and simple labels to teach toddlers shapes, colors, numbers, letters, and opposites.

Katzen, Mollie. *Salad People and More Real Recipes: A New Cookbook for Preschoolers & Up.* Tricycle Press, c2005. 93p. IL K–3 (Non-fiction)
This cookbook for preschoolers includes twenty recipes and lessons on counting, measuring, mixing, and assembling.

Landry, Leo. *Eat Your Peas, Ivy Louise!* Houghton Mifflin, 2005. 30p. IL K–3
Ivy Louise's parents encourage her to eat, unaware that the tiny green peas are performing a circus on her tray.

McFarland, Lyn Rossiter. *Mouse Went out to Get a Snack.* Farrar, Straus and Giroux, 2005. IL K–3, Lexile: 9032p.
A hungry mouse finds a tableful of delectable morsels in quantities that illustrate counting from one to ten.

Rabe, Tish. *Oh, The Things You Can Do That Are Good for You!* Random House, c2001. 44p. IL K–3 (Non-fiction)
The Cat in the Hat leads two children on an adventure that teaches them how to take care of themselves through exercise, good hygiene, plenty of sleep, and a healthy diet.

Rockwell, Lizzy. *The Busy Body Book: A Kid's Guide to Fitness.* Crown Publishers, c2004. 40p. IL K–3 (Non-fiction)
A children's fitness guide that explains how the bones, muscles, heart, and lungs work to keep the body healthy and strong.

Rockwell, Lizzy. *Good Enough to Eat: A Kid's Guide to Food and Nutrition.* HarperCollins, c1999. 32p. IL K–3. Lexile: 570 (Non-fiction)
Explains for young children how to eat a healthy diet, covering such topics as vitamins and nutrients, calories, digestion, and the importance of eating breakfast.

Healthy Eating

Rosenthal, Amy Krouse. *Little Pea.* Chronicle Books, c2005. 32p. IL K–3
Little Pea hates eating candy for dinner, but his parents will not let him have his spinach dessert until he cleans his plate.

Sharmat, Mitchell. *Gregory, the Terrible Eater.* Four Winds Press, Macmillan, 1980. 36p. IL K–3, Lexile: 490
A very picky eater, Gregory the goat refuses the usual goat diet staples of shoes and tin cans in favor of fruits, vegetables, eggs, and orange juice.

Yolen, Jane. *How Do Dinosaurs Eat Their Food?* Blue Sky Press, c2005. 34p. IL K–3, Lexile: 490
An introduction to table manners, written in simple text with illustrations, explaining proper etiquette as a variety of dinosaurs display playful antics at the dinner table.

Books for Children Ages Eight to Twelve

Cobb, Vicki. *Junk Food.* Millbrook Press, c2006. 48p. IL 3–6 (Non-fiction)
An introduction to the science behind the making and packaging of junk food, including popcorn, chocolate, corn chips, and other snacks.

D'Amico, Joan. *The Healthy Body Cookbook: Over 50 Fun Activities and Delicious Recipes for Kids.* Wiley, c1999. 184p. IL 3–6 (Non-fiction)
Discusses the various parts of the human body and what to eat to keep them healthy. Includes recipes that contain nutrients important for the heart, muscles, teeth, skin, nerves, and other parts of the body.

Hollyer, Beatrice. *Let's Eat!: What Children Eat around the World.* Henry Holt, 2003. 41p. IL 3–6 (Non-fiction)
Describes traditional foods around the world, including those consumed in Thailand, South Africa, Mexico, France, and India, and provides a number of recipes.

Kalman, Bobbie. *Super Snacks.* Crabtree Publishing, 2003. 32p. IL 3–6 (Non-fiction)
Explores why and how to have delicious and healthy snacks through nutrition facts and easy recipes for nourishing foods.

Katzen, Mollie. *Honest Pretzels: And 64 Other Amazing Recipes for Cooks Ages 8 & Up.* Tricycle Press, c1999. 177p. IL 3–6 (Non-fiction)
Provides step-by-step instructions for sixty-five easy-to-prepare recipes, arranged in such categories as breakfast specials, soups, desserts, and snacks.

Miller, Edward. *The Monster Health Book: A Guide to Eating Healthy, Being Active, & Feeling Great for Monsters & Kids!* Holiday House, c2006. 40p. IL 3–6, Lexile: 880 (Non-fiction)
An illustrated guide to health and nutrition, providing information on the food pyramid and the five food groups, and including tips and suggestions for eating right, getting enough sleep, and finding ways to exercise.

Healthy Eating

Ray, Rachael. *Cooking Rocks!: Rachael Ray 30-Minute Meals for Kids.* Lake Isle Press, Distributed by National Book Network, c2004. 224p. IL 3–6 (Non-fiction)
A cookbook for kids containing recipes they can make for themselves, including kitchen basics, beverages, snacks, and subs.

Investing

Books for Children of All Ages

Axelrod, Amy. *Pigs Will Be Pigs: Fun with Math and Money.* Simon & Schuster Books for Young Readers, c1994. 34p. IL K–3, Lexile: 490

The hungry Pig family learns about money and buying power as they turn the house upside down looking for enough money to buy dinner at the local restaurant.

Bair, Sheila. *Isabel's Car Wash.* Albert Whitman, 2008. 32p. IL K–3

To earn money to buy a doll that she wants, Isabel starts a car wash business with money invested by her friends, hoping to make a profit for everyone. The book includes information on selling shares in a business.

Brisson, Pat. *Benny's Pennies.* Dell Dragonfly Books, 2002, c1993. 32p. IL K–3, Lexile: 360

Benny sets off in the morning with five shiny new pennies to spend and eventually buys something for his mother, brother, sister, dog, and cat.

Chaconas, Dori. *Pennies in a Jar.* Peachtree, c2007. 36p. IL K–3, Lexile: 690

A young boy whose father is serving overseas during World War II struggles to overcome his fears—especially his fear of the horses that pull trade wagons through his neighborhood—as he works odd jobs for money to buy his father a birthday present.

Chamberlin, Mary. *Mama Panya's Pancakes: A Village Tale from Kenya.* Barefoot Books, 2006, c2005. 38p. IL K–3, Lexile: 700

Mama Panya has just enough money to buy ingredients for a few pancakes, so when her son Adika invites all their friends to join them, she is sure there will not be enough to go around.

Enderle, Dotti. *Grandpa for Sale.* Flash Light, 2007. 32p. IL K–3, Lexile: 620

A young girl dreams of all the things she can buy with the money a wealthy woman offers her in exchange for her grandfather and must decide if he is for sale.

Harris, Trudy. *Jenny Found a Penny.* Millbrook Press, c2008. 32p. IL K–3, Lexile: 650

The reader can help Jenny count her pennies—and nickels and dimes and quarters—as she saves the money to buy herself a very special present.

Herman, Charlotte. *Max Malone Makes a Million.* Holt, 1992, c1991. 76p. IL K–3, Lexile: 500

Max Malone, along with his best friend Gordy, is continually frustrated in his attempts to get rich, while his neighbor, little Austin Healy, makes money at every turn.

Lindsey, Kathleen D. *Sweet Potato Pie.* Lee & Low Books, c2003. 32p. IL K–3, Lexile: 860

During a drought in the early 1900s, a large, loving African American family finds a delicious way to earn the money they need to save their family farm.

Mollel, Tololwa M. *My Rows and Piles of Coins.* Clarion Books, c1999. 32p. IL K–3, Lexile: 700

A Tanzanian boy saves his coins to buy a bicycle so that he can help his parents carry goods to market, but then he discovers that, in spite of all the money he has saved, he still does not have enough.

Investing

Nolen, Jerdine. *Pitching in for Eubie.* Amistad, c2007. 30p. IL K–3, Lexile: 540
   Lily tries to find a way to pitch in and help her family make enough money to send her older sister, Eubie, to college.

Schwartz, David M. *If You Made a Million.* Lothrop, Lee & Shepard Books, c1989. 40p IL K–3, Lexile: 840 (Non-fiction)
   Describes the various forms that money can take, including coins, paper money, and personal checks, and explains how money can be used to make purchases, pay off loans, or build interest in the bank.

Books for Children Ages Eight to Twelve

Bailey, Gerry. *Get Rich Quick?: Earning Money.* Compass Point Books, 2006. 47p. IL 3–6, Lexile: 1000 (Non-fiction)
   An introduction to earning money, presented in simple text with illustrations, that explains banks, inflation, investing, and more.

Bochner, Arthur Berg. *The New Totally Awesome Money Book for Kids (and Their Parents).* Newmarket Press, c2007. 189p. IL 5–8 (Non-fiction)
   Teaches about such topics as budgets, credit cards, saving, investing, and paying for college, and features games, riddles, and quizzes.

Clements, Andrew. *Lunch Money.* Simon & Schuster Books for Young Readers, c2005. 222p. IL 3–6, Lexile: 840
   Twelve-year-old Greg, who has always been good at money-making projects, is surprised to find himself teaming up with his lifelong rival, Maura, to create a series of comic books to sell at school.

Croke, Liam. *I'm Broke!: The Money Handbook.* Crabtree Publishing, 2009. 48p. IL 5–8, Lexile: 1030 (Non-fiction)
   An introduction to personal finances that provides advice, facts, and quizzes on budgeting, saving, banking, the economy, loans, investments, credit cards, and more.

Fradin, Dennis B. *Investing.* Marshall Cavendish Benchmark, c2011. 64p. IL 3–6 (Non-fiction)
   Answers basic questions that students ask when learning about the financial skills needed for adulthood, and discusses investing money in the stock market, bonds and mutual funds, gold, and collectibles.

Holyoke, Nancy. *A Smart Girl's Guide to Money: How to Make It, Save It, and Spend It.* Pleasant Co., c2006. 95p. IL 3–6 (Non-fiction)
   A practical guide to money smarts for girls, offering advice on how to identify spending style, tips on running a business, and information on saving and investing. The book includes 101 money-making ideas.

From *101 Great, Ready-to-Use Book Lists for Children* by Nancy J. Keane. Santa Barbara, CA: Libraries Unlimited. Copyright © 2012.

Investing

Karlitz, Gail. *Growing Money: A Complete Investing Guide for Kids.* Price Stern Sloan, c2010. 143p. IL 3–6 (Non-fiction)

    Explains different types of investing—savings accounts, bonds, stocks, and mutual funds—and provides information to help make decisions on each kind of investment.

McGillian, Jamie Kyle. *The Kids' Money Book: Earning, Saving, Spending, Investing, Donating.* Sterling, 2004, c2003. 96p. IL 3–6 (Non-fiction)

    Introduces ways to manage money, from earning an allowance to budgeting to saving for college.

Minden, Cecilia. *Investing: Making Your Money Work for You.* Cherry Lake Publishing, c2008. 32p. IL 3–6 (Non-fiction)

    An introduction to financial literacy, looking at ways in which people can put their money to work for them through investing. The book includes notes designed to help readers identify the skills needed for success in the twenty-first century in the areas of learning and innovation, business and money, and life and career.

Paulsen, Gary. *Lawn Boy.* Wendy Lamb Books, c2007. 88p. IL 5–8, Lexile: 780

    Things get out of hand for a twelve-year-old boy when a neighbor convinces him to expand his summer lawn mowing business.

Needs versus Wants

Books for Children of All Ages

Caines, Jeannette F. *I Need a New Lunch Box.* Scholastic, 1988. 32 p., IL K–3, Lexile: 530
A little boy yearns for a lunch box, even though he hasn't started school yet.

Crimi, Carolyn. *Don't Need Friends.* Dragonfly Books, 2001, c1999. 32p. IL K–3, Lexile: 290
After his best friend moves away, Rat rudely rebuffs the efforts of the other residents of the junkyard to be friendly, until he and a grouchy old dog decide that they need each other.

Demi. *The Magic Gold Fish: A Russian Folktale.* H. Holt, 1995. 32p. IL K–3
A poor fisherman's greedy wife is never satisfied with the wishes granted her by an enchanted fish. This version is adapted from Louis Zelikoff's translation of Pushkin's tale of the fisherman and the little fish.

Fleming, Candace. *Boxes for Katje.* Farrar, Straus and Giroux, 2003. 36p. IL K–3, Lexile: 460
After a young Dutch girl writes to her new American friend in thanks for the care package sent after World War II, she begins to receive increasingly larger boxes.

Hall, Donald. *Ox-Cart Man.* Viking Press, 1979. 40p. IL K–3, Lexile: 1130
Describes the day-to-day life of an early nineteenth-century New England family over the changing seasons.

Lionni, Leo. *Frederick.* A. Knopf, Distributed by Random House, 1995, c1967. 30p. IL K–3, Lexile: 500
Frederick, the poet mouse, stores up something special for the long, cold winter.

Mills, Lauren A. *The Rag Coat.* Little Brown, c1991. 32p. IL K–3, Lexile: 630
Minna proudly wears her new coat made of clothing scraps to school, where the other children laugh at her until she tells them the stories behind the scraps.

Polacco, Patricia. *Luba and the Wren.* Puffin Books, 2002, c1999. 34p. IL K–3, Lexile: 520
In this variation on the story of "The Fisherman and His Wife," a young Ukrainian girl must repeatedly return to the wren she has rescued to relay her parents' increasingly greedy demands.

Seuss, Dr. *The Lorax.* Random House, c1999. 64p. IL K–3, Lexile: 560
The Once-ler describes the results of the local pollution problem.

Viorst, Judith. *Alexander, Who Used to Be Rich Last Sunday.* Atheneum, 1978. 32p. IL K–3, Lexile: 570,
Although Alexander and his money are soon parted, he comes to realize all the things that can be done with a dollar.

Williams, Vera B. *A Chair for My Mother.* Greenwillow Books, c1982. 32p. IL K–3, Lexile: 640
A child, her waitress mother, and her grandmother save dimes to buy a comfortable armchair after all their furniture is lost in a fire.

Needs versus Wants

Williams, Vera B. *Something Special for Me.* Greenwillow Books, c1983. 32p. IL K–3, Lexile: 760
Rosa has difficulty choosing a special birthday present to buy with the coins her mother and grandmother have saved, until she hears a man playing beautiful music on an accordion.

Ziefert, Harriet. *A New Coat for Anna.* Knopf, Distributed by Random House, c1986. 32p. IL K–3, Lexile: 690
Even though they have no money, Anna's mother finds a way to make Anna a badly needed winter coat, and the pair celebrate a special Christmas as a result.

Outcasts

Books for Children of All Ages

Andersen, H. C. *The Ugly Duckling.* Odyssey Books, 2010. 32p. IL K–3
An ugly duckling is scorned by everyone because he is different, but after a lonely winter he discovers he has grown into a beautiful swan.

Crimi, Carolyn. *Don't Need Friends.* Dragonfly Books, 2001, c1999. 32p. IL K–3, Lexile: 290
After his best friend moves away, Rat rudely rebuffs the efforts of the other residents of the junkyard to be friendly, until he and a grouchy old dog decide that they need each other.

Depken, Kristen L. *Rudolph the Red-Nosed Reindeer.* Random House, c2009. 32p. IL K–3
Rudolph the reindeer, who has an unusual nose, is teased by the other reindeer until his unique trait saves Santa's trip on a foggy Christmas Eve.

Henkes, Kevin. *Chrysanthemum.* Greenwillow, c1991. 32p. IL K–3, Lexile: 460
Chrysanthemum loves her name until she starts going to school and the other children begin to make fun of it.

Hoffman, Mary. *Amazing Grace.* Dial Books for Young Readers, 1991. 26p. IL K–3, Lexile: 680
Although a classmate says that she cannot play Peter Pan in the school play because she is African American, Grace discovers that she can do anything she sets her mind to do.

Howe, James. *Horace and Morris But Mostly Dolores.* Atheneum Books for Young Readers, 2003, c1999. 32p. IL K–3, Lexile: 410
Horace, Morris, and Dolores are very good friends and have always done everything together; however, their friendship may be in trouble when Horace and Morris decide to join a no-girls-allowed club and Dolores joins a no-boys-allowed club.

Lester, Helen. *Hooway for Wodney Wat.* Houghton Mifflin, c1999. 32p. IL K–3, Lexile: 360
All his classmates make fun of Rodney because he cannot pronounce his name, but it is Rodney's speech impediment that drives away the class bully.

Lester, Helen. *Tacky the Penguin.* Houghton Mifflin, c1988. 32p. IL K–3, Lexile: 810
Tacky the penguin does not fit in with his sleek and graceful companions, but his odd behavior comes in handy when hunters come with maps and traps.

Lovell, Patty. *Stand Tall, Molly Lou Melon.* G. P. Putnam's, c2001. 32p. IL K–3, Lexile: 560
Even when the class bully at her new school makes fun of her, Molly remembers what her grandmother told her and she feels good about herself.

Polacco, Patricia. *Thank You, Mr. Falker.* Philomel Books, c1998. 40p. IL K–3, Lexile: 650
At first, Trisha loves school, but her difficulty learning to read makes her feel dumb, until, in the fifth grade, a new teacher helps her understand and overcome her problem.

Polacco, Patricia. *Welcome Comfort.* Philomel Books, c1999. 32p. IL K–3, Lexile: 520
Welcome Comfort, a lonely foster child, is assured by his friend the school custodian that there is a Santa Claus, but he does not discover the truth until one wondrous and surprising Christmas Eve.

Outcasts

Rathmann, Peggy. *Ruby the Copycat.* Scholastic, 2006, c1991. 32p. IL K–3, Lexile: 500
Ruby wants to fit in on her first day at school, so she begins to copy her classmate Angela. Eventually, Ruby's teacher shows her how much fun it is to just be herself.

Wells, Rosemary. *Yoko.* Hyperion Books for Children, c1998. 33p IL K–3, Lexile: 350
When Yoko brings sushi to school for lunch, her classmates make fun of what she eats—until one of them tries it for himself.

Books for Children Ages Eight to Twelve

Cole, Brock. *The Goats.* Square Fish, 2010, c1987. 184p. IL 5–8, Lexile: 550
Stripped and marooned on a small island by their fellow campers, a boy and a girl form an uneasy bond that grows into a deep friendship when they decide to run away and disappear without a trace.

Estes, Eleanor. *The Hundred Dresses.* Harcourt, 2004, c1944. 80p IL 3–6., Lexile: 870
In winning a medal she is no longer there to receive, a tight-lipped little Polish girl teaches her classmates a lesson. The book includes a note from the author's daughter, Helena Estes.

Fenner, Carol. *Randall's Wall.* Aladdin Paperbacks, 2000, c1991. 85p. IL 3–6, Lexile: 730
Artistically talented but socioeconomically underprivileged, a fifth-grade boy has built a wall of defense to protect himself from the pain of human relationships—a wall that begins to crumble when a dynamic and compassionate classmate decides to interfere in his life.

Madonna. *The English Roses.* Callaway, c2003. 46p. IL 3–6, Lexile: 790
Four best friends are jealous of a neighbor girl and refuse to have anything to do with her, until each has a dream in which a fairy godmother reveals what the girl's life is really like.

Swarthout, Glendon Fred. *Bless the Beasts and Children.* Pocket Books, 2004. 196p. IL 5–8, Lexile: 970
Ostracized by their peers at Box Canyon Boys Camp in Arizona, six teenage boys from dysfunctional homes band together to free a herd of buffalo to be used as prey in a state-sanctioned guided hunt. The book includes a reader's guide.

Mermaids

Books for Children of All Ages

Fraser, Mary Ann. *Mermaid Sister.* Walker, 2008. 32p. IL K–3, Lexile: 420

Shelly has always wanted a sister, so when she meets Coral, a mermaid, and brings her home, it seems as if her wish has been granted.

Guillain, Charlotte. *Mermaids.* Raintree, c2011. 32p. IL K–3

Explores how mermaids have been portrayed in the myths of various cultures throughout history, and discusses the beliefs and superstitions surrounding their existence.

Hakala, Marjorie. *Mermaid Dance.* Blue Apple Books, 2009. 32p. IL K–3

The mermaids gather to celebrate the first night of summer, and the high tide allows them to swim closer to the shore where the woodland animals can watch their festivities.

Minarik, Else Holmelund. *Father Bear Comes Home.* HarperCollins Publishers, c1987. 62p. IL K–3, Lexile: 240

Collects four stories featuring Little Bear and his adventures with his family, including "Father Bear Comes Home," in which Little Bear hopes that his father returns from his fishing trip with a mermaid.

Oliver, Narelle. *Mermaids Most Amazing.* G. P. Putnam's Sons, 2005, c2001. 32p. IL K–3

An illustrated exploration of mermaid legends from around the world.

Pitcher, Caroline. *Mariana and the Merchild: A Folk Tale from Chile.* Eerdmans Books for Young Readers, 2000. 26p. IL K–3

A childless old woman is given a merbaby to raise until the child can safely return to the sea.

San Souci, Robert D. *Sukey and the Mermaid.* Aladdin Paperbacks, 1996, c1992. 32p. IL K–3, Lexile: 820

Unhappy with her life at home, Sukey receives kindness and wealth from Mama Jo the mermaid.

Books for Children Ages Eight to Twelve

Andersen, H. C. *The Little Mermaid.* Penguin Young Readers Group, c2004. 42p. IL 3–6

A little sea princess, who longs to be human, trades her mermaid's tail for legs, hoping to win the love of a prince and earn an immortal soul for herself.

Johnson, Gillian. *Thora.* Katherine Tegen Books, 2005, c2003. 229p. IL 3–6

Ten-year-old Thora, daughter of a mermaid mother and a human father, has many adventures at sea until she must return to the English seaside town of Grimli and save her mother, who has been captured by a greedy real estate developer, Frooty de Mare.

Kessler, Liz. *Emily Windsnap and the Castle in the Mist.* Candlewick Press, 2007. 204p. IL 3–6, Lexile: 670

When she incurs Neptune's wrath by finding a diamond ring buried under rocks in the ocean, Emily is put under a curse that will force her to choose to be either a mermaid or a human and split up her parents forever.

Mermaids

Kessler, Liz. *Emily Windsnap and the Monster from the Deep.* Candlewick Press, 2007, c2004. 219p. IL 3–6, Lexile: 570

> Young mermaid Emily Windsnap must turn for help to someone she hoped to never see again, when she awakes the huge and terrifying octopus-like monster known as the kraken.

Kessler, Liz. *The Tail of Emily Windsnap.* Candlewick Press, 2006. 208p. IL 3–6, Lexile: 600

> After finally convincing her mother that she should take swimming lessons, twelve-year-old Emily discovers a terrible and wonderful secret about herself that opens up a whole new world.

Levine, Gail Carson. *Fairy Haven and the Quest for the Wand.* Disney Press, c2007. 191p. IL 3–6, Lexile: 630

> When Soop the mermaid threatens Fairy Haven with a flood, three fairies—Rani, Tinker Bell, and Ree—set out on a perilous journey in search of a magic wand that Soop has demanded in exchange for pulling back the waters.

Selfors, Suzanne. *To Catch a Mermaid.* Little, Brown, 2009, c2007. 245p. IL 3–6, Lexile: 770

> Twelve-year-old Boom Broom thought his life couldn't get any worse, until he stumbles upon a foul-tempered merbaby and must find a way to return her to the world of the merfolk in the hopes of breaking the curse she seems to have put on Boom.

Raised by Animals

Books for Children of All Ages

Balcziak, Bill *Paul Bunyan.* Compass Point Books, c2003. 32p. IL K–3
Presents the life story of the enormous lumberjack, Paul Bunyan, who, along with his blue ox Babe, is said to have made the 10,000 lakes of Minnesota with his footsteps.

Blair, Eric. *Pecos Bill.* Picture Window Books, c2011. 31p IL K–3,
Relates some of the legends of Pecos Bill, a cowboy who was raised by wild animals, once roped a whole herd of cattle at once, and invented Texas chili.

Namm, Diane. *The Jungle Book. #4, Mowgli Knows Best.* Sterling Publishing, c2007. 32p IL K–3
A brief, simplified retelling of the episode in *The Jungle Book*, in which Mowgli, a boy who was raised by wolves and other animals, ignores the advice of his friends Bagheera and Baloo and goes off by himself in the jungle.

Books for Children Ages Eight to Twelve

Burroughs, Edgar Rice. *Tarzan of the Apes.* Signet Classic, 2008. 306p. IL AD
Tarzan, who was abandoned as a baby in the jungle of Africa, is adopted into a tribe of great apes and grows to become Lord of the Jungle. When he becomes a young man, his domain is disturbed by civilized men who cause Tarzan to question his true identity.

Eckert, Allan W. *Incident at Hawk's Hill.* Little, Brown, c1971. 207p. IL 5–8, Lexile: 1200
A shy, lonely six-year-old wanders into the Canadian prairie and spends a summer under the protection of a badger.

Eckert, Allan W. *Return to Hawk's Hill: A Novel.* Little, Brown, c1998. 192p. IL 5–8, Lexile: 1230
Running away from a vicious trapper, seven-year-old Ben MacDonald becomes separated from his family and eventually ends up on the shores of Lake Winnipeg, where he is taken in by a tribe of Metis Indians.

Hesse, Karen. *The Music of Dolphins.* Scholastic, 2005, c1996. 181p. IL 3–6, Lexile: 560
Using sophisticated computer technology, a fifteen-year-old girl who has been raised by dolphins records her thoughts about her reintroduction to the human world.

From *101 Great, Ready-to-Use Book Lists for Children* by Nancy J. Keane. Santa Barbara, CA: Libraries Unlimited. Copyright © 2012.

Remembering September 11, 2001

Books for Children of All Ages

Curtiss, A. B. *The Little Chapel That Stood.* OldCastle Publishing, c2003. 33p. IL K–3 (Non-fiction)
The story of how St. Paul's Chapel, located across the street from the Twin Towers of the World Trade Center, survived the September 11 blast and then served as a service depot for rescuers.

Deedy, Carmen Agra. *14 Cows for America.* Peachtree, c2009. 38p. IL K–3 (Non-fiction)
An illustrated tale of a gift of fourteen cows given by the Maasai people of Kenya to the United States as a gesture of comfort and friendship in the wake of the attacks on September 11, 2001.

Gerstein, Mordicai. *The Man Who Walked Between the Towers.* Roaring Brook Press, c2003. 40p. IL K–3, Lexile: 480 (Non-fiction)
A lyrical evocation of Philippe Petit's 1974 tightrope walk between the World Trade Center towers.

Kalman, Maira. *Fireboat: The Heroic Adventures of the* **John J. Harvey.** G. P. Putnam's Sons, c2002. 42p. IL K–3, Lexile: 280 (Non-fiction)
A fireboat, launched in 1931, is retired after many years of fighting fires along the Hudson River, but is saved from being scrapped and then called into service again on September 11, 2001.

Osborne, Mary Pope. *New York's Bravest.* Dragonfly Books, 2006, c2002. 32p. IL K–3, Lexile: 350
Tells of the heroic deeds of the legendary New York firefighter, Mose Humphreys.

Roth, Susan L. *It's Still a Dog's New York: A Book of Healing.* National Geographic Society, c2001. 32p. IL K–3
Pepper and Rover, two New York City dogs, feel miserable after the tragedy of September 11, 2001. Over time, however, both dogs manage to recover and enjoy life again.

Winter, Jeanette. *September Roses.* Farrar, Straus and Giroux, 2004. 33p. IL K–3
Two sisters find a good use for the roses they have grown when their plane from South Africa is delayed by a storm, causing them to miss a flower show in New York City.

Books for Children of All Ages

Benoit, Peter. *September 11 We Will Never Forget.* Children's Press, 2012. 64p. IL 3–6 (Non-fiction)
Provides an account of the events of September 11, and looks at the lasting effects of this tragedy.

Britton, Tamara L. *The World Trade Center.* ABDO Publishing Co., c2003. 40p. IL 3–6 (Non-fiction)
Describes the history, design, construction, and original controversial nature of the World Trade Center, as well as the terrorist attack that destroyed it on September 11, 2001.

Brown, Don. *America Is under Attack: September 11, 2001: The Day the Towers Fell.* Roaring Brook Press, 2011. IL 3–6, Lexile: 840 (Non-fiction)
Provides a chronological account of September 11, 2001, and the terrorist attacks on the World Trade Center in New York and the Pentagon in Washington, D.C., and the hijacking of a plane that crashed in Pennsylvania.

Remembering September 11, 2001

Louis, Nancy. *Heroes of the Day: The War on Terrorism.* ABDO, c2002. 48p. IL 3–6 (Non-fiction)
Describes the actions of emergency telephone operators, police officers, firefighters, trained dogs, and individual citizens who helped in the aftermath of the terrorist attacks on the World Trade Center and Pentagon on September 11, 2001.

Senzai, N. H *Shooting Kabul.* Simon & Schuster Books for Young Readers, c2010. 262p. IL 3–6, Lexile: 800
Escaping from Taliban-controlled Afghanistan in the summer of 2001, eleven-year-old Fadi and his family immigrate to the San Francisco Bay Area. There, Fadi schemes to return to the Pakistani refugee camp where his little sister was accidentally left behind.

September 11, 2001. Steck-Vaughn, c2002. 48p. IL 3–6 (Non-fiction)
An introduction to the events surrounding the September 11 tragedy for young readers, featuring full-color photographs and maps, and discussing the people and places involved, along with the aftermath of the terrorist attacks.

Slugs, Snails, and Worms

Books for Children of All Ages

Allen, Judy. *Are You a Snail?* Kingfisher, 2000. 31p. IL K–3 (Non-fiction)
Introduces the life cycle of a snail, showing how it changes from an egg to an adult snail.

Bruel, Robert O. *Bob and Otto.* Roaring Brook Press, 2007. 32p. IL K–3
Otto the worm is shocked to discover that his best friend Bob is actually a caterpillar who emerges from a cocoon one day as a butterfly.

Colburn, Mary Palenick. *Rainy Day Slug.* Sasquatch Books, 2008, c2000. 32p. IL K–3.
One rainy day, a slug goes for a walk in the wide, wide world, going scrass, scrass, scrass through the tall, green grass, scuddle, scuddle, scuddle in a deep rain puddle, and scrape, scrape, scrape down a long, pink drape.

Cronin, Doreen. *Diary of a Worm.* Joanna Cotler Books, c2003. 34p. IL K–3, Lexile: 360
A young worm discovers, day by day, that there are some very good things and some not so good things about being a worm in this great big world.

Cutler, Jane. *Mr. Carey's Garden.* Houghton Mifflin, 1996. 32p. IL K–3
All of his neighbors have suggestions about how to get rid of the snails in his garden, but Mr. Carey isn't interested.

Edwards, Pamela Duncan. *Some Smug Slug.* HarperCollins, c1996. 32p. IL K–3, Lexile: 620
A smug slug that will not listen to the animals around it comes to an unexpected end.

Hazen, Lynn E. *The Amazing Trail of Seymour Snail.* Holt, 2009. 64p. IL K–3, Lexile: 410
Hoping to become a famous artist one day, Seymour Snail takes a job in a New York City art gallery, where everyone is buzzing about a "magnificent mystery artist."

Hightower, Susan. *Twelve Snails to One Lizard: A Tale of Mischief and Measurement.* Simon & Schuster Books for Young Readers, c1997. 32p. IL K–3, Lexile: 900
Bubba the bullfrog helps Milo the beaver build a dam by explaining to him the concepts of inches, feet, and yards.

Pearson, Susan. *Slugs in Love.* Marshall Cavendish Children, c2006. 32p. IL K–3, Lexile: 590
Marylou and Herbie, two garden slugs, write love poems in slime to each other, but have trouble actually meeting.

Ryder, Joanne. *The Snail's Spell.* Puffin Books, 1982. 32p. IL K–3, Lexile: 670
A young boy finds himself in the garden. He is now the size of a snail and experiences how it feels to be a snail.

Scarry, Richard. *Richard Scarry's The Adventures of Lowly Worm.* Sterling, 1995. 42p. IL K–3
Lowly Worm takes an unexpected ride in a hot-air balloon, helps Huckle find just the right gift for Mother Cat, and gets lost during a visit to the city.

Stadler, John. *The Adventures of Snail at School.* HarperTrophy, c1993. 64p. IL K–3, Lexile: 280
Snail goes on three errands for his teacher and has amazing adventures.

Slugs, Snails, and Worms

Stadler, John. *Hooray for Snail!* HarperCollins, c1984. 32p. IL K–3, Lexile: 10
Slow Snail hits the ball so hard during a baseball game that it flies to the moon and back—but that still may not be enough time for Snail to slide in for a home run.

Stadler, John. *Snail Saves the Day.* Star Bright Books, c2006. 32p. IL K–3
Snail's team may lose the football game unless he makes it to the stadium in time.

Books for Children of All Ages

Amato, Mary. *The Word Eater.* Holiday House, c2000. 151p. IL 3–6, Lexile: 590
Lerner Chanse, a new student at Cleveland Park Middle School, finds a worm that magically makes things disappear. She hopes the worm will use its powers to help her fit in, or get revenge, at her hated school.

Avi. *A Beginning, a Muddle, and an End: The Right Way to Write Writing.* Harcourt, c2008. 164p. IL 3–6, Lexile: 530
Avon the snail wants to become a writer. He enlists the help of his friend Edward the ant on a series of adventures involving an anteater, a tree frog, and a hungry fish.

Avi. *The End of the Beginning: Being the Adventures of a Small Snail (and an Even Smaller Ant).* Harcourt, c2004. 143p. IL 3–6, Lexile: 620
Avon, a snail, and Edward, a take-charge ant, set off together on a journey to an undetermined destination in search of unspecified adventures.

Day, Trevor. *Body Bugs: Uninvited Guests on Your Body.* Capstone Press, 2008. 32p. IL 3–6, Lexile: 950 (Non-fiction)
Describes microorganisms and insects that live on and in the human body.

Greenburg, J. C. *In the Garbage.* Random House, c2006. 84p. IL 3–6
Ten-year-old inventor Andrew Dubble creates a machine designed to swallow and shrink garbage. He soon finds himself in trouble when the machine shrinks him, his robot Thudd, and his cousin Judy down to the size of beetles and they are carried off to a dangerous dump ruled by worms.

Hipp, Andrew. *The Life Cycle of an Earthworm.* PowerKids Press, 2002. 24p. IL 3–6 (Non-fiction)
Photographs and text follow the life cycle of the earthworm from hatching to adulthood, and provide information about how these worms mate, burrow, eat, and make soil.

Huggins-Cooper, Lynn. *Slimy Sliders.* QEB Publishing, c2008. 32p. IL 3–6 (Non-fiction)
Contains close-up color photographs of slugs, snails, worms, leeches, and other slippery, slimy animals, and provides facts about their habits and behaviors.

Kalman, Bobbie. *The Life Cycle of an Earthworm.* Crabtree, c2004. 32p. IL 3–6, Lexile: 940 (Non-fiction)
Traces the life cycle of an earthworm from cocoon to adult, and includes information about earthworm anatomy, eating, tunneling, and earthworm watching.

Slugs, Snails, and Worms

Katz Cooper, Sharon. *Sewers and Gutters.* Raintree, c2010. 32p. IL 3–6 (Non-fiction)
Text and photographs describe less-than-pleasant and unexpected habitats and the animals that live in them, focusing on sewers and gutters, and discussing rats, cockroaches, bats, snails, and slugs.

Masoff, Joy. *Oh, Yuck!: The Encyclopedia of Everything Nasty.* Workman, c2000. 212p. IL 3–6, Lexile: 950 (Non-fiction)
An alphabetical collection of articles about disgusting things, from acne, ants, and bacteria to worms, x-periments, and zits.

Moore, Heidi. *Giant Tube Worms and Other Interesting Invertebrates.* Raintree, c2012. 32p. IL 3–6 (Non-fiction)
Explores the characteristics of giant tube worms and other marine invertebrates, and presents deep-sea images and fact boxes.

Murray, Julie. *Slowest Animals.* ABDO Publishing, c2010. 32p. IL 3–6 (Non-fiction)
Describes the physical traits, habitats, and behaviors of slow-moving animals, including sloths, spitting spiders, snails, giant tortoises, sea horses, American woodcocks, Gila monsters, and others.

Rosenberg, Pam. *Yuck! Icky, Sticky, Gross Stuff in Your Garden.* Child's World, c2008. 24p. IL 3–6 (Non-fiction)
Describes "gross" things that can be found in gardens, such as bacteria and slugs, as well as some of the distasteful activities of garden insects such as bees and flies.

Simon, Seymour. *Pets in a Jar: Collecting and Caring for Small Wild Animals.* Puffin Books, 1979, c1975. 95p. IL 3–6 (Non-fiction)
Suggestions for collecting and keeping as pets such small animals as snails, toads, worms, ants, butterflies, and starfish.

Toys Come to Life

Books for Children of All Ages

Allison, Catherine. *Brown Paper Teddy Bear.* Scholastic, c2004. 32p. IL K–3
An ancient teddy bear comes to life one night and takes Jess on a magical adventure.

Bianco, Margery Williams. *The Velveteen Rabbit, or, How Toys Become Real.* Courage Books, c1997. 53p. IL K–3
A little velveteen rabbit discovers that he can become real, no matter how dirty and beat-up he might be.

Freeman, Don. *Corduroy.* Viking Press, 2008, c1968. 32p. IL K–3, Lexile: 600
A teddy bear spends his days at a store, waiting for someone to buy him.

Grey, Mini. *Traction Man Is Here!* Knopf, 2005. 32p. IL K–3, Lexile: 730
Traction Man, a boy's courageous action figure, has a variety of adventures with Scrubbing Brush and other objects in the house.

Grey, Mini. *Traction Man Meets Turbodog.* Alfred A. Knopf, c2008. 32p. IL K–3, Lexile: 540
Traction Man braves the evil bin things to save Scrubbing Brush, who had been thrown away by the little boy's father and replaced with a battery-operated dog.

Jenkins, Emily. *Toys Go out: Being the Adventures of a Knowledgeable Stingray, a Toughy Little Buffalo, and Someone Called Plastic.* Schwartz & Wade Books, c2006. 116p. IL K–3, Lexile: 730
Six stories relate the adventures of three best friends, who happen to be toys.

Lionni, Leo. *Alexander and the Wind-up Mouse.* Knopf, c1997. 31p. IL K–3, Lexile: 490
Alexander, a real mouse, makes friends with Willy, a toy mouse, and wants to be just like him—until he discovers that Willy is to be thrown away.

Pinkney, Andrea Davis. *Sleeping Cutie.* Harcourt, c2004. 32p. IL K–3, Lexile: 410
Cutie LaRue is perfect in nearly every way, but her sleeplessness causes problems for her parents—until they send for a new toy that introduces Cutie to the Dreamland Nightclub.

Books for Children Ages Eight to Twelve

Andersen, H. C. *The Steadfast Tin Soldier.* ABDO Publishing, 2006. 40p. IL 3–6
The classic story by Hans Christian Andersen about a one-legged tin soldier who is accidentally launched on a dangerous voyage and finds his way back to his true love—the paper dancing girl.

Banks, Lynne Reid. *The Indian in the Cupboard.* Doubleday, c1980. 181p. IL 3–6, Lexile: 780
A nine-year-old boy receives a plastic Indian, a cupboard, and a little key for his birthday and finds himself involved in adventure when the Indian comes to life in the cupboard and befriends him.

Collodi, Carlo. *The Adventures of Pinocchio.* Creative Editions, 2005. 191p. IL 3–6
A wooden puppet that is full of tricks and mischief, and has a talent for getting into and out of trouble, wants more than anything else to become a real boy.

Toys Come to Life

DiCamillo, Kate. *The Miraculous Journey of Edward Tulane.* Candlewick Press, 2006. 198p. IL 3–6, Lexile: 700

Edward Tulane, a cold-hearted and proud toy rabbit, loves only himself—until he is separated from the little girl who adores him and travels across the country, acquiring new owners and listening to their hopes, dreams, and histories.

Eager, Edward. *Knight's Castle.* Harcourt, 1999, c1956. 198p. IL 5–8, Lexile: 860

Four cousins—Roger, Ann, Eliza, and Jack—have an extraordinary summer when, after an old toy soldier comes to life, they find themselves transported back to the days of Robin Hood and Ivanhoe.

Field, Rachel. *Hitty, Her First Hundred Years.* Macmillan, c1957. 207p. IL 3–6, Lexile: 1180

Hitty, a doll carved from mountain ash in the nineteenth century, has many adventures as she travels around the world with different owners.

Martin, Ann M. *The Doll People.* Hyperion Books for Children, c2000. 256p. IL 3–6, Lexile: 570

A family of porcelain dolls that has lived in the same house for one hundred years is taken aback when a new family of plastic dolls arrives and doesn't follow The Doll Code of Honor.

Milne, A. A. *Winnie-the-Pooh.* Dutton Children's Books, c2006. 147p. IL 3–6

An eightieth-anniversary edition of A. A. Milne's 1926 classic—complete with Ernest H. Shepard's original illustrations—in which a small boy named Christopher Robin embarks on a series of adventures with Piglet, Rabbit, Kanga, Roo, Eeyore, Owl, and the roly-poly Winnie-the-Pooh in the Hundred Acre Wood.

Retiring Principal/Teacher

Agee, Jon. *The Retired Kid.* Hyperion Books for Children, 2008. 32p. IL K–3, Lexile: 560
Although he enjoys some aspects of his retirement, eight-year-old Brian gains a new perspective on his job of being a child after spending time in Florida's Happy Sunset Retirement Community.

Boynton, Sandra. *Yay, You!: Moving out, Moving up, Moving on.* Simon & Schuster, c2001. 32p. IL 3–6
In rhyme, outlines some of the possibilities that life has to offer, from the adventurous to the tranquil.

Cocca-Leffler, Maryann. *Mr. Tanen's Ties.* A. Whitman, 1999. 32p. IL K–3, Lexile: 260
Mr. Tanen, the principal at Lynnhurst Elementary School, is well known for his colorful and unusual ties, but he and his students are saddened when his boss orders him to stop wearing them.

Creech, Sharon. *A Fine, Fine School.* Joanna Cotler Books, c2001. 32p. IL K–3, Lexile: 300
When a principal loves his school so much that he wants the children to attend classes every day of the year, it's up to his students to show him free time is a good thing, too.

Danneberg, Julie. *Last Day Blues.* Charlesbridge, c2006. 32p. IL K–3, Lexile: 740
During the last week of school, the students in Mrs. Hartwell's class try to come up with the perfect present for their teacher.

Grant, Jim. *What Principals Do When No One Is Looking.* Crystal Springs Books, 1998. 24p. IL K–3 (Non-fiction)
A color-illustrated tribute to school principals that lists the many parts of their job that few people ever see.

McKissack, Pat. *Goin' Someplace Special.* Atheneum Books for Young Readers, c2001. 34p. IL K–3, Lexile: 550
In segregated 1950s Nashville, a young African American girl braves a series of indignities and obstacles to get to one of the few integrated places in town: the public library.

Pattou, Edith. *Mrs. Spitzer's Garden.* Harcourt, 2007. 32p. IL K–3
With her sure, loving, gardener's touch, Mrs. Spitzer nurtures the students in her classroom each year.

Polacco, Patricia. *Mr. Lincoln's Way.* Philomel, c2001. 41p. IL K–3, Lexile: 450
When Mr. Lincoln, "the coolest principal in the whole world," discovers that Eugene, the school bully, knows a lot about birds, he uses this interest to help Eugene overcome his intolerance.

Rosenthal, Amy Krouse. *Duck! Rabbit!* Chronicle Books, c2009. 34p. IL K–3
Two unseen characters argue about whether the creature they are looking at is a rabbit or a duck.

Retiring Principal/Teacher

Seuss, Dr. *Oh, the Places You'll Go!* Random House, c1990. 48p. IL K–3, Lexile: 600
Presents humorous, rhyming advice from Dr. Seuss on how to proceed in life; conquer fear, loneliness, and confusion; and take charge of one's own actions.

Thaler, Mike. *The Principal from the Black Lagoon.* Spotlight, Scholastic, 1993. 32p. IL K–3
When a young boy is sent to the principal's office, on his way there he imagines all sorts of horrible things about how bad the visit will be.

Library Skills

Buzzeo, Toni. *No T. Rex in the Library.* Margaret K. McElderry Books, c2010. 32p. IL K–3
A rampaging Tyrannosaurus rex demonstrates to an out-of-control little girl the results of inappropriate, "beastie" behavior in the library.

Buzzeo, Toni. *Our Librarian Won't Tell Us Anything!* Upstart Books, c2006. 32p. IL K–3, Lexile: 720
Robert, a new fourth grader, is warned by a classmate that the librarian, Mrs. Skorupski, will not tell students anything. Robert soon earns the label of "Library Success Story" after Mrs. Skorupski teaches him how to use the library's resources himself.

Morton, Carlene. *The Library Pages.* Upstart Books, c2010. 32p. IL K–3
Mrs. Heath is horrified when she sees the changes the students have made while she is on maternity leave and wonders if her wonderful library will ever be the same.

Series

Berg, Brook. *What Marion Taught Willis.* UpstartBooks, c2005. IL PF
Presents information on the Dewey Decimal System through the story of Marion Hedgehog, who during Mr. Owens's career day class, says she wants to be a librarian. The book includes a story and a second volume of Dewey Decimal System worksheet exercises.

Buzzeo, Toni. *The Great Dewey Hunt.* Upstart Books, c2009. IL PF
Twins Hugh and Louis Abernathy try to cheer up Carmen Rosa Pena—who is unhappy because she cannot locate a book in the library and her younger sister is going to be in the same classroom—while taking part in Mrs. Skorupski's Great Dewey Hunt. The book includes instructional strategies and reproducible pages for a lesson about the Dewey Decimal System.

Hopkins, Jackie. *The Shelf Elf Helps.* Upstart Books, c2006. IL K-3
Skoob, a shelf elf, explains the Dewey Decimal System by which books are shelved in the library, likening the different subject categories to neighborhoods, and the numbers on the book spines to addresses. The book includes lessons designed to familiarize students with the library "neighborhoods."

Hopkins, Jackie. *The Shelf Elf Looks It up!* Upstart Books, c2009. IL K-3
Skoob the Shelf Elf, armed with a single clue, consults the dictionary, encyclopedia, and thesaurus in an effort to solve the mystery of where his friend Skeeter went on vacation. The books includes three book and library lessons.

Book Care

Books for Children of All Ages

Buzzeo, Toni. *No T. Rex in the Library.* Margaret K. McElderry Books, c2010. 32p. IL K–3
A rampaging Tyrannosaurus rex demonstrates to an out-of-control little girl the results of inappropriate, "beastie" behavior in the library.

Fraser, Mary Ann. *I.Q. Goes to the Library.* Walker, 2003. 32p. IL K–3
After going to the library with Mrs. Furber's class every day of Library Week, I.Q., the class pet, hopes to take out a funny book with his own library card.

Hopkins, Jackie. *The Shelf Elf.* Upstart Books, c2004. 32p. IL K–3
Skoob the Shelf Elf learns a valuable lesson in library behavior and book care when he completes his work with the shoemaker and embarks upon a new career in the library.

Thompson, Carol. *Mr. Wiggle's Library.* Waterbird Books, c2004. 32p. IL K–3
Mr. Wiggle describes, in rhyming text and illustrations, his first visit to the library and how he learns about the way it is organized and how to look for what he wants to find.

Part 7

Readalikes

If You Liked *Because of Winn Dixie* by Kate DiCamillo, You Might Like...

Bunting, Eve. *The Summer of Riley.* HarperTrophy, 2002, c2001. 170p. IL 3–6, Lexile: 540
Shortly after he gets Riley, the perfect dog, eleven-year-old William must fight for his dog's life when Riley is taken away after he chases and injures an elderly neighbor's old horse.

Byars, Betsy Cromer. *Wanted—Mud Blossom.* Holiday House, 2008, c1991. 180p. IL 3–6
Convinced that Mud is responsible for the disappearance of the school hamster that was his responsibility for the weekend, Junior Blossom is determined that the dog should be tried for his "crime."

Giff, Patricia Reilly. *Pictures of Hollis Woods.* Wendy Lamb Books, c2002. 166p. IL 5–8, Lexile: 650
A troublesome twelve-year-old orphan, staying with an elderly artist who needs her, remembers the only other time she was happy in a foster home, with a family that truly seemed to care about her.

Hannigan, Katherine. *Ida B—:And Her Plans to Maximize Fun, Avoid Disaster, and (Possibly) Save the World.* Greenwillow Books, c2004. 246p. IL 3–6, Lexile: 970
In Wisconsin, fourth grader Ida B spends happy hours being home-schooled and playing in her family's apple orchard. When her mother begins treatment for breast cancer, however, her parents must sell part of the orchard and send Ida B to public school.

Hesse, Karen. *Just Juice.* Scholastic Signature, 1999, c1998. 138p. IL 3–6, Lexile: 690
Realizing that her father's lack of work has endangered her family, nine-year-old Juice decides that she must return to school and learn to read to help their chances of surviving and keeping their house.

Hill, Kirkpatrick. *The Year of Miss Agnes.* Aladdin Paperbacks, 2002, c2000. 115p. IL 3–6
Ten-year-old Fred (short for Frederika) narrates the story of school and village life among the Athapascans in Alaska in 1948, when Miss Agnes arrived as the new teacher.

Korman, Gordon. *No More Dead Dogs.* Hyperion Paperbacks for Children, 2002, c2000. 180p. IL 3–6, Lexile: 610
Eighth-grade football hero Wallace Wallace is sentenced to detention attending rehearsals of the school play. There, in spite of himself, he becomes wrapped up in the production and begins to suggest changes that improve not only the play but his life as well.

Lisle, Janet Taylor. *Afternoon of the Elves.* Puffin Books, c1989. 122p. IL 3–6, Lexile: 820
As Hillary works in the miniature village, allegedly built by elves, in Sara-Kate's backyard, she becomes ever more curious about Sara-Kate's real life inside her big, gloomy house with her mysterious, silent mother.

Madden, Kerry. *Gentle's Holler.* Viking, 2005. 237p. IL 5–8, Lexile: 950
In the early 1960s, twelve-year-old songwriter Livy Two Weems dreams of seeing the world beyond the Maggie Valley, North Carolina, holler where she lives in poverty with her parents and eight brothers and sisters, but understands that she must put family first.

If You Liked *Because of Winn Dixie* by Kate DiCamillo, You Might Like . . .

Morris, Willie. *My Dog Skip.* Vintage Books, 1996. 118p. IL YA, Lexile: 1380 (Non-fiction)
The story of a dog and his closest companion, the author, during their years growing up in a small town in Mississippi.

O'Connor, Barbara. *Fame and Glory in Freedom,Georgia.* Farrar, Straus and Giroux, 2003. 104p. IL 3–6, Lexile: 740
Unpopular sixth grader Burdette "Bird" Weaver persuades the new boy at school, whom everyone thinks is mean and dumb, to be her partner for a spelling bee that might win her everything she's ever wanted.

Paterson, Katherine. *The Same Stuff as Stars.* Clarion Books, c2002. 242p. IL 5–8, Lexile: 670
When Angel's self-absorbed mother leaves her and her younger brother with their poor great-grandmother, the eleven-year-old girl worries not only about her mother and brother, her imprisoned father, and the frail old woman, but also about a mysterious man who begins sharing with her the wonder of the stars.

Peck, Richard. *A Year Down Yonder.* Dial Books for Young Readers, c2000. 130p. IL 5–8, Lexile: 610
During the recession of 1937, fifteen-year-old Mary Alice is sent to live with her feisty, larger-than-life grandmother in rural Illinois and comes to a better understanding of this fearsome woman.

Wallace, Bill. *A Dog Called Kitty.* Holiday House, c1980. 153p. IL 3–6, Lexile: 710
Afraid of dogs since he was attacked by a mad one, Ricky resists taking in a homeless pup that shows up at the farm.

Wallace, Bill. *Snot Stew.* Aladdin Paperbacks, 2008, c1989. 81p. IL 3–6, Lexile: 500
Brother and sister cats are taken in by a family and learn the pleasures and dangers of living alongside humans.

Welch, Sheila Kelly. *The Shadowed Unicorn.* Front Street/Cricket Books, 2000. 185p. IL 5–8, Lexile: 630
When their father dies suddenly, twelve-year-old twins Brendan and Nick, along with their mother and older sister Ami, move to an isolated old farm in the country. There, the twins find themselves pulled into Ami's obsession with capturing a unicorn.

Wiles, Deborah. *Each Little Bird That Sings.* Harcourt, c2005. 247p. IL 3–6, Lexile: 760
Comfort Snowberger is well acquainted with death—her family runs the funeral parlor in their small Southern town. Even so, the ten-year-old is unprepared for the series of heart-wrenching events that begins on the first day of Easter vacation with the sudden death of her beloved great-uncle Edisto.

Wiles, Deborah. *Love, Ruby Lavender.* Harcourt, c2001. 188p. IL 3–6, Lexile: 570
When her quirky grandmother goes to Hawaii for the summer, nine-year-old Ruby learns to survive on her own in Mississippi by writing letters, befriending chickens as well as the new girl in town, and finally coping with her grandfather's death.

From *101 Great, Ready-to-Use Book Lists for Children* by Nancy J. Keane. Santa Barbara, CA: Libraries Unlimited. Copyright © 2012.

If You Liked *Bud, Not Buddy* by Christopher Paul Curtis, You Might Like . . .

De Young, C. Coco. *A Letter to Mrs. Roosevelt.* Dell Yearling, 2000, c1999. 105p. IL 3–6, Lexile: 690
Eleven-year-old Margo fulfills a class assignment by writing a letter to Eleanor Roosevelt, asking for help to save her family's home during the Great Depression.

Friedrich, Elizabeth. *Leah's Pony.* Boyds Mills Press, 1996. 32p. IL K–3, Lexile: 580
A young girl sells her pony and uses the money to buy back her father's tractor when the family's belongings are put up for auction.

Hesse, Karen. *Out of the Dust.* Scholastic Press, 1997. 227p. IL 3–6, Lexile: NP
In a series of poems, fifteen-year-old Billie Jo relates the hardships of living on her family's wheat farm in Oklahoma during the Dust Bowl years of the Depression.

Levine, Gail Carson. *Dave at Night.* HarperTrophy, 2001, c1999. 281p. IL 3–6, Lexile: 490
When orphaned Dave is sent to the Hebrew Home for Boys, where he is treated cruelly, he sneaks out at night and is welcomed into the music- and culture-filled world of the Harlem Renaissance.

Lied, Kate. *Potato: A Tale from the Great Depression.* National Geographic Society, 1997. 32p. IL K–3, Lexile: 660
During the Great Depression, a family seeking work finds employment for two weeks digging potatoes in Idaho.

Mackall, Dandi Daley. *Rudy Rides the Rails: A Depression Era Story.* Sleeping Bear Press, Thomson/ Gale, c2007. 36p. IL 3–6
In 1932, during the Depression in Ohio, thirteen-year-old Rudy, determined to help his family weather the hard times, hops a train going west to California and experiences the hobo life.

Porter, Tracey. *Billy Creekmore.* Joanna Cotler Books, c2007. 305p. IL 5–8, Lexile: 930
When a stranger comes to claim Billy Creekmore from the Guardian Angels Home for Boys, he embarks on a cross-country journey in search of his past, his future, and his own true self.

Schwartz, Ellen. *Stealing Home.* Tundra Books, c2006. 217p. IL 3–6, Lexile: 630
Nine-year-old Yankees fan and Bronx native Joey Sexton is sent to Brooklyn after his mother's death. There, he finds himself battling prejudice in his own family, trying to win the acceptance of his white, Jewish grandfather, who looks down on him because he is half African American.

If You Liked *Diary of a Wimpy Kid* by Jeff Kinney, You Might Like . . .

Angleberger, Tom. *The Strange Case of Origami Yoda.* Amulet Books, 2010. 141p. IL 3–6, Lexile: 760

Sixth grader Tommy and his friends describe their interactions with a paper finger puppet of Yoda, worn by their weird classmate Dwight, as they try to figure out whether the puppet can really predict the future. The book includes instructions for making an origami Yoda.

Colfer, Eoin. *Eoin Colfer's Legend of—Spud Murphy.* Miramax Books/Hyperion Paperbacks for Children, 2005, c2004. 95p. IL 3–6, Lexile: 580

When their mother starts dropping them off at the library several afternoons each week, nine-year-old William and his brother dread boredom and the overbearing librarian, but they are surprised at how things turn out.

Kowitt, Holly. *The Loser List.* Scholastic Press, c2011. 213p. IL 3–6, Lexile: 480

Danny Shine tries to get his name off the "Loser List" posted in the girls' bathroom and winds up in detention, where the school bullies discover Danny's artistic talents and encourage him to draw tattoos and graffiti. When the bullies steal a book from his favorite store, however, Danny needs to find a way to steal it back, return it, and end his association with the bullies before he gets new reputation.

O'Dell, Kathleen. *Agnes Parker—Girl in Progress.* Puffin Books, 2004, c2003. 156p. IL 5–8, Lexile: 660

As she starts in the sixth grade, Agnes faces challenges with her old best friend, a longtime bully, a wonderful new classmate and neighbor, and herself.

Weeks, Sarah. *Oggie Cooder.* Scholastic Press, 2008. 172p. IL 3–6, Lexile: 880

Quirky fourth grader Oggie Cooder goes from being shunned to being everyone's best friend when his uncanny ability to chew slices of cheese into the shapes of states wins him a slot on a popular television talent show. He soon learns the perils of being a celebrity—and having a neighbor girl as his manager.

Series

Benton, Jim. *Dear Dumb Diary.* Scholastic, c2004– . IL 3–6

Presents the hilarious, candid, and sometimes not-so-nice diaries of Jamie Kelly, who promises that everything she writes is true, or at least as true as it needs to be.

Bruel, Nick. *Bad Kitty Series.* Roaring Brook Press, 2008– . IL K–3

A look at the humorous activities of Bad Kitty. When her owners run out of cat food, she responds by turning into Bad Kitty. From hurling hair balls at their head to actually eating homework, this cat has some very interesting moves for her owners.

If You Liked *Diary of a Wimpy Kid* by Jeff Kinney, You Might Like . . .

Gantos, Jack. *Joey Pigza Series*. Farrar, Straus and Giroux, 1998– . IL 5–8
In this hilarious and emotionally honest series, the hyperactive hero has to deal with problems such as controlling his mood swings when his prescription wears off, dealing with his dysfunctional family, and developing a friendship with Olivia Lapp.

Peirce, Lincoln. *Big Nate Series*. Harper, c2010– . IL 3–6
Meet Nate Wright—sixth grader, class clown, self-described genius, and the all-time record holder for school detentions! In these books featuring black-and-white illustrations, comics, and doodles throughout, Big Nate blazes an unforgettable trail through middle school.

Pilkey, Dav. *The Adventures of Captain Underpants Series*. Blue Sky Press, c1997–2003. IL 3–6
"Faster than a speeding waistband . . . more powerful than boxer shorts . . . " The outrageous adventures of the world's greatest superhero!

Russell, Rachel Renee. *Dork Diaries Series*. Aladdin, c2009– . IL 3–6
These hilarious and heartwarming stories from the personal diary of Nikki Maxwell feature drawings, doodles, and comic strips that chronicle the daily drama of her life in middle school.

Vernon, Ursula. *Dragonbreath Series*. Dial Books, c2009– . IL 3–6
This series is written in the author's trademark hybrid style of comic-book panels and text. Danny Dragonbreath and his friend Wendell get an up-close underwater tour of the Sargasso Sea from Danny's sea-serpent cousin, encountering giant squid and mako sharks during their journey.

If You Liked *Little House on the Prairie* by Laura Ingalls Wilder, You Might Like . . .

Alcott, Louisa May. *Little Women.* Oxford University Press, 2007. 323p. IL 5–8
The story of the four March sisters—Meg, Jo, Beth, and Amy—and their trials growing into young ladies in a very poor home in nineteenth-century New England.

Brink, Carol Ryrie. *Caddie Woodlawn.* Simon & Schuster Books for Young Readers, 1973. 275p. IL 5–8, Lexile: 890
The adventures of an eleven-year-old tomboy growing up on the Wisconsin frontier in the mid-nineteenth century.

Conrad, Pam. *Prairie Songs.* HarperTrophy, 1985. 167p. IL 5–8, Lexile: 780
Louisa's life in a loving pioneer family on the Nebraska prairie is altered by the arrival of a new doctor and his beautiful, tragically frail wife.

Cushman, Karen. *The Ballad of Lucy Whipple.* Clarion Books, c1996. 195p. IL 5–8, Lexile: 1030
In 1849, twelve-year-old California Morning Whipple, who renames herself Lucy, is distraught when her mother moves the family from Massachusetts to a rough California mining town.

Erdrich, Louise. *The Birchbark House.* Hyperion Paperbacks for Children, 1999. 244p. IL 5–8, Lexile: 970
Omakayas, a seven-year-old Native American girl of the Ojibwa tribe, lives through the joys of summer and the perils of winter on an island in Lake Superior in 1847.

Erdrich, Louise. *The Game of Silence.* HarperCollins, c2005. 256p. IL 5–8, Lexile: 900
Nine-year-old Omakayas and her family, who are members of the Ojibwa tribe, are forced to leave their island on Lake Superior in 1850 when white settlers move into the territory. Omakayas soon comes to realize that the things most important to her are her home and way of life.

Gray, Dianne E. *Holding up the Earth.* Houghton Mifflin, c2000. 210p. IL 5–8, Lexile: 880
Fourteen-year-old Hope visits her new foster mother's Nebraska farm. There, through old letters, a diary, and stories, she gets a vivid picture of the past in the voices of four girls her age who lived on the farm in 1869, 1900, 1936, and 1960.

Holm, Jennifer L. *Boston Jane:An Adventure.* Random House, 2001. 247p. IL 3–6
Schooled in the lessons of etiquette for young ladies of 1854, Miss Jane Peck of Philadelphia finds little use for manners during her long sea voyage to the Pacific Northwest and while living among the American traders and Chinook Indians of Washington Territory.

Hurwitz, Johanna. *The Unsigned Valentine and Other Events in the Life of Emma Meade.* HarperCollins, 2006. 167p. IL 3–6, Lexile: 810
In early twentieth-century Vermont, fifteen-year-old Emma confides in her diary both her hopes of becoming a farmer's wife one day and her frustrations with her parents' belief that she is too young to be courted by the handsome Cole Berry.

Ingold, Jeanette. *The Big Burn.* Harcourt, 2002. 301p. IL 5–8, Lexile: 860
Three teenagers battle the flames of the Big Burn of 1910, one of the century's biggest wildfires.

If You Liked *Little House on the Prairie* by Laura Ingalls Wilder, You Might Like . . .

Jocelyn, Marthe. *Mable Riley:A Reliable Record of Humdrum, Peril, and Romance*. Candlewick Press, 2004. 279p. IL 5–8, Lexile: 890

> In 1901, fourteen-year-old Mable Riley dreams of being a writer and having adventures while stuck in Perth County, Ontario, assisting her sister in teaching school. During her stay there, she secretly becomes friends with a neighbor who holds scandalous opinions on women's rights.

Lovelace, Maud Hart. *Betsy-Tacy.* HarperTrophy, c2000. 122p. IL 3–6, Lexile: 650

> After Tacy Kelly moves into the house across the street from Betsy Ray, the five-year-olds become inseparable friends.

MacLachlan, Patricia. *Sarah, Plain and Tall.* Charlotte Zolotow Book, c1985. 58p. IL 3–6, Lexile: 560

> When their father invites a mail-order bride to come live with them in their prairie home, Caleb and Anna are captivated by their new mother and hope that she will stay.

Montgomery, L. M. *Anne of Green Gables*. Knopf, 1995. 396p. IL 5–8

> Anne, an eleven-year-old orphan, is sent by mistake to live with a lonely middle-aged brother and sister on a Prince Edward Island farm. She proceeds to make an indelible impression on everyone around her.

Oswald, Nancy. *Nothing Here But Stones*. H. Holt, 2004. 215p. IL 5–8

> In 1882, ten-year-old Emma and her family, along with other Russian Jewish immigrants, arrive in Cotopaxi, Colorado. They face inhospitable conditions as they attempt to start an agricultural colony there, and lonely Emma is comforted by the horse whose life she saved.

Paterson, Katherine. *Jacob Have I Loved*. HarperCollins, c1980. 216p. IL 5–8, Lexile: 880

> Feeling deprived all her life of schooling, friends, mother, and even her name by her twin sister, Louise finally begins to find her identity.

Peck, Richard. *A Year Down Yonder.* Dial Books for Young Readers, c2000. 130p. IL 5–8, Lexile: 610

> During the recession of 1937, fifteen-year-old Mary Alice is sent to live with her feisty, larger-than-life grandmother in rural Illinois and comes to a better understanding of this fearsome woman.

Stratton-Porter, Gene. *A Girl of the Limberlost.* Indiana University Press, 1984. 479p. IL 5–8, Lexile: 850

> Elnora Comstock, an impoverished young girl growing up on the edge of the Limberlost swamp in Indiana, is a lover of nature who has an opportunity to pay for her education by collecting moths.

If You Liked *A Series of Unfortunate Events* by Lemony Snicket, You Might Like...

Ardagh, Philip *Dreadful Acts*. H. Holt, 2003, c2001. 128p. IL 5–8, Lexile: 910
Twelve-year-old Eddie Dickens survives encounters with an escape artist in a runaway hearse's coffin, a hot-air balloon bearing the escape artist's lovely assistant, a gas explosion, and a jewel thief on the run.

Gliori, Debi. *Pure Dead Magic*. Knopf, c2001. 182p. IL 5–8, Lexile: 920
The Strega-Borgia children, their mysterious new nanny, and a giant tarantula use magic and actual trips through the Internet to bring peace to their Scottish castle after the children's father is kidnapped.

Series

Colfer, Eoin. *Artemis Fowl*. Hyperion Books for Children, c2001– . IL 5–8
When a twelve-year-old evil genius tries to capture a fairy and demands a ransom in gold, the fairies fight back with magic, technology, and a particularly nasty troll.

Kerr, P. B. *Children of the Lamp Series*. Orchard Books, 2004– . IL 5–8
Twins Philippa and John discover they are descended from a long line of Djinn—and then their mysterious adventures begin!

Stewart, Paul. *Edge Chronicles Series*. David Fickling Books, 1998– . IL 5–8
Young Twig lives in the Deepwoods among the Woodtrolls, but he isn't one of them. In a brave attempt to find out where he truly belongs, Twig wanders into the mysterious, dangerous world beyond the Deepwoods.

If You Liked *Magic Tree House* by Mary Pope Osborne, You Might Like . . .

Series

Abbott, Tony. *Secrets of Droon*. Scholastic, 1999– . IL 3–6
Eric and his friends find entry into the mysterious world of Droon by using a staircase in Eric's basement. What fate awaits them there?

Adler, David A. *Cam Jansen Adventure*. Viking, c1980– . IL 3–6
Fifth grader Cam Jansen uses her phenomenal photographic memory to solve mysteries. She's a girl with spunk and a knack for being in the right place.

Delton, Judy. *Pee Wee Scouts.* Bantam Doubleday Dell Books for Young Readers, c1988– . IL K–3
Features boys and girls in the first and second grades who are scouts for the first time, and who have fun doing good deeds for their families and friends.

Deutsch, Stacia. *Blast to the Past Series*. Aladdin Paperbacks, 2005– . IL 3–6
With the help of their time-travel gadget and Mr. Caruthers, their history teacher, the class travels through time to keep history on track.

Hale, Bruce. *Chet Gecko Mystery.* Harcourt, c2001– . IL 3–6
The star of this hilarious mystery series is none other than the green-scaled, smart-aleck fourth grader, Chet Gecko—an intrepid, private-eye lizard.

Kline, Suzy. *Horrible Harry Chapter Books*. Viking, 1989– . IL 3–6
Harry inevitably orchestrates the most horrible things, such as putting a vial of ants into the refrigerator. But Harry isn't always horrible, especially when it comes to Song Lee. His growing devotion to her gets him into some awkward situations.

Sachar, Louis. *Marvin Redpost*. Random House, c1992– . IL 3–6
A boy named Marvin Redpost encounters hilarious problems with school, family, and friends.

If You Liked the Nancy Drew/Hardy Boys Mysteries, You Might Like . . .

Series

Adler, David A. *Cam Jansen Adventure*. Viking, c1980– . IL 3–6
Fifth grader Cam Jansen uses her phenomenal photographic memory to solve mysteries. She's a girl with spunk and a knack for being in the right place.

Byars, Betsy Cromer. *Herculeah Jones Mystery*. Sleuth Puffin, 2006– . IL 5–8
The exciting escapades of supersleuth Herculeah Jones and her best friend, Meat. With a policeman for a father and a private investigator for a mother, could thirteen-year-old Herculeah Jones be anything except a sleuth?

Byng, Georgia. *Molly Moon*. HarperCollins, c2003– . IL 3–6
Molly Moon, who lives in a dreary orphanage in a small English town, discovers a hidden talent for hypnotism and hypnotizes her way from one adventure to another—and from one continent to another!

Campbell, Julie. *Trixie Belden*. Random House, 2003. IL 5–8
This character first appeared more than fifty years ago, and generation after generation of readers grew up with mystery-loving Trixie and her friends. Now Trixie is back to make fans of a new generation.

Van Draaen, Wendelin. *Sammy Keyes*. Alfred A. Knopf, c1998– . IL 5–8
These exciting mysteries star the feisty and funny, smart and spunky, seventh-grade ace detective, Samantha Keyes. Sammy is illegally living with her grandmother in a senior apartment building while her mother is off the Hollywood trying to fulfill her dreams. She and her friends solve mysteries around her town of Santa Martina, California.

If You Liked *Ranger's Apprentice* by Joseph Delaney, You Might Like . . .

Barry, Dave. *Peter and the Starcatchers.* Disney Editions/Hyperion Books for Children, c2004. 451p. IL 5–8, Lexile: 770

Peter, an orphan boy, and his friend Molly fight off thieves and pirates to keep a secret safe away from the diabolical Black Stache and his evil associate Mister Grin.

Collins, Suzanne. *Gregor the Overlander.* Scholastic, c2003. 312p. IL 3–6

Eleven-year-old Gregor and his two-year-old sister are pulled into a strange underground world populated by humans, giant spiders, bats, cockroaches, and rats. Gregor's anxiety about finding his way home is quelled, however, when he finds a prophecy that foretells of his role in the Underland's future.

L'Homme, Erik. *Quadehar the Sorcerer.* Scholastic, 2006, c2003. 275p. IL 3–6, Lexile: 780

Robin Penmarch lives a regular life in the Lost Isle, where he and his friends are protected from an ever-present danger by magic and knights in armor—until one day Robin's rare, magical potential is accidentally revealed in the presence of Quadehar the Sorcerer.

Paver, Michelle. *Wolf Brother.* HarperCollins, c2004. 295p. IL 5–8, Lexile: 660

Twelve-year-old Tarak and his guide, a wolf cub, set out on a dangerous journey to fulfill an oath the boy made to his dying father—to travel to the Mountain of the World Spirit and find a way to destroy a demon-possessed bear that threatens all the clans.

Series

MacHale, D. J. *Pendragon.* Aladdin Paperbacks, 2002–2004. IL 5–8

Fourteen-year-old Bobby Pendragon is apprenticed to his Uncle Press, a Traveler responsible for solving interdimensional conflict. The pair must travel from one territory to another to stop an evil enemy named Saint Dane.

Sage, Angie. *Septimus Heap.* Katherine Tegen Books, c2005– . IL 3–6

Jenna learns that she is a princess who found abandoned as a baby. Now she and Septimus, who was taken at birth by the midwife, are being threatened by the evil wizard, DomDaniel, who intends to finish off the entire royal line.

Stewart, Paul. *Edge Chronicles.* David Fickling Books, 1998– . IL 5–8

Young Twig lives in the Deepwoods among the Woodtrolls, but he isn't one of them. In a brave attempt to find out where he truly belongs, Twig wanders into the mysterious, dangerous world beyond the Deepwoods.

From *101 Great, Ready-to-Use Book Lists for Children* by Nancy J. Keane. Santa Barbara, CA: Libraries Unlimited. Copyright © 2012.

If You Liked *Warriors* by Erin Hunter, You Might Like . . .

Avi. *Poppy.* HarperTrophy, 1995. 159p. IL 3–6, Lexile: 670
Poppy, a deer mouse, urges her family to move next to a field of corn big enough to feed them all forever—but Mr. Ocax, a terrifying owl, has other ideas.

Clement-Davies, David. *Fire Bringer.* Firebird, 1999. 498p. IL 5–8, Lexile: 840
Rannoch, who was born with a fawn mark the shape of an oak leaf on his forehead, is destined to lead the deer out of the Lord of the Herd's tyranny. First, however, he must complete a journey through the Great Land.

DiCamillo, Kate. *The Tale of Despereaux: Being the Story of a Mouse, a Princess, Some Soup, and a Spool of Thread.* Candlewick Press, 2003. 267p. IL 3–6, Lexile: 670
The adventures of Despereaux Tilling, a small mouse of unusual talents; the princess whom he loves; the servant girl who longs to be a princess; and a devious rat determined to bring them all to ruin.

Jacques, Brian. *Redwall.* Philomel Books, 2007, c1986. 351p. IL 5–8, Lexile: 800
In this series, a young mouse named Matthias but overcome his fears to save his friends. The rats, led by Cluny by Scourage, want to take ownership of Redwall Abbey but the mice who live there are determined to defend it at all costs.

O'Brien, Robert C. *Mrs. Frisby and the Rats of NIMH.* Atheneum, 1971. 233p. IL 3–6, Lexile: 790
With nowhere else to turn, a field mouse asks the clever escaped lab rats living under the rosebush to help save her son, who lies in the path of the farmer's tractor, too ill to be moved.

Oppel, Kenneth. *Silverwing.* Aladdin Paperbacks, 2007, c1997. 216p. IL 5–8, Lexile: 660
When a newborn bat named Shade (but sometimes called "Runt") becomes separated from his colony during migration, he grows in ways that prepare him for even greater journeys.

Said, S. F. *Varjak Paw.* Yearling, c2003. 254p. IL 3–6, Lexile: 500
Guided by the spirit of his legendary Mesopotamian ancestor Jalal, a pure-bred cat named Varjak Paw leaves his home and pampered existence, and sets out to save his family from the evil Gentleman who took their owner, the Contessa, away.

Wallace, Bill. *The Legend of Thunderfoot.* Simon & Schuster Books for Young Readers, c2006. 150p. IL 3–6, Lexile: 610
Humiliated by the name given to him after a rattlesnake bite left him with gigantic, swollen feet, Thunderfoot, a roadrunner, takes the advice of Berland, a wise gopher tortoise, and sets out to prove a name doesn't mean everything.

White, E. B. *Stuart Little.* HarperTrophy, c1973. 131p. IL 3–6, Lexile: 920
The debonair mouse Stuart Little sets out in the world to seek out his dearest friend, a little bird who stayed a few days in his family's garden.

If You Liked *Warriors* by Erin Hunter, You Might Like...

Series

Collins, Suzanne. *Underland Chronicles.* Scholastic Press, 2004– . IL 3–6
When eleven-year-old Gregor is pulled into a strange underground world, he triggers an epic battle involving humans, bats, rats, cockroaches, and spiders while on a quest foretold by ancient prophecy.

Lasky, Kathryn. *Guardiansof Ga'Hoole.* Scholastic, c2004– . IL 3–6
A band of owls go on a quest for the mythic Great Ga'Hoole Tree in an attempt to acquire the powers that will enable them to defeat the evil that threatens their kingdom.

Professional Titles

Professional Reading Lists

Barr, Catherine. *Best Books for Children: Preschool through Grade 6.* Libraries Unlimited, c2010. 1901p.

> Collects information on nearly 25,000 fiction and nonfiction titles—covering topics such as biographies, history, science, and recreation—for children from prekindergarten through the sixth grade, with brief annotations, bibliographic data, grade level appropriateness, and review citations.

Barr, Catherine. *Best Books for Children: Supplement to the Eighth Edition: Preschool through Grade 6.* Libraries Unlimited, 2007. 445p.

> Presents details on more than 4,200 books for children from prekindergarten through sixth grade, providing bibliographic information, brief summaries, and review citations. The book also includes author/illustrator, title, and subject/grade level indexes.

Barr, Catherine. *Best Books for High School Readers: Grades 9–12.* Libraries Unlimited, 2009. 1075p.

> Contains annotated listings of approximately 15,000 recommended books for high school readers, including fiction and nonfiction titles published through 2008. Each entry includes the book's ISBN, length and price, grade level, review citations, audio availability, and more.

Barr, Catherine. *Best Books for Middle School and Junior High Readers: Grades 6–9.* Libraries Unlimited, 2009. 1242p.

> Contains annotated listings of approximately 15,000 recommended books for middle school and junior high readers, including fiction, plays, literary history and criticism, biographies, philosophy and religion, guidance and personal development, and other genres. Each entry includes the book's ISBN, length and price, grade level, and review citations.

Bartel, Julie. *Annotated Book Lists for Every Teen Reader: The Best from the Experts at YALSA.* Neal-Schuman Publishers, c2011. 270p.

> Presents annotated lists of books for young adults, with lists separated by genre, reading level, theme, and format.

Best Books for Young Adults. American Library Association, 2007. 346p.

> Presents twenty-seven themed, annotated lists of fiction and nonfiction books for young adults and an annotated list of the Best Books for Young Adults Committee selections spanning 1966–2007, and discusses contemporary trends in teen literature.

Bodart, Joni Richards. *Radical Reads 2: Working with the Newest Edgy Titles for Teens.* Scarecrow Press, 2010. 479p.

> Provides information on approximately one hundred controversial books for teen readers, with each entry including publication data, character descriptions, and a booktalk; lists of subject areas and major themes; ideas for book reports and booktalks; risks, strengths, and awards; and excerpts from reviews.

Professional Titles

Drew, Bernard A. *100 Most Popular Nonfiction Authors: Biographical Sketches and Bibliographies.* Libraries Unlimited, 2008. 438p.

> Profiles one hundred of today's most popular nonfiction writers, with an overview of each author's personal and professional lives, literary accomplishments, genre, and awards, with reading lists and contact information for each entry.

Fry, Edward Bernard. *The Reading Teacher's Book of Lists.* Jossey-Bass, c2006. 524p.

> Presents more than two hundred lists for elementary and secondary reading teachers, providing exercises, vocabulary, and other teaching tools in eighteen topic areas, including phonics, word play, study skills, and assessment.

The Librarian's Book of Lists. American Library Association, 2010. 118p.

> A collection of library-related lists, including "10 Commandments for Borrowers of Books," "15 Favorite Library Postcards," "Stephen Leary's Top 10 Ways to Exit a Library," and "10 Intriguing Paper Defects," among others.

McElmeel, Sharron L. *The Best Teen Reads 2010.* Hi Willow Research & Publishing, 2010. 153p.

> An annotated listing of reads for teens drawn from the pool of books that have been tapped as award winners or that have received star reviews from professional reviewing sources or endorsements from professional teenagers. This reference features overviews of several genres, each with notes on representative books, and includes lists of recommended audio materials, award winners, theme books, and book packages.

Nieuwenhuizen, Agnes. *Right Book, Right Time: 500 Great Books for Teenagers.* Allen & Unwin, 2007. 355p.

> Contains reviews and recommendations of five hundred books for teenagers, including Australian and international titles. The recommendations are grouped by genre.

Pearl, Nancy. *Book Crush: For Kids and Teens: Recommended Reading for Every Mood, Moment, and Interest.* Sasquatch Books, c2007. 288p.

> Presents lists of recommended book titles in 118 categories, including dogs, girl power, family, boys, dolls, friends, dancing, love, and many others.

Quick and Popular Reads for Teens. American Library Association, 2009. 228p.

> Contains annotated lists of recommended young adult books for reluctant readers and provides advice on library programming, displays, and readers' advisories.

Reisner, Rosalind. *Read On—Life Stories: Reading Lists for Every Taste.* Libraries Unlimited, c2009. 175p.

> Contains brief summaries of nearly 450 published memoirs from throughout history, grouped in the categories of story, character, setting, language, and mood.

Schwedt, Rachel E. *Core Collection for Children and Young Adults.* Scarecrow Press, 2008. 207p.

> Presents a book list of selected children's and young adult literature, and provides annotations while also listing awards, subjects, and character themes. The lists cover the classics, fantasy, historical, non-fiction, picture books, poetry, and more.

Professional Titles

Strouf, Judie L. H. *The Literature Teacher's Book of Lists*. Jossey-Bass, c2005. 553p.
Contains 254 lists that literature teachers can use to develop instructional materials and plan lessons for middle school, secondary, and college students. Information is provided on a variety of topics under the headings of literature, books, genres, poetry, drama, themes, literary periods, potpourri, and student activities and teacher tips.

Thomas, Rebecca L. *Popular Series Fiction for Middle School and Teen Readers: A Reading and Selection Guide*. Libraries Unlimited, 2009. 710p.
A comprehensive fiction resource guide for middle and high school readers covering more than eight hundred series, along with annotations, character lists, grade levels, genre, and more.

Trupe, Alice. *Thematic Guide to Young Adult Literature*. Greenwood Press, 2006. 259p.
Identifies thirty-two themes in young adult literature and features critical discussions of three or more representative novels in each category. Includes lists of additional recommended titles.

Zbaracki, Matthew D. *Best Books for Boys: A Resource for Educators*. Libraries Unlimited, 2008. 189p.
Profiles five hundred fiction and non-fiction books that will be interesting and motivating for boys, with entries organized by genre. Information is provided on each book's plot, reading level, and author.

Children's Book Awards

Alex Awards http://www.ala.org/ala/yalsa/booklistsawards/alexawards/alexawards.htm
From YALSA. The top adult books enjoyed by young adults.

Best Books for Young Adults http://www.ala.org/ala/yalsa/booklistsawards/bestbooksya/bestbooksyoung.htm
Books published in the past sixteen months that are recommended reading for young adults (ages twelve to eighteen).

Book Sense Book of the Year Award (formerly ABBY Award) http://www.bookweb.org/news/awards/3433.html
American Booksellers Children's Book of the Year. From BookWeb. For earlier ABBY Awards, see ABBYs.

***Boston Globe–Horn Book* Awards** http://www.hbook.com/awards/bghb/default.asp
Given annually since 1967 by the *Boston Globe* and *Horn Book* magazine. Through 1975, two awards were given—for outstanding text and for outstanding illustrations. Since 1976, the awards have included those for outstanding fiction or poetry; outstanding nonfiction; and outstanding illustration.

Caldecott Medal http://www.ala.org/alsc/caldecott.html
Sponsored by the Association for Library Service to Children's Division of the American Library Association. Given to the illustrator of the most distinguished picture book for children published in the United States during the preceding year. Only U.S. citizens or residents are eligible.

Professional Titles

Charlotte Zolotow Award http://www.soemadison.wisc.edu/ccbc/books/zolotow.asp

Given annually to the author of the best picture book text published in the United States in the preceding year. Established in 1998 and administered by the Cooperative Children's Book Center.

Children's Notable Lists http://www.ala.org/ala/alsc/awardsscholarships/childrensnotable/Default1888.htm

Each year, the American Library Association selects, annotates, and presents for publication its list of notable children's books of the preceding year. "Notable" is defined as "worthy of note or notice, important, distinguished, outstanding." As applied to children's books, this term should be thought to include books of especially commendable quality, books that exhibit venturesome creativity, and books of fiction, information, poetry and pictures for all age levels (through age fourteen) that reflect and encourage children's interests in exemplary ways.

Golden Kite Award http://www.scbwi.org/awards/gk_main.htm

Presented by the Society of Children's Book Writers and Illustrators to children's book authors and illustrators by their fellows.

International Reading Association Children's Book Awards http://www.reading.org/association/awards/childrens_ira.html

Given for an author's first or second published book. Four awards are given for fiction and non-fiction in two age categories: younger readers (ages four to ten) and older readers (ages ten to seventeen). Books from any country and in any language copyrighted during the award year are considered.

Laura Ingalls Wilder Medal http://www.ala.org/ala/alsc/awardsscholarships/literaryawds/wildermedal/wildermedal.htm

Honors an author or illustrator whose books, published in the United States, have made, over a period of years, a substantial and lasting contribution to literature for children.

Margaret A. Edwards Award http://www.ala.org/ala/yalsa/booklistsawards/margaretedwards/margaretedwards.htm

Given annually to an author whose book or books, over a period of time, have been accepted by young adults as an authentic voice that continues to illuminate their experiences and emotions, giving insight into their lives.

Michael Printz Award http://www.ala.org/ala/yalsa/booklistsawards/printzaward/Printz_Michael_L__Award.htm

Award for a book that exemplifies literary excellence in young adult literature. From Young Adult Services Division of the American Library Association.

Mildred L. Batchelder Award http://www.ala.org/ala/alsc/awardsscholarships/literaryawds/batchelderaward/batchelderaward.htm

Awarded to an American publisher for a children's book considered to be the most outstanding of those books originally published in a foreign language in a foreign country, and subsequently translated into English and published in the United States.

Professional Titles

Newbery Medal http://www.ala.org/alsc/newbery.html
> Sponsored by the American Library Association. Given to the author of the most distinguished contribution to children's literature published during the preceding year. Only U.S. citizens or residents are eligible.

Outstanding Books for the College Bound http://www.ala.org/ala/yalsa/booklistsawards/outstanding books/outstandingbooks.htm
> The books on this list offer opportunities to discover new ideas, and provide an introduction to the fascinating variety of subjects within an academic discipline. Readers will gain an understanding of our diverse world and build a foundation to deepen their response to that world.

Parents' Choice Awards http://www.parents-choice.org/get_direct.cfm?cat=p_boo
> Awards in print and nonprint categories.

Popular Paperbacks for Young Adults http://www.ala.org/ala/yalsa/booklistsawards/popularpaper back/popularpaperbacks.htm
> Intended to encourage young adults to read for pleasure, by presenting them with lists of popular or topical titles that are widely available in paperback and that represent a broad variety of accessible themes and genres.

Pura Belpre Award http://www.ala.org/Template.cfm?Section=bookmediaawards&template=/ ContentManagement/ContentDisplay.cfm&ContentID=87993
> Awarded to a Latino/Latina writer and illustrator whose work best portrays, affirms, and celebrates the Latino cultural experience in an outstanding work of literature for children and youth.

Quick Picks for Reluctant Young Adult Readers http://www.ala.org/ala/yalsa/booklistsawards/quick picks/quickpicksreluctant.htm
> The list is intended for young adults (ages twelve to eighteen) who, for whatever reasons, do not like to read. The list seeks to identify titles for recreational reading, not for curricular or remedial use.

Robert F. Sibert Informational Book Medal http://www.ala.org/ala/alsc/awardsscholarships/literary awds/sibertmedal/Sibert_Medal.htm
> Awarded annually to the author of the most distinguished informational book published in English during the preceding year.

Sneider Family Book Award http://www.ala.org/ala/awardsbucket/schneideraward/schneiderawardrecipients .htm
> Honors an author or illustrator for a book that embodies an artistic expression of the disability experience for child and adolescent audiences.

From *101 Great, Ready-to-Use Book Lists for Children* by Nancy J. Keane. Santa Barbara, CA: Libraries Unlimited. Copyright © 2012.

Index

About the Author

NANCY J. KEANE is a school librarian whose goal is to get students reading. In addition to her work in the school, Nancy has hosted a children's literature television show that featured children from the area talking about their favorite books. The show also showcased local authors and storytellers. Nancy has authored several books on creating and using booktalks.

Nancy is the author of an award-winning website *Booktalks: Quick and Simple* (http://www.nancykeane.com/booktalks). This site has proved to be indispensable to librarians and teachers. The database includes more than 5,000 ready-to-use booktalks, and additional contributions from educators are welcomed. Additionally, Nancy's wiki, *ATN Reading Lists*, consists of nearly 2,000 thematic lists culled from suggestions from several professional e-mail discussion lists. The wiki is an open collaborative through which educators from around the world can share their lists.

Nancy received a BA from the University of Massachusetts, Amherst; an MLS from the University of Rhode Island; and an MA in educational technology from George Washington University. She is currently an EdD candidate at Rivier College. She is an adjunct faculty member at New Hampshire Technical Institute, Plymouth State University, and University of Rhode Island and teaches workshops around the country.